EQUAL
TO THE
TASK

Men & Women
In Partnership

Ruth Haley Barton

InterVarsity Press
Downers Grove, Illinois

InterVarsity Press
P.O. Box 1400, Downers Grove, IL 60515
World Wide Web: www.ivpress.com
E-mail: mail@ivpress.com

InterVarsity Press® is the book-publishing division of InterVarsity Christian Fellowship/USA®, a student movement active on campus at hundreds of universities, colleges and schools of nursing in the United States of America, and a member movement of the International Fellowship of Evangelical Students. For information about local and regional activities, write Public Relations Dept., InterVarsity Christian Fellowship/USA, 6400 Schroeder Rd., P.O. Box 7895, Madison, WI 53707-7895.

All Scripture quotations, unless otherwise indicated, are taken from the New Revised Standard Version of the Bible, *copyright 1989 by the Division of Christian Education of the National Council of the Churches of Christ in the USA. Used by permission. All rights reserved.*

Cover photograph: C/B Productions ©1996/The Stock Market

ISBN 0-8308-1357-8

Printed in the United States of America ♻

Library of Congress Cataloging-in-Publication Data

Barton, Ruth Haley, 1960-
    Equal to the task : men and women in partnership / Ruth Haley
Barton.
      p.   cm.
    Includes bibliographical references.
    ISBN 0-8308-1357-8 (pbk. : alk. paper)
    1. Man-woman relationships—Religious aspects—Christianity.
  2. Sex role—Religious aspects—Christianity.   I. Title.
BT705.8.B37   1998
261.8'343—dc21   *98-11313*
                                                            CIP

20	19	18	17	16	15	14	13	12	11	10	9	8	7	6	5	4	3	2	1
15	14	13	12	11	10	09	08	07	06	05	04	03	02	01	00	99	98		

To my brothers
Jonathan Taylor Haley and William (Bill) R. L. Haley
Your presence in my life as kindred spirit friends and ministry partners
has been the inspiration for the vision that is set forth in this book

And to Chris
my partner in life and love

Foreword

Every so often a landmark book hits the shelves. Such books stand above the myriad wordy texts that promise the reader so much but deliver so little. Breakthrough books provoke deep thinking and reflection and force the reader to wrestle with the profound. Such books are rarely read in one sitting. They demand action in the face of complacency, change in the midst of comfort.

I believe you are holding a landmark book. It is a risky book, because it dares to present the truth about who we are as men and women in Christ, without shame, fear, insecurity or apology. Bold in its assertions but winsome in its approach, this piece of writing is one of the finest attempts I have seen at challenging men and women to live out the God-honoring mandate of becoming a community in Christ. Not a reactionary community guarded by stereotypical gender roles uninformed by Scripture; not an offending community where truth is used to break down rather than build up. No, in these pages you will find Ruth Barton makes the appeal—and it is a compelling appeal—for true community, teamwork and partnership among men and women that delights the God who created both genders in his image.

This book is a must read for men and women who want to team up to do ministry, raise a family or lead in the marketplace, Ruth makes a fresh and sound appeal to developing trust and building bridges. Sentimental calls to community that do not take into account the struggles and barriers that can arise will only cause frustration between the sexes. Ruth offers no wishy-washy idealism. Instead she both acknowledges the challenges and risks of bringing the genders together and holds out a vision for authentic partnership.

No longer do we have to retreat into men-only or women-only friendships and groups because of fear or misunderstanding. In the world and in the church, men and women must learn to work together, and Ruth Barton tells us how. But don't be deceived. It is not an easy 1-2-3 step plan. It will require courage, truthfulness, the presence of Christ and the commitment of godly men and women to work it out together with integrity and trust. But if we truly want to be the church, there are no other options. Let's not go through life building Christ-honoring relationships and working in ministry with only half the body of Christ. There is so much more to the kingdom!

Dr. Bill Donahue
Executive Director, Small Group Ministries, Willow Creek Association

Acknowledgments

Truth, to be understood, must be lived. We can only possess what we experience. CHARLIE PEACOCK

It is in light of this reality that I wish to express my gratitude to the communities of faith and to the individuals with whom I have experienced the truths presented in this book.

To Willow Creek Community Church, for being a church home in which the equal partnership of women and men in ministry is affirmed and lived out as a crucial component of community life. The opportunity to be "in process" with godly brothers and sisters who are committed to the values associated with partnership has brought me great joy, inspiration and practical insight. I am especially grateful to Bill Donahue, Rex Minor, Lynne Hybels and Bill Hybels, who have supported me in this work and helped to pull me over the finish line.

To Northern Baptist Theological Seminary, for being a haven for me and other women who seek theological training in an environment that receives them with joy and supports them fully in their preparation for pastoral ministry. Special thanks to Emma Justes, professor of pastoral care, whose insightful teaching in the area of gender relations has greatly impacted my thinking and growing.

To my colleagues from Christians for Biblical Equality, especially those on the steering committee in the Chicagoland area. We have lived the message of this book, contributing to each other and to the kingdom of God according to our spiritual gifts and calling without regard to gender. Truly this is a taste of heaven on earth.

To Gareth Icenogle, Stan Grenz and Gilbert Bilezikian, for the scholarship, practical wisdom and openhearted encouragement that each of you made available to me throughout the writing of this book.

To Cindy Bunch-Hotaling, for your patience with the time that it takes for me to write, for your skill as an editor and for your willingness to engage personally with the issues as we shaped this work for publication.

To my parents, Charles and JoAnn Haley, for watching and praying.

To Sis, for your spiritual guidance and support through the risks associated with growing.

To Chris, Charity, Bethany and Haley. Thanks for enduring, for loving me so much, for never letting me forget that you need me and I need you.

Introduction

*The wounds inflicted by men and women on each other
constitute the fundamental fault line running beneath all other
human conflict. . . . It is the biggest reconciliation issue
of all outside of our need to be reconciled to God.*[1]
JOHN DAWSON

If there is any area in which reconciliation is needed in our world, it is the area of gender relations. Not only does the need for reconciliation between men and women cut across lines of race, religion, economic status and age, it affects every sphere, both public and private, in which we function.

When I first started writing this book, I was not looking for personal transformation; I was looking to set men and women straight about what needed to be done in this matter of men and women relating and working together. I was convinced that if I could prove my point theologically, present it logically and say it forcefully, perhaps people would begin to believe that men and women could be partners in the truest sense of the word. Perhaps we really would pull together and include each other in all facets of life and service.

But as I studied the issues, shared experiences with the men in my life and opened my heart to God for what he wanted to do in me, I realized how much I did not know. I became aware of just how complex things really are between men and women, and my heart was moved with love and compassion for men as well as women. All of this was confusing, and

I was forced to face the fact that the avenues I had been relying upon—most of which had to do with the cognitive realm—would never provide full answers to the pains and difficulties associated with male-female relationships.

I could feel myself entering a dark place in which previous answers would not be adequate. I became aware of how much more I needed to listen and learn and how much there was within me that had yet to be transformed. When I surrendered to the learning process, I found that what I was experiencing was beyond my ability to capture in words, and even if I had words, I wondered if I should write them. I was afraid that if I wrote too personally and with too much passion, the whole project would turn into a "woman's book" in which men's voices and concerns would be drowned out. Things only got more complicated when I realized that if I silenced my own voice due to fear, all that would remain would be a collection of words with no heart. During the confusion that ensued I wondered if I should just walk away.

Instead I remembered that God is faithful, and what emerged from that crisis was a strong directive: I was to let my true voice speak with all of the passion and love and hope I hold in my heart about the possibilities for men and women pulling together. But I was to strengthen the male voice as well and allow men to speak from their hearts the stories, experiences and longings that move in places that are beyond words. I had spent years trying to make sense out of my own journey as a woman; but now I was to listen to the men in my life, not to judge them or convince them or change them but to enter into their experiences in the same way that I had been asking them to enter into mine. I was to be available for anything they wanted to say or ask. In partnership with God, I was being led to create a quiet, hospitable space where we could listen—to ourselves, to each other, to our desire for community and oneness, to God himself. We were to speak honestly about what it means to be man and woman, brother and sister. It would be another baby step toward creating a common life, a life that we can all share.

As Henri Nouwen says, "We cannot . . . change other people by our convictions . . . advice and proposals, but we can offer a space where people are encouraged to disarm themselves . . . to listen with attention and care to the voices speaking in their own center."[2] Disarm ourselves we did—in one-to-one conversations, in small groups, in larger groups, with spouses over dinner. In the safety created by this disarmament, we were able to talk about the pain of being excluded from each other's lives, our yearning to come to a place of peace with each other, the difficulty associated with change, our fears and struggles regarding sexual dynamics, the hard work of trying to understand those who seem so different from ourselves, the awkwardness of those less-than-perfect moments, the confusion of trying to find all the fine lines. In the process tears were shed and laughter was shared. Hearts were opened and confessions made. Love, care and empathy were given and received, and true transformation began to take place. Never would I have guessed that the writing of this book would take me to this kind of place.

Now I understand that the process of men and women's coming into community and partnership is no academic exercise (although you will find plenty of theology, reasoned arguments and practical ideas in this book). Instead it is a journey of the heart into an unknown, an opening to a transforming power that we have rarely experienced. It is the admission that before men and women can *accomplish* things together, we must learn to *be together* in love, in compassion, in truth, in body, in strength, in vulnerability—in God.

While there is a wealth of theology to support us, the walk of faith requires sometimes that we push beyond head knowledge to a place that is beyond words, where the moving and groaning of the Spirit guides us into truth. That place is darker than the well-lit place that contains easy answers. In this darker place, we find that we can no longer rely on the ways of "seeing" that have served us so well in the past. We are reduced to listening intently for the softest whispers and feeling our way for a path that is less traveled and thus not as clearly marked.

These softest whispers say this: *Men and women alike share a deep desire to be in community and partnership with each other.* We want to be in each other's lives in meaningful ways, and when we do not know how to accomplish that, we miss each other. We know that when our relationships are not working, we are not yet all we were created to be.

Eventually, if we follow our yearnings through the darkness of the questions and the unknown, we emerge blinking into the light of clarity once more. Most often we find that the answers discovered in the darkness are not inconsistent with much of the head knowledge that we have; it is just that head knowledge is not what transforms us. The living out of that knowledge with real people in real life brings about life-change in ways that are complex and risky, but at the same time richer and more deeply satisfying than we would ever have imagined. In fact, sometimes we are called to *live into* the answers before we have words, trusting that if we are willing to do so, the words will come when we need them. That is the kind of adventurous journey that the writing of this book has been: a journey that started with words, that went beyond words and came back to words again.

I am still on the journey of listening and learning and finding myself changed in the process. I cannot think of myself as anything but a learner and an adventurer, because "true community," as M. Scott Peck says, "is always, among other things, an adventure. You will always be going into the unknown, and you will often be scared, particularly at the beginning. But you will not be alone. You will be entering this adventure with others as scared as you, and you will be able to share not only your fear but your talents and strengths. Out of the strength of your community you will be able to do things you never thought you were capable of."[3]

My prayer is that all of us—men and women alike—who engage with the ideas presented in this book will not back away from the adventure of community and partnership, but will lean into it in faith that God is leading us there.

1

Created for Life Together

The truth is that we are lonely for each other
because we were created to need each other.[1]
KAREN MAINS

Several years ago my daughter Bethany, then seven years old, decided to join a soccer program and ended up being the only girl on her team. I was concerned about how the boys would react to her. Would they welcome and include her, or would they make her feel uncomfortable and strange? Would they take her seriously as a player, or would they coddle her? Would they trust her abilities, or would they pass the ball only among themselves? Would the boys really accept her as a teammate, or would they find subtle ways to leave her out?

At the same time I realized that the responsibility for the success of this experience rested not only with the boys and coaches but also with Bethany. Would she give in to feelings of intimidation and fail to offer her best to the team? Would she hang back in fear and let the boys do most of the hard work? Or would she be strong enough to get in there and take risks even though it was a little uncomfortable being the only girl? Clearly this would require more gumption than I had when I was seven years old!

As it turned out, my concerns were quickly alleviated. I was pleasantly surprised at the ease with which the boys and coaches accepted her and with the lessons she learned about being part of a team. She tried all the positions and learned about her own abilities. She cheered the strengths of her teammates and they cheered hers. She learned how much she and her teammates needed to rely on each other to defend their goal and move the ball down the field. By the time the season was over, her love of the game, her determination and her natural ability caused her teammates to respect and appreciate her just as she respected and appreciated them.

The beauty and effectiveness of a girl and boys working together as equally valued members of a team was a joy to behold. As I observed the camaraderie they exhibited, I could not help but wonder, what happens on the way from childhood to adulthood that makes it so difficult for men and women to include each other?

Stories of manipulation, misunderstanding, harassment and power struggles between men and women are constant in the larger-than-life scenarios of the popular media. While we may distance ourselves from such obvious dysfunction, these stories are really exaggerated reflections of the private pains that many of us struggle with. The objects in the mirror are closer than they appear.

A marriage that ends in violence and death may remind us that we have our own methods of using power in abusive ways in marriage, even if we have not gone that far in trying to control our spouse's destiny. We too have moments when feelings of rage and frustration over issues long unresolved seem to overwhelm us.

A woman decides to confront a boss about his sexual innuendoes and suggestive comments and finds her story and her life splashed all over the local news. We breathe a sigh of relief, knowing that it could just as well have happened to us, and wonder if we would have had enough courage to confront it if it had.

Celebrities divorce, and we contemplate how hard marriage really is. If we resist the urge to be self-righteous, we might admit to our own disappointments or difficulties in marriage, which may help us understand better the painful experience of a broken relationship.

A respected teacher or coach is fired for supposed sexual misconduct, and men wonder, *Is it better to just back off and not get close to anyone? Is that the only way for me to keep myself safe?*

A single mother neglects her children to the point that government officials intervene, and we are aware of how overwhelming the demands of parenting can be when parents are not full partners in the raising of their children.

A church leader falls prey to sexual temptation, inflaming our own deep fears regarding the sexual passions that we feel. We wonder, *Who would I be if I were in a truly tempting situation?*

Women in a corporation or church denomination dare to speak up about discriminatory practices. Perhaps the women lash out in anger; perhaps the men do not know how to listen. Everyone feels misunderstood. Eventually the women may "win" from a legal standpoint, but relationships are no longer intact, and we are tempted to despair about the possibilities for men and women to communicate, work out their problems and come together with mutual respect and regard.

Where Is the Answer?

I would like to be able to say that the church has offered answers to the pains and questions that men and women experience in relation to each other, but in this area in particular the church often has contributed to the problem. Rather than living out God's ideal of women and men in equal partnership in such a way that our presence in society begins to transform it, we have created elaborate systems, rules and structures that segregate and limit us. For many religious women, their deepest wounds have been inflicted by a church that has silenced them and excluded them from full participation in the life of the church. Florence Nightingale, acknowledged before her death as a world authority on the scientific care of the sick, was not the first nor the last woman to express these sentiments in relation to the church: "I would have given her my head, my heart, my hand. She would not have them . . . she told me to go back and do crochet in my mother's drawing room."[2]

While we are not sending women back to the drawing room today, women who are gifted and called by God to speak prophetically to the church, to provide pastoral care and to offer visionary leadership as elders are often sent back to the Sunday school, the women's Bible study or even the foreign mission field rather than being invited to share their gifts with full congregations. The privilege of serving as pastors, priests and elders in many churches is still reserved for men alone.

At the same time as women are silenced and excluded from full participation in the life of the church, many men feel squeezed by stereotypes that leave them feeling like misfits rather than valued members of the team. As one man put it, "People keep pushing me to be an elder, and that's just not who I am. I am much more comfortable working behind the scenes. But when I don't fit into the role that everyone else feels is right for me, I wonder what I am worth around here."

In addition to the difficulty we experience in sharing power and allowing full expression of each other's giftedness, our discomfort and fear about the sexual dynamic between women and men has severely hampered our ability to be together the way God intended, not only as husbands and wives in the safety of marriage but as brothers and sisters in the safety of community. Neither the misuse of sexuality nor segregation into male-only or female-only friendships and small groups has served us well. Both patterns leave us starving for healing and community.

Created for Community

One of the things that used to bother me as a young wife was the pattern that women and men often fell into after sharing a communal meal together in a home. Inevitably, it seemed, the men would retire to the living room to relax while the women would immediately begin to clear the table, do the dishes and keep an ear open for any mischief the children might be getting into. Aside from the obvious unfairness of the situation (after all, the women usually prepared and served the meal as well), I always wanted to be in the living room with the men. Especially if the occasion was Sunday dinner following a church service, their conversation often turned to issues relating to God, church business or the sermon we had just heard. Since I was drawn to these subjects myself and very much enjoyed the conversation of mixed groups, I began to feel downright resentful at being relegated to the kitchen. I couldn't get those dishes done fast enough!

At the same time, though, I felt a little ashamed. Was I betraying my own sex by wanting so much to join the men's conversation? Why did I find myself participating in the kitchen conversation with one ear always tuned to the conversation going on in the next room? If I were a true servant (a much-emphasized role for women), wouldn't I be willing to do the dishes and serve the coffee before participating in conversation with the men?

I admit that servanthood is not always my strongest suit. However, today I realize that there was (and is) more to my longings than questions about servanthood and solidarity with my members of my own sex. Today I understand that my frustrations were really evidence of a great creational truth: Women and men are created to be together in community. My desire to be in the living room or anyplace else where men might be discussing issues of life, faith and kingdom work was really the hunger to live and work as God intended—in community with my brothers.

The creation of humankind in two sexes was intended to reflect God's eternal existence in community—God the Creator, God the Word and God the Life-giving Spirit—functioning together in perfect mutuality and interdependence. Two individuals who were exactly the same could not adequately form the community that would show us who God is. It would take maleness and femaleness together to fully round out the image.

The God who exists as a community of equals (the "us" in "Let us make humankind in our image, according to our likeness" [Gen 1:26]) recognized that it was not good for the man to have as his only companions the animals he had been given the responsibility to oversee. Even Adam's relationship with his Creator could not provide the experience of community that comes when two or more peers commit themselves to share the journey together. As Julie Gorman notes, "'It is not good,' [God] assessed. 'The creature is alone' (Gen 2:18). The Hebrew concept means 'acting independently' or being separate. Adam was not meant to be self-sufficient! The *image* [of God] is not one of aloneness. . . . A helper, an equal one, would complete the community design that God had in mind."[3]

Not only were men and women created to reflect the relational aspects of God's character, we were also placed on this earth to accomplish certain tasks. At the conclusion of the sixth day of creation according to Genesis 1, God blesses the male and female he has just created in his image and gives them these instructions: "Be fruitful and multiply, and fill the earth and subdue it; and have dominion over the fish of the sea and over the birds of the air and over every living thing that moves upon the earth" (Gen 1:28).

Just as Adam or Eve alone could not fully reflect the image of God, neither one of them alone could effectively accomplish the tasks God had given. So God provided Adam with Eve as a helper *(ezer)* who would bring additional strength and resources to the tasks at hand. The Hebrew word *ezer* is often used to refer to God himself[4] and is translated in Scripture by a variety of words such as *succorer, rescuer, helper, deliverer, strength* and *power.* The word *kenegedo,* which modifies *ezer,* means "corresponding to" or "equivalent." When taken together, these words yield a translation such as "a power equal or corresponding to man."[5]

The male-female team that God created was not characterized by hierarchical authority structures but by an equal sharing of power, strength and helpfulness. Neither the man nor the woman was given the option of standing on the sidelines cheering while the other one did all the work. Neither was given the option of reneging on responsibilities that had been given to both of them together. They would both bear equal responsibility for being fruitful and nurturing life, for stewardship of the earth's resources and for exercising appropriate leadership and dominion. Now, in addition to the animals that Adam was responsible to oversee and a God to worship and serve, Adam had an equal, one whose strength and resources corresponded perfectly to his own. Adam and Eve were called to keep building their relationship (community) as they worked together (teamwork).

Thereafter, recognizing their fundamental unity and valuing their diversity, men and women down through the ages have been given the opportunity to reflect the relational (community) aspects of God's character and also the reality of a God who accomplishes creative tasks through a team effort. Both of these facets of humanity's godlikeness are in evidence when together women and men "open up the possibilities latent in creation."[6] It was only after this male-female team was put in place that God, for the first time in the entire creation story, commented that the creation was "very good" (Gen 1:31).

God's Continuing Effort to Build Community

The hints about God's intentions regarding community in the creation account are just the beginning of a full-blown effort on God's part to continue to create community among us. Even though the introduction of sin into our world took us far from God's created ideal for unity and oneness, it has always been God's task to bring us back into community with himself and with each other. It has been his continuing creative effort to redeem us from the effects of the Fall and to create a larger community of those who share not only their humanity but also their covenant relationship with the living God. Through Abraham, God brought forth a "covenant community"—men and women who lived and journeyed toward the Promised Land together. In support of this covenant community, God provided the children of Israel (as they came to be known) with his presence to fill their spiritual hunger, with food for their physical sustenance and with parameters for preserving community (the Law). However, in the words of Gareth Icenogle, Israel's leaders

> were terribly bound by the existing images and shadows of tyrannical pharaohs and kings who led systems of pyramids and hierarchies. No refined community-building model had been developed or demonstrated that could help leaders give away such personal and communal power from generation to generation. For humanity to find a way back to the Garden, there had to be a leader who could incarnate the character of God in human form and lead a community to be transformed by the power of the Spirit.[7]

That leader was Jesus Christ.

God's visit to earth in the person of Christ was a pivotal event for the human community. Not only was it a powerful expression of God's desire for a restored relationship with us, it became the opportunity to form community around the person and work of Christ, the leader who could fully incarnate God's character. Christ's choice to invite twelve individuals to be with him during his earthly life transformed the individuals he chose, challenged ineffective religious systems and ultimately changed the world.

After Christ's work on this earth was completed, God continued to work through the Holy Spirit to create and empower a new community characterized by mutual servanthood, radical equality and an unprecedented sharing of power and resources. Their experience demonstrates that spiritual life and power is to be found only in community. From the book of Acts we learn that when we open ourselves to the experience of being together in this way, God visits us; he moves and works in ways that are powerful and transforming. The men and women who huddled together to pray in the upper room after Christ's death stayed together in their darkest moment because Christ had taught them that they could not go it alone. He had shown them by his own commitment to a small group of disciples that there is no life outside the community of faith. So they waited together until God practically overwhelmed them with his presence. This happened over and over again when they were together; God's presence and power were poured out on the men and women who gathered, he answered the prayers that men and women prayed in community, he taught them, he grew them and he used them all to accomplish great things. This is the power that women and men are meant to experience as they "do life" together. It is what we were created for and it is what Christ came to perfect among us.

As we trace the concept of community through creation, the Israelite journey, the life of Christ and the formation of the early church, a major scriptural theme emerges: Biblical community is a commitment to take the spiritual journey together, to be present (in face-to-face relationship) with each other as we are transformed by an increasing connection with God and with each other.

" 'Community' should be understood as the movement between persons to experience 'common' life. . . . Community is about the interpersonal connections between two of more beings. . . . Community is the process of individual persons coming together into unity (*com + unity*)."[8]

To create a common life and to come together in unity presents an incredible challenge to men and women today. More often than not, women and men have been segregated from each other, or we have segregated ourselves, in direct opposition to the partnering relationships for which we were created. Women have often used their sexuality in manipulative ways, have failed to tell men the truth and have reneged on sharing important responsibilities with them. Men have often treated women with disrespect, limiting them and exploiting them rather than empowering them to become all they are created to be. Because we have wounded each other over generations, our stance toward each other is often characterized by suspicion, guardedness and defensiveness.

As difficult as it might seem to overcome these dynamics, only a radical return to community will take men and women beyond sinful patterns of wrongful domination, exclusion and disrespect to the mutuality and interdependence for which we were created. In fact, the impact of biblical community and the context it provides for teamwork and partnership is so crucial that chapters two and three are devoted to the disciplines that will make it possible.

The Power of Oneness

The Wisdom of Teams, a popular management book by Jon R. Katzenbach and Douglas K. Smith, outlines the powerful results that can be achieved when people with complementary skills commit themselves to a common purpose, set goals together and decide on an approach for which they hold themselves mutually accountable.[9] Teams "get the job done" in ways that far exceed anything that an individual can accomplish alone. Head coach Phil Jackson of the Chicago Bulls observed that "the real reason the Bulls won three straight NBA championships from 1991 to 1993 was that we plugged into the power of *oneness* instead of the power of one man, and transcended the divisive forces of the ego that have crippled far more gifted teams."[10] Even a player as talented as Michael Jordan had to grow in his understanding that it is not brilliant individual performances that make a great team "but the energy that is unleashed when players put aside their egos and work toward a common goal."[11]

A writer for *Fortune* magazine spent time with a variety of elite teams—U.S. Navy SEALS, the Dallas Cowboys offensive line, the Tokyo String Quartet, a team of firefighters and an emergency-trauma team—and summarized his observations this way:

> We are talking here about teamwork at a rarefied level, a swarm of people acting as one. These folks have checked their self-interest in the garage somewhere and moved to another zone. It's a state in which team members—be they musicians, commandos or athletes—create a collective ego, one that gets results unattainable by people merely working side by side.[12]

Katzenbach and Smith identify several phenomena that explain why teams perform so well:

> First, [teams] bring together complementary skills and experiences that, by definition, exceed those of any individual on the team. . . . Second, in jointly developing clear goals and approaches, teams establish communications that support real-time problem solving and initiative. . . . Third, teams provide a unique social dimension that enhances economic and administrative aspects of work. . . . Finally, teams have more fun . . . [and] inevitably we hear that the deepest most satisfying source of enjoyment comes from "having been part of something larger than myself."[13]

This strategy bears an uncanny resemblance to the team approach that God initiated when he created Adam and Eve to function as partners in accomplishing his purposes. As the Scriptures unfold, partnership between men and women is carried out in the context of a larger community—the people of Israel in the Old Testament and the Christian community in the New Testament. Within the context of a community of faith, men and women with a variety of God-given gifts form smaller work teams for the purpose of achieving common goals such as spiritual growth, helping the poor, planting churches or working for racial reconciliation. Their relationships and their work together build their community life.

The question that immediately presents itself in light of our present concerns is, Why are there still so many areas in which women and men are not yet fully living out the partnership that God intended? Consider the area of being fruitful and nurturing life, for instance. Aside from the partnership that is required for a man and a woman to conceive a child, the actual care of children is still largely a female responsibility. As I observe PTA meetings and activities, mothers' groups and the day-to-day care of children, I notice that women carry a vast majority of the responsibilities related to the nurturing of children. In fact, the care of children is still understood in our culture as primarily a women's issue to the point that presidential candidates in the 1996 campaign used family issues as a major tactic for wooing women voters. In the words of presidential candidate Bob Dole to a group of women voters, "You are the ones who are out there raising the families. The future's all about what's going to happen with your children, your grandchildren, your business."[14]

Does the assumption that women are the ones who are single-handedly raising families offend anyone besides me? More specifically, does it offend any of my male readers who think of themselves as being meaningfully involved in the parenting process? Are women really the only ones who care about issues facing children? I don't think so. Yet in the 1996 presidential campaign, all of these issues were framed as women's issues that, if addressed effectively by the candidates, would win the female vote.

One reason this supposed gender gap is so offensive is that the assumption that women are much better-suited to be in the home caring for children (and if not the mother, then female hired help) leaves many men in the position of adjunct parent, one who fills in the gaps when the mother is not available. This pattern of "almost exclusive mothering and marginal fathering"[15] is a far cry from true teamwork in such a crucial area, and it belies men's capacity for caring for their children.

Many men are so weighted down with the burden of being sole provider for their families that they have given up all hope of being as connected with their families as they would like to be. A 1993 poll revealed that almost three-quarters of fathers identified spending more time with their children as the area of their lives they would like most to change. Their role as primary breadwinner exacerbates the conflict that fathers experience. Statistics from 1991 show that among married couples with preschool children, 77 percent of all fathers had full-time, year-round employment, while only 28 percent of mothers were so employed.[16]

Through the men's movement and other means of spiritual growth, many men are experiencing a new awareness of their own need for relationships and meaning in life beyond the daily grind. But at the same time, the economic realities of inflation, longer workweeks and corporate downsizings make the idea of a balanced lifestyle seem like the impossible dream. Many go through periods of depression as they contemplate a lifetime of working hard at a job that seems pointless. Some silence their fondest dreams ("I have always wanted to be a writer" or "I would really like to go to seminary" or "I have always dreamed of starting my own business and being my own boss"), feeling that for economic reasons they could not make a change even if they wanted to. One man expressed his frustration with this comment: "Women have choices, men have responsibilities."

If a husband and wife were to work toward true teamwork in generating income for their family and seeking creative alternatives, rather than seeing this as primarily the man's responsibility, men and women alike might find that they have healthier options over the long haul.

Ruling, subduing and having dominion is another area in which one wonders why women and men are not more intentional about doing it together. The meaning of these biblical words is hard for us to pin down in the context of a modern culture in which most of us have never had the need or the opportunity to break in a horse, carve out a town in the middle of an untamed wilderness or harness the power of a river. But if the essence of these mandates involves wise and stewardly decision-making in all facets of human activity, one wonders why women and men seem to be so segregated in some of the key arenas where such work takes place. Upper management teams of many corporations include so few women that when a woman does break into these ranks, it is a major news story. In many evangelical churches, women are routinely excluded from the ruling bodies such as elder teams and sessions and are rarely, if ever, seen in the pulpit. The Roman Catholic Church still maintains that women cannot serve as priests, much to the chagrin of women who have committed themselves to the religious life in the same way their male counterparts have.

The fact that it took a long and arduous fight for women to win the right to participate in the democratic process by voting here in the United States demonstrates what a major paradigm shift is often needed for women and men to become a team in the truest sense of the word. Even now, seventy-five years after women won the right to vote, they still hold only 8 percent of the Senate seats, 11 percent of the House seats and 20 percent of the state legislature slots. When it comes to national leadership and finding solutions to the huge problems facing the global community, true teamwork is still a thing of the future. It is coming and it has been coming for a long time, but it is surprisingly slow for a truth that is, in some ways, quite simple and foundational.

A Spiritual Struggle

Ultimately, the struggle that women and men experience as they try to live, work and minister together is spiritual in nature; it is one result of the terrible tearing that occurred in the community of two that God created in the beginning. God was not the only one who realized how effective true teamwork can be; Satan must have also understood how effective the male-female partnership would be in accomplishing God's purposes, for he wasted no time in attempting to undermine it.

Soon after God created the first team and gave them their assignment, Satan approached Eve in an effort to convince her that God had less than honorable motives in instructing her and Adam not to eat from one of the trees in the Garden. In fact, he accused God of lying when he said, "You will not die; for God knows that when you eat of it your eyes will be opened, and you will be like God, knowing good and evil" (Gen 3:4-5). Eve, who was attracted to the forbidden fruit, tried to argue, but to no avail. Even though Adam was right there with her, it seems she failed to ask for Adam's input and he failed to give it. Furthermore, when Eve offered the fruit to Adam, he took it without any argument at all.

This was not a failure in male leadership or female submission, as some would argue. This was a failure to function effectively as the team God created. When Adam and Eve grew lax in inviting each other's feedback, being accountable to each other, offering their strength freely and being influenced by each other, the teamworking relationship that God had initiated broke down, and grave mistakes were made. Rather than exercising appropriate dominion together and subduing this creature who was seeking to destroy their relationship with God and each other, they acted without conferring together and were the weaker for it.

The Fall, as we have come to identify this pivotal event in human history, caused dire consequences for the human race. The most immediate was the introduction of sin and guilt, shame and blame into the male-female relationship. Now, rather than experiencing the respect, mutuality, shared responsibility and enjoyment that comes from being part of a true team, Adam and Eve blamed each other, felt ashamed regarding their sexuality and hid from each other. Even as God called them out of their hiding place and promised them a Savior, he predicted that men and women would continue to struggle with the relational issues that sin had introduced. God alludes to these difficulties in Genesis 3:16 when he says to Eve, "Your desire shall be for your husband, and he shall rule over you."

Seeking to clarify these words, sociologist Mary Stewart Van Leeuwen suggests that

> there are two opposite ways we can abuse our God-given exercise of accountable dominion. The first (man's sin) is to try to exercise dominion without regard for God's original plan for male/female relationships. . . . As a result of the Fall there will be a propensity in men to let their dominion run wild, to impose it in cavalier and illegitimate ways not only on the earth and on other men, but also upon the person who is bone of his bones and flesh of his flesh—upon the helper corresponding to his very self. Legitimate, accountable dominion all too easily becomes male domination.
>
> But the second—peculiarly female sin—is to use the preservation of those relationships as an excuse not to exercise accountable dominion in the first place. . . . The woman's analogue to the man's congenital flaw, in light of Genesis 3:16, is the temptation to avoid taking risks

that might upset relationships. It is the temptation to let creational sociability become fallen "social enmeshment."[17]

Even though true teamwork is what men and women were created for, the consequences of sin—shame, blame, wrongful domination, avoidance of personal responsibility—began to work mightily against it. Many of the difficulties we experience in relationships between men and women today can be traced right back to that fateful moment when the first team floundered. When we peruse the Old Testament we do not have to read far before we observe problems between men and women that are surprisingly similar to the struggles we have today.

Rebekah and Isaac's marriage and family were threatened by deception and manipulation. Dinah was raped while visiting friends in a neighboring town. Potiphar's wife sexually harassed Joseph. Hagar epitomizes the economic vulnerability of women from Bible times to the present. Abigail endured an abusive marriage. Miriam allowed her jealousy regarding Moses' position of leadership to get the best of her. Jephthah abused the power inherent in his role as the father of his daughter. The daughters of Zelophehad confronted discrimination against their sex when it came time to dispose of their dead father's property. Unfortunately, the relational unhealth that these incidents represent went unchecked for so long that many of these abuses have become cultural norms that only in the past century have we begun to question. And we are still a long way from true teamwork in some crucial areas.

Making Our Way Back

Our fallenness will always present us with problems as men and women seek to become the team they were created to be. The only answer for our sin and brokenness is repentance: for those times when we have dominated others rather than inviting them to share responsible dominion with us; for those times when we have left to others the responsibilities that were also given to us at creation; for failing to include each other in all aspects of life, love and kingdom work.

Repentance will lead us to turn away from our fallenness to make that radical return to community mentioned earlier. The word *radical* means "arising from or going to a root source; fundamental, basic." If we are to deal adequately with the difficulties that we experience in gender relations, it will take such a return to the root source. It will take a commitment to certain basic disciplines of biblical community for us to create the context in which true teamwork can become a reality.

I use the word *discipline* because most of the behaviors and attitudes that are required do not come naturally to us as human beings living in a world that has been tainted by sin. They come even less naturally to us as men and women who struggle with centuries of cultural and personal baggage. But the good news is that the disciplines of biblical community can be learned and practiced until they become more natural to us than the ineffective relational patterns to which we have grown accustomed.

We also need to wrestle with the ways cultural influences and stereotypes support us in maintaining our separateness and hampering our ability to develop effective partnerships. The middle-class Victorian ideal of family life (revived after the Industrial Revolution) separated human experience into "the man's world" of work and governance and "the woman's world" of motherhood and homemaking, with women totally dependent on men for their financial support. This has made it difficult for women and men to experience themselves as full partners in the work of church and business life, raising children, generating income and taking care of the home. These responsibilities have been so carefully divvied up that we are hard-pressed to know how to take them on as partners.

The cultural myth that our sexual urges are so powerful that we cannot control them has us convinced that if women and men partner together in workplace projects, church ministries or mentoring relationships, they will ipso facto end up in bed together. Even trends in the religious community that send us forever traipsing off to male-only and female-only conferences and small groups can foster an unconscious belief that men and women do not need each other in the process of growing and wrestling with the challenges of life. These and many other cultural messages need to be unpacked and examined in light of the biblical patterns of relating that are governed by teamwork and community.

Once we acknowledge the sinful relational patterns and cultural conditioning that are so destructive to unity and effectiveness in male-female relationships, we are ready to develop the skills and disciplines for moving beyond these difficulties. A woman may come to understand that she has failed to participate fully in "having dominion" in some area of her life, such as in sharing the responsibility for the spiritual formation of her children, taking responsibility within her church setting, or preparing for her future. While it is important for her to gain this new insight, she will also need to learn new ways of moving in her relationships that will enable her to follow God more fully and also partner effectively with men. Similarly, a man might recognize ways in which he has bought into cultural myths and gender stereotypes; he may be genuinely saddened as he observes the way these stereotypes have caused him to limit, prejudge or even harass women. He will need to learn new mental disciplines and relational skills in order to move beyond stereotypes toward intimacy and partnership with women.

It becomes apparent that an intentional move toward partnership will require us to work on several levels simultaneously. First, we will need to understand and apply a biblically based theology of gender relations. We will need to critique our culture in light of that understanding. We will also need to develop new skills. And we will be called to open ourselves to the kind of personal transformation that is nothing short of miraculous. Our exploration will revolve around several key questions:

☐ What will it look like when women and men function as those who are equally sinful, equally redeemed for all facets of love and priestly service, equally graced with spiritual gifts, equally empowered by the Spirit?

☐ How might we transform our world if men and women deeply honored each other as equal reflections of God's image rather than using gender as a means of limiting, exploiting and stereotyping?

☐ What are the skills and disciplines that will take us toward personal and corporate transformation?

This book is for those with enough strength and courage to find out.

Questions for Individuals or Groups

1. What are some of the joys you have experienced in partnership with members of the other sex, such as a coworker, boss, someone you are dating, spouse or pastor? What are some of the pains or difficulties?

2. Do you think it is possible for men and women today to experience community together? Why or why not?

3. In what areas of your life would you like to see more effective partnerships between women and men?

2

The Disciplines of Biblical Community

The goal of biblical history is the establishment
of a new people among whom outward distinctions
no longer govern interpersonal relationships.
The New Testament testifies that through Jesus Christ,
God has inaugurated just such a people.[1]
STANLEY GRENZ AND DENISE MUIR KJESBO

It was quite a few years ago that my struggles regarding the exclusion of women from full participation in the life of the church came to the fore. As my husband, Chris, and I began realizing that we could no longer be spiritually healthy in a religious system that limited people based on their sex, we also realized that we did not want to raise our three daughters in a setting where being female was a major liability if you were called and gifted to be a pastor, priest or elder. (In the church we were a part of at that time, women were not permitted to serve as pastors or elders.) Eventually Chris and I decided that it was time to make a change, so we sat our girls down for a family council. We explained to them that the policy of our church would not allow women to serve as elders and teaching pastors and that this was inconsistent with our understanding of God's view of women.

This prompted a reply from our daughter Charity. "Oh, that's a lockout. At our school, we're not allowed to have lockouts."

My curiosity piqued, I asked, "What's a lockout?"

With the conviction of all eleven of her years, Charity answered, "It's when the boys won't let the girls play. But we're not allowed to have lockouts, and I'm really glad, because then we can get in there and show them what we can do!"

The Discipline of Inclusiveness
Interestingly enough, "no lockouts allowed" is one of the first and most basic lessons that the new community of first-century Christians had to learn. In Acts 10 we read of Cornelius, a Gentile whose heart was alive to God and to the needs of others. However, the Jewish Christians were still under the impression that the new community was reserved for them alone—no Gentiles allowed. They were convinced that only Jews could experience "the repentance that leads to life" (11:18). Even though Cornelius's heart was full of worship and spiritual yearning, he was outside the community of faith where the presence and the teaching of the Holy Spirit were being experienced so strongly. How painful to experience such yearning and yet be excluded from the very fellowship where this yearning could be filled!

Cornelius prayed constantly about his situation, and one day God answered him by telling him to send for the apostle Peter, who was ministering in a nearby town. In the meantime God was preparing Peter through a dream in which a large sheet descended from heaven full of different kinds of animals that Jews were forbidden to eat because they were considered unclean. In the dream, God told Peter not once but three times, "What God has made clean, you must not call profane" (11:9). As he was considering the meaning of his dream, Cornelius's servants knocked on the door and asked Peter to come and visit Cornelius, a Gentile. Obviously, this was no coincidence!

In the course of Peter's visit with Cornelius, he grew in his understanding of what God was doing in the community. He began to understand "that God shows no partiality, but in every nation anyone who fears him and does what is right is acceptable to him" (10:34-35). While Peter was speaking, the Holy Spirit was poured out on everyone present, the Jews who had accompanied Peter *and* the Gentiles of Cornelius's household. This caused the Jewish Christians to realize that the new community was for everyone in whom the Spirit of God was working.

Later, as Peter described his learning process to the rest of the apostles in Jerusalem, he said, "The Spirit told me to go with them and not to make a distinction between them and us. . . . If then God gave them the same gift that he gave us when we believed in the Lord Jesus Christ, who was I that I could hinder God?" (11:12, 17).

Although this learning experience involved race, not sex, the apostle Paul understood that the same principle applies to all the lines that usually divide us as human beings—race, class and sex: "There is no longer Jew or Greek, there is no longer slave or free, there is no longer male and female; for all of you are one in Christ Jesus" (Gal 3:28). According to Paul, individuals become part of the faith community because of the spiritual reality of their connectedness with God. In this community, perhaps for the first time for some of us, we are defined not by outward characteristics such as sex, race, age or economic status but by our new life in Christ. Here all polarizing distinctions are left at the door.

This basic principle of biblical community is so radical on so many levels (spiritual, cultural, economic, relational) that we have yet to realize it as a culture or as a spiritual community. In the Jewish context, this learning represented a significant departure from long-accepted norms regarding relationships between Gentiles and Jews. Peter is a compelling example of one whose willingness to learn and change in the context of community life resulted in great good for many. He was willing to get on board with this new thing that the Holy Spirit was doing among them.

It will take this same teachable spirit among those in our own faith communities if we are to get on board with what the Holy Spirit wants to do among men and women today. For not only are we to welcome each other into community based on spiritual realities, we are also to function in the community based on the spiritual reality of the gifts that the Holy Spirit gives to each one. While some would say that the scope of Galatians 3:28 is limited to inclusiveness as far as salvation is concerned, Klyne Snodgrass points out that "there is nothing in the Christian faith that is merely *coram Deo* [before God]. All of our faith engages all of our lives."[2] The spiritual reality of man and woman's equal standing before God is reflected in the practical reality of our equal opportunity to serve God and each other.

The implications for contemporary relationships are obvious but far from being achieved. Practically speaking, in the biblically functioning community (whether it be the community of marriage, the family, the local church or the church universal) women and men will share the responsibilities of preaching, caring for children, providing all sorts of pastoral care, feeding one another physically and spiritually, administrating practical details and participating in visionary leadership. This will be true not only in our theology but also in the reality of what is seen week to week in our homes, pulpits, nurseries and board meetings. But in order for this kind of sharing to become the norm, we must diligently apply a second discipline of biblical community.

The Discipline of Mutual Empowerment

As a writer, I rely heavily on my computer, and one of my greatest fears is an unexpected power outage. I experienced one of these again recently, and since I do not save my files as often as I should, I was reduced to wandering around the house waiting for the power to return and wondering how much work I had lost. To make matters worse, I had only a short time to work that day. It was extremely frustrating to know that there was plenty of power to be had but that some blockage or brokenness was preventing that power from flowing into my home to fire up my computer.

This is our situation as the household of God. According to 1 Corinthians 12, we have unlimited power at our disposal. Each individual has gifts and graces that God has already activated, is activating or wants to activate for the common good: "Now there are varieties of gifts, but the same Spirit; and there are varieties of services, but the same Lord; and there are varieties of activities, but it is the same God who activates all of them in everyone. To each is given the manifestation of the Spirit for the common good" (vv. 4-7).

This passage is about the power, the energy, the activity that God is making available to the body of Christ through each one of us. This power—the capacity to act and to have influence—is already available to us. It is like the electricity that is waiting to be unleashed and come pulsing through the electrical wires to warm our homes, turn on our lights and run our computers. The question for us as the people of God, then, is: How can we be the house with all the lights on? How can we be the house where the spiritual power and energy that is available to each woman and each man is free to flow?

There are blockages in the household of God where we have turned off the switch or cut the line by saying, "The power of the Holy Spirit cannot come to us through a woman in the pulpit. It cannot come through teams of men and women serving together as elders and shepherds. It cannot come through male-female friendships and mutual accountability, because that would be too dangerous."

Mutual empowerment, on the other hand, is the discipline by which we help each other recognize our strength and potential and then do whatever we can to encourage and guide the development of those qualities. Mutually empowering relationships are those in which we enable or permit others to be powerful in our lives and in the lives of others in good, kingdom-building ways. In such relationships we invite strength and spiritual influence to flow unblocked from one to the other.

The Discipline of Interdependence

I visited a local church recently on a Sunday morning, and my heart was warmed by many aspects of their worship. But one thing grieved me: there were no women who had a speaking responsibility, and all the elders and pastoral staff members listed in the bulletin were men. I was grieved because what I observed there in one hour on a randomly chosen Sunday morning did not reflect a belief that men and women are interdependent, that we need each other. Sadly, I knew that this was not an isolated situation but rather a way of structuring ourselves that is repeated in church after church throughout the world.

One of the most powerful ways women and men can empower each other is by acknowledging the fact that we need each other. When I believe deep in my soul that I need you, that I need whatever gift or strength God has given the body of Christ through you, am I not giving you permission to be powerful in my life? But when I say either by words or actions that I do not need you in the pulpit or the elder board, or to keep me accountable in a small group community or to help me care for children, isn't that completely disempowering? According to 1 Corinthians 12, none of us has the right to say, "I have no need of you."

Biblically functioning community calls us back from our lack of respect, our anger and our beliefs that we can do without each other, and offers us a radical commitment to respect and healthy interdependence. Paul was a model of this interdependence of man and woman not only in his words but also in the way that he carried out his ministry. Romans 16 offers an extraordinary example of Paul's reliance on his female and male coworkers. This passage is a testimony to his commitment to a team approach to ministry. Of the thirteen references to coworkers in the New Testament, twelve are from the writings of Paul. He uses the term *coworker* to signify colleagues who are worthy of obedience and recognition (1 Cor 16:16, 18). Throughout his writings Paul includes many women in this category of close colleagues—Priscilla (or Prisca), Junia, Tryphaena, Tryphosa, Euodia and Syntyche, to name a few.

Paul begins his list of greetings in Romans 16 by commending Phoebe, a minister from the church in Cenchreae. Since Paul could not be everywhere at once, he sent Phoebe to deliver a letter to the Romans and to minister among them. He emphasized her spiritual qualifications because, since there were no telephones and mail had to be sent by traveler, she would no doubt be the one responsible for explaining to them anything that they did not understand regarding this significant doctrinal statement. Paul wanted the Romans to know that Phoebe was qualified to minister to them in this way.

One word used to describe Phoebe in this passage has often been translated *helper* or *benefactor;* however, the word Paul uses to describe his coworker is actually the noun form of the verb "to be at the head of, rule, care for."[3] It combines the ideas of caring and leadership. It is used in other New Testament references to refer to governance and leadership in the context of the community of faith (as in Romans 12:8 and 1 Thessalonians 5:12). Thus Paul was asking the Roman believers to follow her leadership and assist her "in whatever she may require from you." Paul could commend her with such confidence because "she has been a [caring leader] of many and of myself as well" (Rom 16:2).

Paul knew what it was to share leadership with women and to benefit from their caring direction without any diminishment of his own leadership contributions. This commitment to interdependence is reflected over and over again in Paul's life. The lack of partnership in many churches today stands in stark contrast to the teamwork that was modeled in the early church and taught by Paul and Peter. It is time for Christians to work more proactively for true teamwork among the brothers and sisters in the family of God. Those of us who wish to be part of a biblically functioning community will be careful to do whatever we can to foster this kind of interdependence. We will be careful to look around the nursery and Sunday school, the elders' meeting, the prayer group, the platform on Sunday morning and ask, Does the way we are functioning demonstrate that men and women are interdependent? Are we demonstrating on as many levels as possible that we really do need each other? How many church services or board meetings or evenings at home would someone have to sit through before they would see clear evidence of partnership between men and women?

Disciplines for Navigating Times of Transition

The process of achieving true teamwork is not a bump-free ride. The men and women in the early church encountered some significant roadblocks along the way to true teamwork because they too were dealing with deeply entrenched cultural patterns and biases along with many of the same sinful relational patterns that we experience today.

The early church had to work through the problem of how to include women more fully when, up to that point, boys and men had been the only recipients of theological training. In such a context, explains Aida Besançon Spencer,

> Jewish women were discouraged from having formal higher education in the Law. They were not required to pursue religious training nor did they receive any merit in study. Furthermore, no one was required or encouraged to teach them. They were not admitted to religious schools. Even in the synagogue service they were not to "study fully." These exemptions [from the commands to study the Law] were made for woman because she was primarily to be a homemaker and to be protected against unchastity. Consequently, women were often treated as persons who had little edification to share in conversation and who had little preparation to withstand the temptations of public life.[4]

Since it was not forbidden for women to study the Law, there were some women who did have a considerable grasp on spiritual truth, perhaps because of training they received from their parents or through personal study. Passages such as 1 Corinthians 11:5 and Acts 18:24-26 confirm that women were participating fully in the life of the church through praying, prophesying (preaching), expounding the Scriptures, evangelizing and helping to plant churches. Two churches in particular, however, ran into some problems.

The first was the church in Corinth, where the women were getting a little boisterous in their newfound freedom, praying and prophesying in ways that were offensive to cultural sensitivities and monopolizing the worship service with their disorderly ways. Paul's teaching related to this situation was that the women should remain sensitive to cultural mores by covering their heads when they were praying and prophesying in the church service. Since it was already a stretch in that culture for men and women to be worshiping and learning together and the lack of a head covering symbolized a woman's loose morals, the new community needed to be sensitive to the possibility of misperceptions about what was going on when they got together.

In addition, the lack of self-control and the impropriety that characterized some women's participation were resulting in chaos and a great deal of interruption. Their lack of theological training left them with many questions which, evidently, they blurted out during the service rather than waiting to pursue their questions at a more appropriate time. In answer to this Paul emphasized the interdependence of women and men (11:11-12) and the necessity of honoring all the spiritual gifts that had been given to the community (12:4-26). By doing things decently and in order, the community could honor God and make room for everyone to contribute by praying, prophesying, suggesting a hymn, speaking in or interpreting tongues. Women who had not had the opportunity to learn were encouraged, for the good of the entire community, to be quiet and ask their questions at a more appropriate time rather than monopolizing the teaching portion of the meeting with their questions (14:34-35).[5]

The church in Ephesus had to deal with similar issues in a slightly different context. At the time Paul wrote to Timothy, who was ministering as a pastor/elder to the believers there, Ephesus stood as a bastion of feminine supremacy in religion. The shrine of the great mother goddess Artemis (or Diana, as the Romans knew her) was located in Ephesus, and there she was worshiped as the mother of gods and humans. She was believed to be the originator of life, and her presence or intervention was thought to guarantee economic and political security. It was in this religious climate that Gnosticism, with its radical distortions of biblical stories, began to develop and infiltrate the church.

One such distortion twisted the story of Eve to say that she was the one who brought life to Adam. She was further regarded as the one who brought true knowledge to humankind.[6] The veneration of Eve that grew out of this distortion dovetailed perfectly with the practice of goddess worship that was already firmly entrenched in the religious psyche of those living in the first century. It was a logical progression to mythologize and deify Eve as the mediator of truth and special hidden knowledge. Gnostics developed an entire belief system which claimed that mystic knowledge resided not only in feminine figures of sacred literature (such as Eve and Mary the mother of Jesus) but also in actual Gnostic women who were willing to share their divine secrets. These secrets were often conveyed through the use of repetitious nonsensical syllables, riddles and paradoxes that apparently made sense to Gnostics themselves but were very difficult for anyone else to understand and refute.

Paul wrote to his young protégé, Timothy, for the express purpose of encouraging him to stay at the church in Ephesus to combat such false teaching: "I urge you . . . to remain in Ephesus so that you may instruct certain people not to teach any different doctrine, and not to occupy themselves with myths and endless genealogies that promote speculations rather than the divine training that is known by faith" (1 Tim 1:3-4).

The church in Ephesus was not a healthy church; it was a church in crisis due in part to confusion about the woman's role as mediator of religious truth. This problem was layered on top of the issue already mentioned about how to best include women who up to this point had been basically untaught. Guidelines that were more stringent than normal were needed to give these women an opportunity to learn and submit themselves—not to men, as has often been assumed, but to the sound teaching, the divine revelation that is mentioned so frequently throughout the book of 2 Timothy.

In her book *Beyond the Curse,* Aida Besançon Spencer makes a strong case for the fact that Paul's instruction in 1 Timothy 2 is uplifting for women because, for the first time in Jewish religious culture, women are actually commanded not just to listen but to learn.

> Silence, first of all, was a positive attribute for adults, male as well as female. Second, silence was, as well, a positive attribute for rabbinic students. Paul's words were declaring to his Jewish friends that at this time women were to be learning in the same manner as did rabbinic students. . . . The ancient Jews esteemed silence as a state of calm, restraint at the proper time, respect and affirmation of a speaker because the Bible esteems such silence.[7]

Spencer's observations are consistent with W. E. Vine's definition of the word *hēsuchia* (translated "silence" in verse 11). Vine, a well-respected Greek scholar, translates *hēsuchia* as "quietness" or "tranquillity arising from within."[8] (Interestingly, he does not even list "silence" as a possible translation![9]) It is understandable then that while Paul commands the women to learn quietly as is expected of any rabbinical student learning from a respected teacher, he employs the present active indicative tense for the word *allow* to indicate that during this transitional phase (when the women are just beginning to learn) "I am not presently allowing a woman to teach."[10]

Spencer concludes that this instruction represents an attempt by Paul to slow the pace of a movement that was headed toward full participation of both women and men.

> Before people are "liberated" in Christ, they need to recognize and understand the nature of that liberation. . . . Instruction in the faith has to precede the living out of that faith. Women were not prepared to withstand unorthodox learning since they were not required to learn the Torah. Probably they were among those who desired to be teachers of the law without understanding what they were saying (1 Tim 1:7). . . . If anything, the development of Paul's work at Ephesus should culminate in the authoritative leadership of schooled orthodox women today. Paul never meant for women to remain at the beginning stage of growth exemplified by the women in Ephesus. It was his design to have them mature as heirs according to God's promise (Gal 3:26-29).[11]

In addition, the Greek word *authentein* (translated "authority" in 1 Timothy 2:12: "I permit no woman to teach or to have authority over a man") is worthy of note. Although there are several other Greek words translated "authority" in the New Testament,[12] this is the only time *authentein* appears in the entire New Testament. W. E. Vine, Richard and Catherine Kroeger, and Aida Spencer (to name a few) agree that this little-used word carries with it connotations of violence, wrongful domination and the usurping of someone else's legitimate rights. In fact, in classical Greek literature *authentein* is often used to describe religious activity characterized by promiscuity and the reversal of gender roles, the mingling together of sex and death in cultic practice, murder and the claiming by women of a monopoly on religious power (as among the Amazons). In addition, the Kroegers have found several older dictionaries in which the word *authentein* is defined "to represent oneself as the author, originator, or source of something."[13] This definition is particularly interesting in light of the fact that in the ancient world of Asia Minor, many viewed women as the ultimate source of life.

Since there are at least three other Greek words that Paul and Jesus used frequently to signify legitimate authority, it is doubtful that Paul is barring women from exercising legitimate authority. Paul was a scholarly writer, and if he meant to bar women from all legitimate authority, he could have used any of the other words that are much more straightforward in their meaning. Given that women such as Phoebe and Priscilla were already functioning with authority in the New Testament church, it is more likely that Paul is instructing women not to be domineering in their relationships with men or to get caught up in the false teaching of that day that placed women in a position of superiority over men.

The point of this careful work with passages from 1 Corinthians and 1 Timothy is to demonstrate that Paul's teaching is not contradictory to the partnership model that he himself modeled and encouraged. Rather it represents his instruction to churches that were "in process" in culturally specific situations. It is our task, then, to distinguish between what Paul was saying to the specific people to whom he was writing and the timeless principles that we are to apply to our situation today.

One timeless truth that presents itself through the experiences of the Corinthian and Ephesian churches is that developing partnership models across lines that have traditionally been dividing lines is never a one-time decision. The commitment to partnership is always only the beginning of a process that is worked out over time.

We are at a different stage in the process of moving toward full partnership between men and women than our New Testament counterparts were, but the same timeless principles apply: we are to honor God and each other by doing things decently and in order, to be responsive to cultural sensitivities, to organize our gatherings in such a way that we make room for everyone's gifts, and to respectfully submit ourselves to sound doctrine rather than false teaching. These are the instructions that are meant for the community to adhere to even today. The disciplines of biblical community lived out with an openness to what the Holy Spirit is doing among us will help us to navigate the rough spots in the team-building process.

The Discipline of Truth-Telling

It was the first day of a seminary class on small groups, and we had been asked to find three individuals whom we did not know and interview them briefly. One of the questions we were to ask was "What brought you to seminary?" One of my interviewers (a Methodist pastor, I found out later) listened intently as I described the long and rather painful process I had been through in finding the freedom to follow God's call to the pastorate. When I finished, he commented on my apparent lack of anger. Then he said very quietly, "You know, so many of my female colleagues in ministry are so angry. I'm tired of being their punching bag."

I assured him that I had indeed experienced periods of anger in this process; then I asked him to elaborate on his comment. This quiet and gentle man went on to say that even though he believed in full equality for women and tried to empower the women in his life, many were so angry from their past experiences that their anger seemed to spill out all over him no matter what he did. This was a continuing source of sadness for him, but he was encouraged that he and I had been able to speak of these issues in a healing way. I was encouraged too that this man had chosen to share the truth of his experience, because it was a truth I needed to hear and respond to. I had been so caught up in my own pain that I had been oblivious to what men were going through. Now I began to understand that just as it had been very important for me to have some men in my life who were able to listen to the truth of my experiences, it was important for me to listen to my brothers as well. Without mutual listening and sharing, there would never be a true coming together in unity and understanding.

Gareth Icenogle observes that even the strongest of communities cannot endure lasting periods of unrest in which the truth is avoided: "Disintegration of a small group is the result of trying to live in community without the delicate marriage of truth with intimacy. Truth cannot be shared without intimacy, and intimacy cannot be sustained without truth. Truth, love and justice must all work together in group life."[14]

Icenogle's comments help us begin to understand why God dealt with the sin of untruthfulness so quickly and severely in the life of the early church. As Acts 5 recounts, Ananias and Sapphira tried to deceive the community into thinking that they were making an offering of all the money they had received from the sale of a piece of property. When Peter confronted them over this, they were struck dead immediately. Why? It was not because they had kept some of the proceeds of the sale for themselves. Peter was careful to point out that they were free to do whatever they wished with their property. The issue was that they had lied to the community of faith, and in so doing had lied to God.

Why was this lack of honesty such a problem? When we fail to be honest, we strike at the heart of community and undermine its viability. It is not possible to be in community with each other without the discipline of truth-telling. The implications of this reality are astonishing in our present context, because truth and justice have so rarely been the pattern or the norm for male-female relations. Manipulation, deception, betrayal and power struggles have been much more the relational norms from Bible times to the present. In fact, the reality that "men and women lie to each other all the time" prompted *Glamour* magazine to compile a list of the nineteen lies men tell women and the nineteen lies women tell men. The lies from women include "I didn't get the message," "If I wanted to sleep with anyone right now, it would be you," "I won't get mad as long as you're being honest," "Don't worry, I'd never discuss this kind of thing with my girlfriends," "I love baseball!" Men's lies include "I could fall in love with you in a minute," "But I tried to call," "I didn't notice what she looked like," "Sex is not the most important thing," "I just want to hold you," "I love you too."[15]

Ephesians 4:15, on the other hand, states that it is only as we speak the truth in love that we grow up in relation to each other, that we become knit together and that each person offers his or her own unique strength to the process of working together. Since the truth has so often been absent in our dealings with one another, is it any wonder that, in many cases, true community between women and men is still a thing of the future?

Truth-telling can be frightening and difficult, especially in relations between the sexes, where there are many barriers such as different life experiences and differences in communication styles, and where ineffective communication patterns are already entrenched. But there is no other way for men and women to grow up in relation to each other and to become partners in growing and ministering together. There are many skills and insights that will help us to be effective in our truth-telling. We will consider some of these later (see chapters four and six). But for now we must understand that only as we work toward telling the truth in love and hearing the truth with open hearts, no matter how hard it is, will community begin to be forged among us. As we engage in truth-telling, we need to be prepared to exercise another discipline.

The Discipline of Repentance

I recently read an editorial in *Prism* magazine in which editor Dwight Ozard confesses, "I am utterly convinced that gender equality—in privilege, responsibility, service and ministry—is as essential to Biblical faith as is the conviction of racial equality."[16]

That's nice, I thought. I had heard that kind of sentiment from men before and I was glad.

But then he went beyond the normal discussions of theological, social and contextual reasons for being "a Christian feminist" to this powerful admission:

> I am a feminist because failing that, I surrender to the very worst in my nature. You see, when I am alone with myself, I know that I am a chauvinist. Despite all my protestations, rationalizations, and arguments, despite my best intentions, deep convictions, my mother and even my new wife, I am a man capable of the most vile objectification, abuse and hatred of women. I have ogled, fondled, betrayed, and ignored. I have cursed women for not fulfilling me, then cursed again for their demands on me. I have not listened. I have, in so many ways, refused to treat women as "neighbors" to "love as myself" and in so doing I have betrayed my Lord.[17]

I was eating breakfast as I read this editorial, and by the time I was finished, I was crying in my Cheerios! I had never heard or read of a man uttering those kinds of words before. I had heard men (and women) talk the theology of equality and justice, I had heard them preach through the Bible from beginning to end. I had been part of debates, discussions and planning sessions. I had heard many excuses for why things could not be changed. I had witnessed the invalidation of women's experiences of being excluded with comments such as "Well, at least women are allowed to do [fill in the blank]," or "It's not that bad," or "You have to be patient; at least we're making progress." But I had never once heard the language of confession. Never once had a man shed tears of repentance and said, "I'm sorry."

Later that week a friend gave me a copy of John Dawson's book *Healing America's Wounds,* which helped me understand my own emotional response to Ozard's editorial. Dawson describes what he calls "identificational repentance," a missing piece that has long been neglected in our attempts at reconciliation, whether between races, sexes or classes:

> If we have broken our covenants with God and violated our relationships with one another, the path to reconciliation must begin with the act of confession. The greatest wounds in human history, the greatest injustices, have not happened through the acts of some individual perpetrator, rather through the institutions, systems, philosophies, cultures, religions and governments of mankind. Because of this, we, as individuals, are tempted to absolve ourselves of all individual responsibility.
>
> Unless someone identifies themselves with corporate entities, such as the nation of our citizenship, or the subculture of our ancestors [or, I might add, our church denomination], the act of honest confession will never take place. This leaves us in a world of injury and offense in which no corporate sin is ever acknowledged, reconciliation never begins and old hatreds deepen.
>
> The followers of Jesus are to step into this impasse as agents of healing.[18]

It is important for men and women to acknowledge that we have violated God's community design for our relationships; we have sinned against each other in our individual relationships and also in the systems we have created. Our failure to confess our sins as Ozard did in his editorial has left us in "a world of injury and offense" that theological discussion alone cannot touch.

If women and men really do begin telling the truth to each other, sometimes it will take more than theological concepts and intellectual assent to take us where we need to go in our relationships. Too often, in moments when pain and injustice are uncovered, we resort to intellectualizing, making excuses and problem-solving when what the human soul needs is the cleansing tears of repentance and the opportunity to participate in the healing process by uttering the words "I am sorry." In the face of such humility and repentance, those who had been wronged are given the opportunity to extend forgiveness and to heal their own souls.

I only wish that I had the insight I have now during my interview with the Methodist pastor whose heart was wounded by the anger of the women around him. Without denying that women have good reason to be angry, I would have admitted that we have often taken it out on the men who love us. I would have identified myself with my sisters who have worked out their anger in destructive ways, and I would have said to this brother, "I am sorry."

There will be moments for all of us, as individuals and churches and institutions, when the "godly grief" that leads to repentance (2 Cor 7:10) will also be the pathway that leads to true reconciliation and partnership. May God grant us the grace to humble ourselves, to ask forgiveness and forgive. Perhaps one of the most crucial areas for us to seek true reconciliation is the area of our sexuality.

Questions for Individuals or Groups

1. Have you ever been "locked out" of something you really wanted to be a part of? How did it feel? What did you do about it?

2. What could members of the other sex bring to your life that is different from what members of the same sex bring? In what ways do you foster interdependency in these areas?

3. In what areas do you need to be more truthful in your dealings with the other sex?

4. Is there any relationship with a member of the other sex where you sense a need for repentance and reconciliation? What steps are you willing to take to bring this about?

3

The Discipline of Honoring Sexuality

*This is a society where, for the most part, men know only how
to use women, control them, or possess them;
where women manipulate men.
Intimacy seems possible only in the sex act. . . .
[But] there's a better way a few of us with strength enough,
with wisdom enough, must forge.*[1]
KAREN MAINS

I still remember the day I heard that a prominent Christian leader whom I greatly respected had had an affair. I was a young wife at the time, intent on doing everything "right" as it related to my marriage and ministry. Now I was wandering around in a daze, trying to grasp what I had heard, wishing it wasn't so, wondering what to do with this bit of reality that had intruded on my otherwise tidy life. I remember thinking *This sexuality thing is beyond our control; there is no hope for any of us.* I was truly afraid.

For several years after that I lived out of my fear, busily building hedges around my marriage and my sexuality—no lunches alone with members of the other sex for myself or my husband, office doors open in meetings with male colleagues, and relationships with men that were very limited, if they were allowed to develop at all. Eventually I discovered that the hedges I had built were so tall and so wide that they only served to strenghten my fears, keep my awareness of the goodness of sexuality in embryonic form and weaken my relationships with my brothers in Christ.

Most of us have experienced moments like this, moments when the news of someone else's infidelity and our awareness of our own temptability threaten to illuminate realities we would rather not face. In such moments the fear can feel pretty overwhelming. We may wonder, *If women and men get close to each other, won't they end up in bed together?* If we are honest, it is this fear more than any other factor that prevents us from entering the partnerships for which we were created.

In the midst of a culture in which it is often assumed that sexual urges can overtake us at any time and that close relationships between men and women inevitably end up in the bedroom, it is understandable that we would be concerned as men and women form partnering relationships. The presence of women in places of power and authority previously dominated by men—church leadership, civic and political organizations, and the workplace—can be very unsettling, because we are not accustomed to dealing with sexuality in these settings. However, the biblical mandate that men and women fully include each other in all aspects of community life requires that we face our fears about the relationship between our sexual stirrings and the spiritual passions within us.

Our fears stem, in part, from the fact that most of us have not opened up this area of our lives for careful thought and learning. Consequently, we feel ill-prepared to deal with feelings that might arise when we are in close association with persons of the other sex. If we are honest with ourselves, we are not at all convinced that we will have the strength to do the right thing when such feelings are present. The fact is, many *are* ill-prepared to deal in healthy, wholesome ways with the sexual dynamic that is present when women and men partner together, and the results are disastrous.

I would be less than honest if I did not admit that I still experience remnants of the fear that caused me to build hedges around myself. But I am now willing to make this admission: I enjoy men. I enjoy the similarities. I enjoy the differences. There is a chemistry that is produced when male and female—the core elements of the human race—get together.

Yes, there is good reason to be cautious about cross-gender relationships in a society where affairs are commonplace, divorce is no longer frowned upon and accusations of sexual harassment fly. However, it is time that we look beyond the pathology of our culture and ask, Are relationships ruled by fear and mistrust all we can hope for in the family of God? Our fears and failures point to our great need for biblically functioning community in which sexuality, or "genderedness," rather than being used to limit and exploit others, is honored, respected and even celebrated as the great gift that it is. In order to get to that point, we will need to face our fears, acknowledge their sad results and move intentionally toward wholeness.

Facing Our Fears

It was a variation on a conversation that I have had many times when interacting with people about the possibilities for close partnerships between men and women. This time it was a long-time friend whose honesty and vulnerability touched me deeply. He said, "Ruth, I don't think you understand the pull that men feel in relation to women. When I feel that pull, I just have to run because I'm not sure what would happen if I didn't. And isn't that what the Bible says—to flee temptation? I don't know what else to do with everything that I feel."

Of course my friend is not alone in his consternation about such powerful sexual yearnings. Many Christians respond to their sexuality with a mixture of denial, judgment, fear and guilt. This is not surprising, considering the fact that part of our religious heritage as Protestant Christians, and that of Catholics in particular, is an image of spirituality in which true spirituality is viewed as sexless, celibacy is the ultimate commitment to God, and bodily mortification and pain are conducive to spiritual purification.

Women as the object of men's sexual yearnings became particularly suspect. Tertullian, one of the church fathers (A.D. 160-230), wrote: "Women . . . do you not know that you are (each) an Eve? The sentence of God on this sex of yours lives in this age: the guilt must of necessity live too. *You* are the devil's gateway; *you* are the unsealer of that (forbidden) tree: *you* are the first deserter of the divine law: *you* are she who persuaded him whom the devil was not valiant to attack."[2] Augustine was "puzzled, revolted, and possibly also frightened by the power of his sexual desire. It gave women tremendous power, a power that could be neutralized by the labels *inferior* and *evil*."[3]

While we may not be familiar with the perspectives of these early theologians, their influence is very much present among us. The result is that we have inherited a dualistic approach to life that is very powerful, made more so by the fact that we hold these beliefs at an subconscious level. Just as male has been understood throughout history to be essentially different from and superior to female, so the spirit has been believed to be essentially different from and superior to the body. "The sexual dualisms, though more consciously challenged in recent years, continue to have their formidable grip on our personal lives, on our communal ethos, and on our institutional structures. One [result] is that churches simply shy away from dealing vigorously with sexuality because it seems incidental to 'the life of the spirit.' "[4]

Christian men in particular "carry a heavy load of guilt about sex and sexuality, because Christian piety values an asexual environment.... They are reminded of sex by women, as all men are, but they feel guilty about it, perhaps more than the average man, because the church has taught them that sex is evil."[5] While that may be a bit overstated, it is true that men have been socialized to view women almost exclusively as sexual objects, to the point that learning to be with women as equal partners requires a radical shift in thinking and behavior.

Some men are not aware of the fact that their fears about sexual dynamics cause them to back away from meaningful contacts with women. Others are aware of the ways in which they keep their distance, but they don't know what else to do. While their desire to live with integrity is admirable, the result is that rather than being invited into partnership, women find themselves kept at arm's length by men who have not dealt with their fears. Since the "powers that be" are still predominantly male in most churches, businesses and social organizations, women will continue to find themselves on the outside of the circles of power as long as sexual issues are ignored.

Not only is it painful to be excluded for reasons that are unstated, but women functioning in the "man's world" of work and church often experience painful feelings of self-doubt when they encounter such resistance. Most women go through moments when they entertain thoughts like *Maybe I am the problem. Maybe it is somehow my fault that my presence causes men to struggle. Maybe it would be better if I weren't around.* As a result, women learn to "manage their gender" in order to make it more comfortable for men to have them around. They are constantly concerned with finding the fine line between owning and being comfortable with their sexuality and not leaving themselves open to other (undesirable) interpretations. In addition, they cannot avoid the awareness that they are judged by aspects of their sexuality more than men are and that the judging is not always consistent.

Women may also find themselves tempted to use their sexuality in manipulative ways and/or to place too much significance on it. Being attractive can help (some men enjoy and are comfortable around attractive women), but it can also hurt (some men would rather surround themselves with plainer women so they don't have to deal with their sexual response). One never knows.

The problems I have described here are only a start, yet they help us sense the urgency of our need to move toward health and wholeness regarding the male-female dynamic. It is of utmost importance that each of us—men and women alike—take responsibility for learning what it means to honor the gift of sexuality so that we can come together in ways that are life-giving and pleasing to God. It is not necessary for us to remain victims of sin and cultural pathologies. In fact, *we stop being victims when we refuse to blame others and take responsibility for our own transformation.*

Being honest about our fears and the ways our fears have limited our ability to partner together as God intended is an important first step. It is easier to face our fears and move beyond them when we understand the connections between sexuality and spirituality.

Making the Connection

From a clinical standpoint, sexuality is "the entire range of feelings and behaviors which human beings have and use as embodied persons created male and female. Sexuality is expressed in relationship to ourselves and others through look, touch, word, and action. It includes the combinations of our gender (identity and role) and sex (anatomy and physiology)."[6] Our sexuality, while connected to all facets of ourselves, is a bodily thing.

But sexuality is so much more than just a physical reality. When considered from a psychospiritual standpoint, we understand it as our capacity for community and connectedness. "Sexuality always leads us beyond the physical stage to a far more personal need: we are driven inexorably into a desire for personal, intimate involvement with another person. The glandular urge, it turns out, is the undercurrent of a need for sharing ourselves with another person. Sexuality throbs within us as the movement toward relationship, intimacy and companionship."[7] God, who created us out of his own desire for fellowship and intimacy, placed that same capacity and desire within us and said, "It is very good" (see Gen 1:31).

Our ability to appreciate the gift of being in the world as embodied, gendered people begins with some understanding and acceptance of the fact that "sexuality is not merely some physical impulse contained in a safe-box to be let out on special, appropriate occasions. Humans are not sexual only when they participate in sexual acts, and asexual at all other times. Rather, sexuality is part of the total personality and has at least four dimensions—biological, psychological, ethical and cultural."[8]

We need to allow the realities of creation to sink deeply into our understanding. Our differentiation as male and female is very good. The fact that we have the capacity to connect deeply with others and that we have been created with bodies that can express that intimacy in physical ways is very good. Our experience of ourselves as sexual beings is very good. The sexual energy between men and women is very good. Yes, we can take that gift and use it in ways that are contrary to God's intention for the gift, and in so doing create problems for ourselves and others. *But* that doesn't mean that the gift has ceased to be good.

Most of us have arrived at the point where we can accept and perhaps even feel good about the sexuality that "throbs within us" when it is in response to our spouse or our spouse-to-be (although even then sexuality can be experienced as more of a problem that anything else). However, if we experience any hint of longing in relation to anyone else, we are quick to clamp down on ourselves with judgment and controlling measures. We pummel ourselves with verses like "Everyone who looks at a woman with lust [and it works the other way around, too] has already committed adultery with her in his heart" (Mt 5:28) and then wonder why we don't experience sexuality as a gift.

One problem with our traditional approach to managing sexuality is that we have failed to distinguish between lust and the stirrings that come from the fact that all the parts of ourselves—spiritual, relational, physical, emotional—are interconnected. The lust to which Jesus was referring in this oft-quoted passage is impulsive and anxiously self-seeking,[9] willing to take whatever it can get. Lust is hurtful and dehumanizing, because it reduces people to a single element of their personhood—their sexuality—rather than responding to them as multidimensional persons functioning in the context of many relationships and commitments. Lust doesn't care who or what it destroys to get what it wants.

The antidote to lust is love, as Paul points out in Romans 13:8-10. When there are sexual sparks in a relationship in which individuals are valued for the many facets of who they are, it is a call to love—the kind of love that would never dream of harming another person or those close to him or her. These sparks must generate energy that finds its expression in behavior that is loving, respectful and wise. It can actually become an occasion for being joyful about the fact that we are alive in all the ways that God has made us alive and cause us to be truly thankful for the beauty he has brought into our lives through other people.

It is also helpful to distinguish, as Stanley Grenz does, "between sexual desire and the desire for sex, both of which arise out of our basic sexuality." Grenz continues:

"Sexual desire" refers to the need we all share to experience wholeness and intimacy through relationships with others. It relates to the dimension often called *eros*. . . . For many people the desire for sex, the longing to express one's sexuality through genital acts *(venus)* is psychologically inseparable from sexual desire. Nevertheless, for the development of true sexual maturity, a person must come to terms with the differences between these two dimensions.[10]

The Bible tells us that our bodies are the temple of the Holy Spirit (1 Cor 6:19). In some unexplainable way God inhabits our bodies, making them a place where we can meet and know him. Since sexuality is such an important aspect of our bodily selves, this too can become an area of our lives where we meet and know God in unique ways. All of human experience is somehow connected, and all of it holds the possibility for abundant living, for the experience of grace and for the imprint of the divine. Many spiritually awake people have noticed that "our sexual feelings intensify as we are made more whole. Many think that sexuality will go away or at least become quiescent as we grow spiritually. On the contrary! As we abide more closely to the God who is the source of all creative energy, the God of the Incarnation, we begin to experience sexual energy in a new way, as a holy, inalienable, generative force."[11]

The Reverend Alice Peterson explores the connection between sexuality and spirituality when she writes,

There is a fine line between sexuality and spirituality. I believe the *experiences* of both come not from our heads but from deep within our beings. (Check out the mystics like Julian of Norwich, John of the Cross.) For many people, when they tap into these gut, primal feelings, it is very scary. Thus we tend to keep these two arenas separate. So when men and women partner together, if they are open, if they are in touch with their inner lives, the sexual part will be touched as well. And basically it is *energy*. My questions to myself revolve around how the energy will be harnessed and used to the glory of God and to my well being and those around me.[12]

Opening Our Longings to God

As we begin to awaken fully to the spiritual, social and sexual dimensions of ourselves, we find that they are inseparably intertwined and not to be compartmentalized. One of the reasons male-female relationships and the sexual energy within them are so powerful is that they have the capacity to bring us face to face with the places in the human soul where the longings of body, soul and spirit all come together. It is tremendously important that we come to understand, to grow comfortable with and to live wisely with ourselves as beings who need and desire intimacy with others.

We need to stop judging ourselves for the desires and capacities that God created within us. But this is hard because we have been taught to be ashamed of such experiences of our humanness. Shame in this context is not helpful. What *is* helpful is to bring our longings to God and say to him, "Can you touch me here in this place where I am responding to the beauty of a another human being, where an emotional/spiritual connection is causing me to long for physical expression?"

While it may seem frightening to allow ourselves such awareness and spiritual openness regarding such powerful longings, this approach actually affords us more safety than we might imagine. Why? Because opening up to our longings in the presence of God gives us the opportunity to take care of ourselves so that we will not express our sexuality in inappropriate sexual behavior. Being honest with God keeps us safe in moments when we are vulnerable.

When we sense a strong sexual attraction to a colleague, when we are feeling the need for affirmation, when we are not too thrilled with our spouse, when longings for connection stir in the context of a male-female friendship, we can open ourselves to experience God's loving, caring presence and become clearer about what is really going on inside. We might become aware that it really isn't sex we want but maybe just a hug or a meaningful connection with someone who cares about us. Maybe we will recognize an old pattern of looking for affirmation from people when we need to learn to receive it from God. Maybe we are entangled in a cultural pattern of sexualizing love, intimacy and beauty, when we need to enjoy God's gift of meaningful relationships just the way they are. There is a great deal of insight that can come to us when we are open before God in this way.

It is also important for us to realize that relational needs are legitimate, but all of them cannot possibly be met in one relationship (such as marriage). In moments when we are aware of our need for human connection and realize that we may be a bit vulnerable, we can give ourselves the gift of making a strong connection with a same-sex friend or a friend of the other gender with whom there is not a lot of sexual tension. Reaching out to someone who can provide care without the added complications of sexual tension is a much better experience than being in denial or being ruled by fear. It is about self-awareness, loving care for ourselves and others, and wisdom.

Cultivating Self-Awareness

Taking responsibility for our own transformation also involves a willingness to become aware of the issues that affect our way of being in the world and taking the initiative to work through them. An excellent example of this kind of personal responsibility came from a thirtysomething married man, who described what it was like to go back to school for an advanced degree and have young coeds flirt with him. He said, "I loved it, but it scared me so bad that I ran away—into counseling!"

We chuckled together, but I was delighted by this man's self-awareness—his willingness to recognize and name his fear—and the responsibility he demonstrated in seeking additional insight. It would have been just as easy (if not easier) for him to blame his fear on the behavior of the women who were flirting with him, to go along with the flirtation to see how far it would go or to repress his awareness of his own sexual response by becoming cold and aloof. Instead, he used it as an opportunity to learn more about himself and to deal with some of his own issues more intentionally. In the process, he came to understand his own need for affirmation from women, how he often attached sexual meaning to that need and how that pattern left him vulnerable to responding in a sexual manner to any woman who affirmed him. He realized that he tended to view sexuality as a moral sledgehammer and began exploring the possibilities for how he might retain an appropriate moral voice without pounding himself into a pulp. He also arrived at the conclusion that it is more appropriate to be genuinely loving than to be flirtatious and decided that he wanted to consciously bring that kind of an influence into his secular, academic setting.

None of us are perfectly well-adjusted sexually, and we all have areas where greater insight is needed. Therefore, it is important for us to sort through the messages we received about sexuality when we were young and to understand the patterns that we developed in response to these messages. The ways in which our needs for love, intimacy and self-esteem have or have not been met throughout our lives influence how we respond to the dynamics of male-female relationships. Unresolved difficulties in our current sexual lives can make us vulnerable to making unwise choices. Cultivating awareness along these lines gives us an expanded range of choices; rather than being captive to our unconscious needs and desires, we are able to make conscious choices to respond in ways that are life-giving to ourselves and others.

Our willingness to know and understand ourselves may also lead us to take an honest look at our marriages. As one pastor pointed out in conversation recently, "We think of adultery as being the big sin, to the point that we ignore the sin that precedes it—the sin of our passionless marriages." If the passion in our marriages has flickered and gone out, we are seriously vulnerable to misusing the sexual energy that might be present in other relationships. All marriages go through seasons when passion is the last thing that seems to characterize the relationship; this is normal, given the demands of marriage, family and the daily busyness of life. However, once we realize that the passion has dissipated, the discipline of honoring sexuality demands that we attend to ourselves and to the marriage. If it is just a matter of time and energy, the solutions may be as simple as reworking schedules and priorities. If there are deeper issues, such as unresolved conflict, issues of power and control, guilt from the past, depression or ineffective relational patterns, we may be in for a longer season of working carefully on some deeper levels—perhaps with the help of a qualified counselor. There is no price that is too great for us to pay in working to restore passion to our marriages.

We also need to be aware that men's and women's experience of their sexuality is often very different; in order to honor each other as sexual beings, we will need to listen and be sensitive to each other's needs. Because of cultural stereotypes, women often don't experience themselves as strongly sexual beings and so are not fully awake to their own needs and desires. This can leave them vulnerable to men who awaken those longings and seem capable of filling them. Many women are also unaware of their own sexual energy and how others are experiencing it, so they may find themselves sending messages that they don't wish to send. It would be much safer for women, and the men with whom they interact, if they acknowledged their sexual power and made more conscious decisions about the messages they wish to send.

Rather than being out of touch with their sexuality, men experience their sexuality as being powerful and almost uncontrollable. Many men I spoke with experienced sexuality primarily in terms of pain and struggle, guilt and fear rather than joy. Several even went so far as to say that they felt victimized by the availability of pornography, sex in the media and women who dress and act seductively. They acknowledged that they have been conditioned to view women almost exclusively as sex objects, and so relating with women as multidimensional human beings requires conscious discipline. In order to cope with their powerful sex drives in a world that seems intent on providing constant sensual stimulation, many men try to cope by distancing themselves from their sexuality. This too is a pattern of repression that sets them up for being ambushed by the sexual energy that they try to shove down. Only when a man takes personal responsibility for dealing with his sexual issues on a more conscious level will he become safer in relation to himself and the women with whom he interacts.

Becoming more self-aware and taking the initiative to work through unresolved issues does not mean we all have to run to the nearest therapist, although that may not a bad idea for some. It does mean being awake to the questions raised in the context of our relationships and seeking out resources that will help us grow. When we connect with others on a spiritual or an emotional level, when we experience their beauty, we may experience a longing for physical connection as well. Self-awareness gives us the opportunity to accept this as a natural phenomenon rather than judging ourselves harshly. We can then more fully integrate our sexuality into the whole of who we are, responding with gratitude that we are alive and able to connect meaningfully with others, without crossing the boundary of inappropriate sexual behavior.

Respecting the Power
Sexuality is one of the most powerful forces in the human experience; that is why fear has so often been our response. But sexuality is not the uncontrollable force that we sometimes experience it to be or that the popular media would have us believe that it is. Furthermore, the fear that results from this belief is inadequate as a means of managing sexuality, because it only leads us to deny our sexuality, giving it a greater power over us. Repressing our sexuality by refusing to acknowledge it or accept it or enjoy it is much like trying to push a beach ball down in the water: no matter how hard you push, when you let up on it for just a moment, it inevitably pops back up somewhere—probably where you least expect it and when you are the most unprepared to handle it.

When we experience a sexual stirring in relationship with someone of the other sex (and this happens to all of us at one time or another if we are at all alive), there are many responses we can make that are consistent with our understanding that our creation as sexual beings is both good and powerful. In addition to acceptance of and gratitude for the gift of sexuality, we respect its power by using our awareness of sexual feelings as an opportunity to lovingly care for this vulnerable part of ourselves. We harness the power by using it as a reminder of our commitment to biblical values and to doing that which is truly loving for ourselves and others.

Another way of acknowledging and living respectfully with the power of our sexuality is to bring it into the light of community. I know of one church staff team that is very intentional about fostering male-female partnerships. They deal regularly and directly with one another (and their spouses) about the sexual dynamics among them. Realizing that whenever realities are left unnamed they become much more powerful and confusing, the team members talk about sexual feelings toward others on the team. They invite each other's input and observations regarding their relationships. They have learned that intimacy that is isolated from the accountability of community can be dangerous, so they keep short accounts interpersonally and as a group. The open and disciplined way in which they manage sexual dynamics gives them a great deal of safety and thus more freedom to enter more fully into partnership.

Those of us who are willing to take the risk of greater self-awareness, opening up to the connections between sexuality and spirituality and participating in deeper-level, cross-gender relationships, need to structure a system of support and accountability for ourselves, especially when the territory is new. Such a support system might include books, classes, counseling, spiritual direction and meaningful connections with others who are biblically responsible and aware of their own sexuality. Whatever resources we choose, *it is important to choose something.* It is all a part of the "vigorous dealings" which are necessary for real growth.

Beyond Fear

We live in a culture that tends to sexualize everything that happens between men and women, whether it's friendship, love, intimacy or even fun. Men in particular have a hard time separating intimacy from "the desire for sex." Since the development of community involves increasing intimacy, it is easy to see how things can become confused if we are not careful.

Throughout Jesus' life, he demonstrated a remarkable ability to interact with women in ways that were intimate, comfortable and life-giving. He was never inappropriate, but he also wasn't prudish or overly concerned about appearances. How healing it is when—like Christ—we are able to be fully present in relationships with the other gender while seeing the best in each other *and* maintaining boundaries.

Friendliness, intimacy and even appropriate sexual energy are normal elements of deepening relationships and should not be confused with openness to a sexual encounter. Unless there is good reason to question someone's intent to do right, it is much more helpful to assume that both the man and the woman in the relationship want to do what is godly. When we think of our relationships within the community of faith in terms of our responsibility to call forth the best in each other, our number one concern is how we can help each other stay faithful to our commitments and live lives of integrity.

I am not recommending that we remain naive in situations where mixed signals are causing confusion or anxiety, or where truly seductive or manipulative behavior is in evidence. In such situations, honest communication needs to take place and guidelines about what is appropriate need to be set or clarified. If these are not honored, then perhaps there is a need for disciplinary action or a third-person intervention. But in partnering relationships between people who have been clear about their intentions and are committed to each other's best, we need to "believe all things" and act accordingly.

There is a fine line between respecting the power of sexuality and refusing to live out of our fears. It is the line that Christ walked, and it is the line that women and men today need to find together as they move toward partnership. The willingness to move beyond fear and paranoia but to do so with wisdom and purity is contrary to what we see in secular culture and also in much of the religious subculture. Celia Allison Hahn speaks of the call for men and women to partner together in the context of biblical community as a call to live faithfully in "the tension of two realities: awareness of our feelings and drives and also the call to behave in responsible ways. Sexual paradox invites us to live where the currents of energy spark back and forth. People discover new sources of vitality when they hold opposites together in tension. And there is a lot of good energy in male-female collaboration—energy that is one of the most precious gifts of God for the people of God!"[13]

Questions for Individuals or Groups

1. When have you observed or experienced a situation in which sexuality or fears about sexuality hampered partnership between men and women? What do you think might have remedied the situation?

2. How do you respond to the idea of making the connection between sexuality and spirituality? (Is it new? uncomfortable? freeing?)

3. Are you able to open your spiritual, relational and sexual longings to God? Why or why not?

4. What fears are most pressing for you right now in relation to sexuality?

5. In what area(s) of your sexuality do you need to work toward greater wholeness so that you can partner fully and appropriately with those of the other gender?

4

Tearing Down Walls, Building Bridges

The overall purpose of human communication is—or should be—
reconciliation. It should ultimately serve to lower or remove
the walls and barriers of misunderstanding that unduly
separate us human beings from each other.[1]
M. SCOTT PECK

In the introduction to his book *The Different Drum,* M. Scott Peck recounts a mythic tale about a monastery that had fallen on hard times. What had once been a great order had, for several different reasons, deteriorated to the point that there were only five monks left in a decaying main house: the abbot and four others, all over seventy years old. However, in the deep woods surrounding the monastery there was a little hut that a rabbi from a neighboring town occasionally used for personal retreats. As the abbot agonized over the fact that his order would likely die with the five monks who were left, it occurred to him that maybe the rabbi could offer some insight that might lead to a revival of the order.

The abbot decided to pay a visit to the rabbi. The rabbi welcomed his visitor but could only commiserate with him: "I know how it is. The spirit has gone out of the people. It is the same in my town. Almost no one comes to the synagogue anymore." And so the two old men wept together and spoke quietly of spiritual things. When it came time for the abbot to leave, the two men embraced each other, and the abbot asked one last time,

"Is there nothing you can tell me, no piece of advice you can give me that would help me save my dying order?" With apologies the rabbi responded that he had no advice to give. "The only thing I can tell you," he said, "is that the Messiah is one of you."

When the abbot returned to the monastery, the monks were anxious to hear what the rabbi had had to say.

"He couldn't help," the abbot answered. "We just wept and read the Torah together. The only thing he did say, just as I was leaving—it was something cryptic—was that the Messiah is one of us. I don't know what he meant."

In the weeks and months that followed the old monks pondered the rabbi's enigmatic words and wondered whether there was any significance to them. *The Messiah is one of us? Could he possibly have meant one of us monks here at the monastery? If that's the case, which one? Do you suppose he meant the abbot? Or perhaps Brother Thomas, who has always been a man of light? Certainly he could not have meant crotchety old Brother Elred or Brother Phillip. But come to think of it, Brother Elred does have a great deal of insight, and Brother Phillip does have a gift for somehow always being there when you need him. Maybe one of them is the Messiah. Of course he couldn't possibly have meant me. I'm just an ordinary person. But what if I am the Messiah? O God, not me. I couldn't be that much for You, could I?*

As they contemplated in this manner, the old monks began to treat each other with extraordinary respect on the off chance that one of them might be the Messiah. And on the off, off chance that each monk himself might be the Messiah, they began to treat *themselves* with extraordinary respect.

And so it happened that, without even being conscious of it, the people who occasionally visited the monastery began to sense an atmosphere of extraordinary respect that now surrounded the five old monks and seemed to radiate out from them. There was something strangely attractive, even compelling, about it. Hardly knowing why, they began to come back to the monastery more frequently to picnic, to play, to pray. They began to bring their friends to show them this special place. And their friends brought their friends.

Then it happened that some of the younger men who came to visit the monastery started to talk more and more with the old monks. After a while one asked if he could join them. Then another, and another. Within a few years the monastery had once again become a thriving order and, thanks to the rabbi's gift, a vibrant center of life and spirituality in the realm.[2]

A Question of Respect

Allow yourself for a moment to enter this story and imagine a setting where respect for fellow human beings is so vibrant and so real that it feeds people's souls. What would it be like to have others treat you with the kind of regard that these old monks began to extend to one another? What kind of person would you be if you were to treat others as though they were sacred and precious? What difference would it make if women and men were to approach each other with this kind of wonder and care? Though it may sound simplistic, there is a real possibility that if women and men learned to respect each other deeply—to see each other as the ones through whom God is made present among us—little else would be needed.

The story of the rabbi's gift is so moving because it answers a deep and universal human longing—to know that we are valued and truly worthwhile. For those of us who have experienced respect on some level from parents, a brother or a sister, a friend, a teacher or a mentor, we know it to be transforming. Intangible though it is, we can all sense when respect is present and when it is not. And it makes all the difference in the world.

Much of the hurt that is present in male-female relationships has disrespect (or lack of understanding about how to communicate respect) at its core. When women lump all men together as power-hungry fools and view them with thinly veiled disdain or suspicion, we are disrespecting individual men who are willing and able to share power and relate effectively. Furthermore, we close our hearts to the potential within each man to move into more effective partnership with us. When men exclude or overlook women in the process of filling leadership positions in the workplace or in the church, they are disrespecting women's identity as those who are gifted and called of God to exercise responsible dominion. When we use sexuality as a means to limit, harass or manipulate, we are disrespecting the significance of this sacred gift. When we prejudge each other and jump to negative conclusions about each other's words and behaviors without putting forth loving efforts to understand, we are not treating each other in the way that we ourselves wish to be treated.

We do not have to wonder and imagine, as the monks did, who is the special one among us. According to Scripture, each one of us is a priest charged with the responsibility of offering up spiritual sacrifices and proclaiming the excellencies of Christ (1 Pet 2:9). The tragedy in the Christian community is that our pattern of limiting up-front communication to men while women labor in relative silence and subordination behind the scenes has obscured the fact that *together* women and men are a community of priests. We cannot see it because we never have the opportunity to see it! However, when we hold ourselves in conscious awareness that we are all royal priests and when we live it out in actual partnering relationships, there will be a shift in attitudes that will begin to transform our relationships.

Cultivating Community Through Effective Communication

The words *community* and *communicate* come from the same root word meaning "to come together." Highlighting the relationship between these two words, Scott Peck points out that "the principles of good communication are the basic principles of community-building. Because people do not naturally know how to communicate, because humans have not yet learned how to talk with each other, they remain ignorant of the laws or rules of genuine community."[3] That is the bad news.

The good news, Peck continues, is that "the rules of communication and community-building can be simply taught and learned with relative ease. . . . The vast majority of people are capable of learning the rules of communication and community-building and are willing to follow them. In other words, if they know what they are doing, virtually any group of people can form themselves into a genuine community."[4]

In this chapter we will consider principles of effective communication as the primary vehicles for helping us come together in unity, especially as men and women in relationship together. We want to understand how adherence to these principles can undergird us as we move more intentionally toward partnership. But we must be clear that skills are no substitute for love and true openheartedness.

We have all been around people who have used their skills on us, making us feel like projects rather than peers. Most of us have been in at least one relationship in which there was no sense that both individuals had something to give as well as receive. In such relationships learning is not perceived as a result of partnership but rather one party always teaching and "talking at" the other. This pattern usually plays itself out among men and women in one of two ways. In situations where public communication is taking place, the men usually have the floor and talk at women without giving them equal opportunity to speak. (If you are inclined to be skeptical, think about the church services, public lectures or corporate meetings you attended in the last month. Which sex was given the most opportunities for public, planned speaking?) Women, on the other hand, seem to dominate the interpersonal communication that takes place in more intimate gatherings with family, friends and small groups. In such settings, women often talk at men without paying attention to ways they could encourage more give-and-take. In neither case is effective communication taking place.

We must be careful not to practice the laws of effective communication in a pretending sort of way in order to more effectively manipulate others, become the experts in their lives or get more work out of them. This is a subtle trap that we must constantly guard against, because the human soul seems to have special sensors that pick up on this kind of mixed message. As Stephen Covey points out, "If I sense that you're using some technique, I sense duplicity, manipulation. I wonder why you're doing it, what your motives are. And I don't feel safe enough to open myself to you."[5]

Gerard Egan, in his book *Interpersonal Living,* discusses respect as "an attitude that is expressed behaviorally,"[6] especially as it relates to the communication process. To put it more strongly: Our communication patterns and practices are primary vehicles for expressing respect or the lack of it. We learn the laws of communication and community building so that the love, respect and openness of our hearts can be experienced by others in practical ways. If technique—rather than love and openheartedness—is all we have to offer, this will eventually become apparent and communication will break down. But if we practice these skills because we want to be open to the experience of appropriately influencing others and allowing others to influence us, then they will serve us well.

Acceptance
One key component of respect is acceptance, simply recognizing the other

person as a worthy individual entitled to his or her own experiences or opinions. Men and women often have very different perceptions of and opinions about situations, ideas, experiences—even theology! When one or both assume that their thoughts and feelings are more valid than the other's, communication dies quickly. On the other hand, when we see diversity as valuable for our lives, we support others in their uniqueness. We understand that if we can resist the urge to squeeze others into our own image we will have much to learn from the knowledge and perspective they have to offer.

One way to gauge our ability to truly accept others is to observe our own responses, spoken and unspoken, as someone else shares a thought or an opinion.

☐ Is my first response to begin formulating an argument or a counterpoint to what they are saying?

☐ Am I distracted from listening to what they are saying because I am concerned about what I'm going to say next?

☐ Do I make judgments about the validity of what someone else is saying based on my own experience?

☐ When someone states an opinion that is different from my own or reflects poorly on something in which I have a vested interest (my family, the church where I serve on staff, the corporation where I am one of the executive officers, a commitee I am chairing), is my first impulse to defend my opinion or my territory?

Chances are, most of us can respond affirmatively to at least one of these questions. For some of us it takes a great deal of mental and emotional discipline to put aside our tendencies to argue, to judge, to defend and to be self-absorbed in our communication with others. Just recently, I had to confront these tendencies within myself through an interaction with my husband that was so silly it is embarrassing to mention. Yet it gave me such a clear picture of myself that I could not ignore it.

Several family members were wondering what Chris wanted for Christmas, so I asked him for a few ideas as he was getting ready to leave for work one morning. As he mused out loud about things he wanted, I found myself criticizing his choices, judging them based on my experiences and opinions. Camping gear? You haven't even been able to get away for a bike ride this season; what makes you think you'll find time to go camping? A sports Walkman? What's wrong with the Walkman you've got? And on it went.

At the time I knew the conversation was taking on a negative tone, but it was early enough in the morning (before coffee) that I was not completely clear about what was going on. However, after Chris left and I sat quietly with God before starting my day, I saw myself so clearly that it was shocking. In a matter as simple as Christmas presents, I had not been able to accept my husband's desires as valid. Rather than listening to who he was, I had judged his choices based on my own thoughts and experiences. I recognized in this small, fairly nonthreatening incident a pattern of nonacceptance that operates in other interactions in my life as well. Ironically enough, a wise friend had lovingly tried to heighten my awareness of this pattern earlier that very week, but I had yet to see it with my own eyes and feel its sad result. What a gift it was, to Chris and to me, to finally be able to see and admit to this pattern and begin consciously to move in new ways that gave him more freedom to be himself with me.

One way to develop a more accepting attitude is to acknowledge that someone else's ideas and opinions make sense to them in their context. If increased effectiveness in communication is our desire, we will seek to understand how the content of someone else's communication makes sense to them rather than arguing, offering counterpoints or defending our position. Instead of criticizing Chris's Christmas wish list, I could have easily recalled his previously expressed interest in outdoor activity. I could then have supported his desire with a response such as "I know you really want to get away more often on the weekends to camp and hike. If you do get camping gear for Christmas, I hope we can find some ways for you to get out and use it."

If men and women are to progress toward community and partnership, we will need to accept each other and support each other in our communication efforts over and over again. When women talk about their experiences in the church, home or the workplace, men need to accept these admissions rather than offer arguments, counterpoints and reasons why they do not matter. A recent cover story in *Business Week* describes a scenario in which eighty women, all partners in a large accounting firm, sat down with eight senior members—all men—of the management committee. This meeting had been called because the women wanted to know why, after a decade of gender-neutral hiring at the firm, females still made up just 8 percent of the 1,300-person partnership. Why weren't women responsible for more of the firm's key clients? Why did they head just three of the seventy regional offices?

It quickly became evident that there were differing perspectives between the women and the men. Some men believed female partners did not want to travel. Astounded, the women countered that they were eager to get out and meet clients. Even though men said they were open to lunching with female counterparts, women said they felt excluded from such informal gatherings. Opinions also diverged over whether the road to partnership favored men. "If you're in an environment mostly dominated by a male culture, many of the things you must do to succeed are more comfortable for men than women," said a female partner who chaired the gathering. The chair of the board recalls that the woman's description surprised him "but there were enough women who said it that I believe it's an issue."[7] Accepting someone else's experience as real and valid is the starting place for effective communication.

One of the reasons it is hard for us to extend this kind of acceptance or understanding—especially when we are communicating about issues on which we do not agree—is that we feel we are giving up a point in the argument. We might feel that if we acknowledge that what another person is saying makes sense on some level, that will mean we have to give up our own perspective and agree with that person. This is not the case. Acceptance does not necessarily mean that two parties agree or that change is not needed. We can still hold our own experience of a situation or our own view while acknowledging the validity of someone else's.

Acceptance means that both individuals are received as persons with valid thoughts, ideas and perspectives. As Deborah Tannen observes in her book *You Just Don't Understand,* "We all want, above all, to be heard. We want to be understood—heard for what we think we are saying, for what we know we meant."[8] When this happens through the validation inherent in phrases like "That makes sense" or "I can see why you feel that way," it can be very settling and provide some common ground as we move into the further challenges of effective communication.

Active Listening
With respect and acceptance comes a genuine desire to understand the

persons we encounter and support them as they try to make themselves known. We may be unsure, however, how to express this. Active listening provides us with several different avenues for communicating meaningfully with others.

The first and most immediate way that we show our regard and openness is through our body language. We all communicate with our bodies and read other people's body language without even knowing it. In his book *Interpersonal Living,* Gerard Egan offers an acronym that outlines some of the basic ways our bodies can communicate our attention to others as they speak. I have adapted it for our use here:

S—Face the other person *squarely,* as this is the basic posture of involvement.

O—Maintain an *open* posture. Crossed arms and legs are often a sign of defensiveness or minimal involvement.

L—*Lean* toward the other person as they speak. This is another sign of availability, presence or involvement.

E—Maintain good *eye* contact, not for the purpose of intruding or "staring them down" but to demonstrate your continued interest in what they are saying.

R—Be at home and relatively *relaxed* in this position but also in your own body. "Relative relaxation says to the other person 'I'm at home with you.' . . . An effective communicator *is* relatively comfortable with involvement and intimacy, and therefore will be relatively relaxed even in this attending position."[9]

Men and women alike sometimes experience a level of nervousness and discomfort when they are with members of the other sex. Since we are not that used to being together—as ministry peers, business colleagues or even friends—we are not "at home" with each other, and it shows. I remember many occasions in my early ministry years when I would notice that some men seemed unable to look me in the eye when they talked to me. They would look right over my head or try to work things out so that they could talk with Chris instead. It is not that bad today, but I still often sense nervousness from others, and I sometimes feel nervous myself.

It can be helpful to be aware of any nervousness, tension, defensiveness or boredom you are feeling and how you might be holding that in your body. If your fists are clenched, your arms or legs are crossed tightly, or you are having a hard time maintaining eye contact, sometimes a shift in your body position (such as opening your hands or your arms, putting both feet on the floor, moving your shoulders into a more relaxed position, reestablishing eye contact) can release some of the tension and provide renewed energy. Remembering to breathe deeply can also alleviate nervousness.

An active listener also provides timely feedback. My husband still recalls one of our earliest experiences in a small group when he shared about his struggle for balance between work, family, church and spiritual life—and nothing happened! Nobody said anything or did anything to support him. They left him, as we affectionately refer to it now, "standing there naked in the middle of the room." One of the men prayed a pious prayer that made Chris feel like he was the only one who struggled with this particular issue. It was a long time before he shared that openly in a group again.

This was a prime example of people who had loving hearts but lacked the skill to make their love and regard known. Had individuals in the group been aware of the need for timely feedback, someone might have leaned forward in their seat and said, "I'm glad you mentioned that because it's a really important issue that a lot of us struggle with," or "It sounds like you are feeling overwhelmed with all of your responsibilities in life," or "It makes sense that you are struggling with that right now. The years when you have young children, you're building a career and you're trying to contribute in your church are really intense." When we reflect someone's words back to them, we are letting them know that they have been heard and understood, that we are with them and for them in the human struggle.

Generally, women and men are still uncertain about whether the other sex is with them and for them or just tolerating them. I was aware of this dynamic as I interviewed some of my male friends and colleagues for this book. As we got into some personal issues, it was important for me to offer timely feedback rather than leave them feeling exposed. When one man shared his ongoing struggle with an addictive behavior, it was crucial for me to maintain eye contact so that he could somehow sense the love and acceptance I felt for him in that moment. As the conversation became more intense, it felt very natural for me to lean forward, with both feet on the floor, elbows on my knees, hands open as an expression of the fact that I was for him and with him in his struggle.

Another man was insightful enough about his feelings of vulnerability to say at a couple of different points in the interview, "It would really help me if you would share some of your thoughts on this question first." This was not feedback in the purest sense of the word, but it was another form of support similar to that which timely feedback provides as we risk a greater sharing of ourselves.

Another piece of the active listening process is to speak up if you are not sure what the other person means or if you are picking up emotion or body language that you do not understand. This is the process described in Proverbs 20:5 by which a person of understanding draws out the true meaning of what is in someone else's heart: "The purposes in the human mind are like deep water, but the intelligent will draw them out." Rather than assuming that we have understood the person who is speaking, we check it out to make sure that what we heard is what they really meant. The process of clarifying will include such questions as:

☐ Are you saying that? I heard you say _____.

☐ Did I understand you correctly?

☐ What do you mean when you use the word _____?

☐ I'm not quite clear on that. Could you say it differently?

When we clarify rather than assume that we understand, the speaker then knows that he or she has been heard accurately or has the opportunity to say, "Well, not exactly. What I really meant was . . ." Over time, a trust develops between people who take the time to clarify; they communicate more freely because they know that if a misunderstanding occurs, there is a process in place in the relationship for making the necessary adjustments. Not only do clarifying questions demonstrate our desire to understand, they also give the one speaking an opportunity to become clearer within themselves about their true meaning.

Empathic Listening

While the skills listed above are helpful, empathy is really the highest form of listening, as Stephen Covey points out in *The Seven Habits of Highly Effective People.* He encourages the practice of disciplining ourselves to seek first to understand, then to be understood:

Seeking first to understand involves a very deep shift in paradigm. We typically seek first to be understood. Most people do not listen with the intent to understand; they listen with the intent to reply. They're either speaking or preparing to speak. They're filtering everything through their own paradigms, reading their autobiography into other people's lives. . . . Empathic listening [on the other hand] gets inside the other person's frame of reference. You look through it, you see the world the way they see the world, you understand their paradigm, you understand how they feel.[10]

The discipline of empathy requires us to move away from our own experience as the measure of all things and to learn about life and perhaps even ourselves from someone else's vantage point. It takes a very secure person to set aside his or her own beliefs and feelings long enough to fully enter into someone else's. Covey continues:

Empathic listening is . . . risky. It takes a great deal of security to go into a deep listening experience because you open yourself up to be influenced. You become vulnerable. It's a paradox, in a sense, because in order to have influence, you have to be influenced. That means you have to really understand.[11]

Empathy is an especially important element in relationships between men and women because our experiences in our families, our churches, our society and even our bodies are so different. Our understanding of each other will be inadequate unless we know, to some degree, what it feels like to be in another's situation. When a man enters into a woman's experience by asking what it would be like to be barred—in subtle ways and not-so-subtle ways—from activities just because of one's sex, he will be changed on some level. If, after listening, he insists on holding to a view that limits women based on their sex, hopefully he will at the very least hold his views with greater sensitivity. He might even find that it becomes a starting point for seeing certain issues in new ways.

Likewise, when a woman imagines how unsettling it would be to have all of her guidelines for relating with men turned upside down, she might sense God's direction to discipline herself in taking a more compassionate approach as she communicates with the men in her life about the changes she seeks.

It is a rare and beautiful thing when men and women are willing to listen empathically before moving to the other types of communication, problem-solving and policymaking. It is hard to suspend our task orientation and our urge to problem-solve long enough to listen. Husbands and wives are probably more empathic with one another than men and women in most other settings because they have deep love and commitment; however, empathy can be a challenge even for them. In organizations and institutions the situation is often much worse. We are much more interested in unilateral communication or policymaking than we are in truly listening. In some cases, this stems from an unacknowledged fear of what might happen within us and what may be required of us if we were to put ourselves in someone else's shoes. We do not necessarily want to change or be moved, and we certainly do not want to confront new issues for which we may or may not have the answers.

At certain times we may feel that we already have all the insight we need, so listening is unnecessary. In some cases that may be true, but in the area of gender relations we are nowhere near the point where men and women understand each other so well that empathic listening is no longer necessary.

Another reason we do not avail ourselves of opportunities to listen to each other is that we believe (erroneously) that change will happen if some respected person just gets up and pronounces it so. We fail to understand real change as a process that requires empathy and understanding before we move to dialogue, discussion, large group communication, problem-solving and policymaking. Only in the context of empathic listening can we even begin to identify what the real problems are, let alone the solutions.

In order to understand each other's unique life experience more fully, Chris and I try not only to imagine what it would be like to be in each other's shoes but to actually find ways to share our worlds more fully. As I have moved into the world of work and professional life, I find that I am much more sensitive to the unremitting pressure that he experiences; I am more compassionate about the dilemmas he faces, and I am slower to offer simplistic solutions to the complexities of his life. By the same token, our efforts to share the responsibilities of home and children more fully have given him the experience of trying to schedule his own work around school hours and kids' schedules, making last-minute arrangements when a child is sick on a day he has an important meeting to go to, and dealing with the wear and tear on his patience and perspective when he has been around quarreling children all day. Because of this, Chris too has become more apt to listen than to offer the quick solutions to the stresses of my life as he often did when he had had no experience managing the home front.

As men and women begin to share more fully in each other's worlds, it will be easier for them to empathize with each other's life situations. But in the meantime, we must make the extra effort to weep with those who weep, rejoice with those who rejoice, feel frustration with those who are frustrated, pain with those who are excluded and confusion with those who are trying to understand.

Direct Communication

Recently the senior pastor of a local church called me with an invitation. He planned to initiate at his church a process for the purpose of working through the issue of women in leadership and wanted to bring in four speakers, two presenting the more traditional view and two presenting an egalitarian perspective. He wondered if this was something I would be interested in and if I could recommend any others. I told him that I enjoyed speaking on this subject and that I was just finishing a book on it; then I described the approach I would take if I were to participate in this series. I recommended several other speakers in the area as well and he said he would get back to me.

About a month later, he called back and informed me that he had invited four men to present the theological teaching. He was wondering if I would like to come on the fifth Sunday and "share about my experiences" and did I have "a lady friend" who could do the presentation with me. I was floored. I could not believe that he would invite me to take such a stereotypical role in his church's process, and I could feel the physical sensations of outrage rising up from my gut. I knew that I was facing a decision. Should I tell him how offensive his invitation was and risk having him misunderstand me? Or should I just respond politely to him and share my outrage later with women who would understand immediately how insulting this was?

It is amazing how many thoughts can go through one's mind in a split second. Crammed into one moment of silence on the phone were several levels of awareness. First of all, I was aware of how passionate I am about people telling each other the truth. I was also painfully aware of how often women do not tell the truth about their experiences in the church and society and how strongly I believe that until men and women start speaking the truth and hearing the truth, we will not progress in our personal relationships or organized structures. At the same time, my female tendencies to want to please and to be accepted were alive and kicking. That longing to be included and to have a voice in those places where men were discussing issues of life, faith and kingdom building was stirred. I knew that if I withheld the truth about how insulting this pastor's decision was, I would at least be included on some level. If I told the truth, I would probably be on the outside once again. It is a dilemma that women face all the time.

It did not take long, though, for truth to prevail. My voice shaking with emotion, I said, "I'm very disappointed that you have taken such a stereotypical approach to your series. To be honest, I am offended. I am a Bible teacher, and so even though I always include experience, I also speak from the Word. I will not put myself in a situation where the men are invited to teach authoritatively from Scripture and I am invited to share experiences. That's the way it usually is in the Christian community, and it's sad that your congregation will not have the experience of hearing a woman teach Scripture with authority." I did not even address the fact that he thought I would need or want "a lady friend" to present with me while all the male speakers, presumably, could stand on their own two feet!

To his credit, after a moment of silence this pastor said, "Well, I guess I'm not as sensitive to the issues as I thought. [Pause.] Would you be willing to come and teach from the Scriptures?" Although I had told him that I was willing to do this during our first conversation, I replied, "Yes. It's what I do."

With the assurance that he would think about what to do and get back to me, we hung up. But somehow I knew that he probably would not call me back; this sort of honest encounter can be a little hard to take. After two weeks I called him back to say that I did not want our last communication to be our last communication. I told him that I am committed to two things: I am committed to women speaking the truth about what it is like to be a part of the Christian community at this time, but I am also committed to men and women "hanging with each other" in accomplishing the changes that need to take place. I acknowledged that it is tempting for women to just walk away but that if we believe that the fundamental theological community is man, woman and God together, we need to try to continue working on our relationships.

In a somewhat tired voice he responded, "I felt duly chastened. I'm not very good with conflict—it's something the Lord is working with me on. But at this point, I need to keep the balance of two speakers for each point of view. There's nothing I can do to change the way the series is set up."

With compassion toward this man in a tender moment—a moment I had helped create—and the familiar sadness of not being able to "do what I do" within the community of faith that I love so much, I assured him that I would pray for his church as they went through this process, that I would love to hear about the outcome, that I hoped our paths would cross again. Amazingly enough, I meant it.

In these days of change and transition it is a great temptation for men and women to retreat into the safety of communicating with members of our own sex when things get a little tense. Many times it seems easier to avoid situations that involve conflict or, if conflict does occur, to talk with members of our own sex because the chances of being understood and agreed with seem higher. While these approaches may keep us within our own comfort zones, if we persist in surrounding ourselves only with members of our own sex, we will not learn anything new about the other.

Gerard Egan refers to this kind of direct communication as *immediacy,* the ability to discuss with another person directly where the two of you stand in your relationship to each other generally or to discuss what is happening between you in the here-and-now of an interpersonal transaction. He says immediacy "is one of the most important, but also one of the most difficult, of the interpersonal skills" because "it is a complex skill that involves a fair degree of social intelligence," including perception (knowing what is happening), technology (the skills we have already described, such as empathy), and courage or assertiveness.[12]

Since honest and direct communication is such a complex process, one thing is for sure: we will not always do it perfectly. No doubt one can look at the interchange I just described and make suggestions about how I could have done it differently or better and I would probably agree. But that is not the point. The point is that, without direct communication, the gulf between men and women struggling to work together will only widen.

We may not always know where direct communication of the truth will take us; I still do not know everything about what the interaction I described here accomplished. But I do know that if I had not spoken honestly with this man, he might have remained unaware of the way he had fallen into a stereotypical way of functioning that robs women of the opportunity to have a voice. Were such an approach to continue, the gulf between him and other competent women who would like to be included more equitably would only widen. Perhaps our interaction has prevented him from making the same mistake again.

I also know that if I had failed to be direct and had chosen instead to complain to my female friends about this man's lack of perceptivity, I would have violated Scripture's consistent message that we go to one another when we are hurt or offended (Mt 5:23-25; 18:15-20; Eph 4:15-16). I would have held my anger in my heart rather than opening my heart to the experience of love that did eventually come. I might have fallen into the trap of criticizing and ridiculing a brother in Christ rather than working productively for change.

We cannot wait until we are perfect to initiate the communication that needs to take place among us. While opening our hearts to the miracle of divine love, we need to step out of our comfort zones and take the risk of communicating directly with each other and of being open to others' direct communication with us. We need to bear with each other even when we do not get it quite right. For as we do, we will get better at it, and we will find over time that we are joined and knit together, building ourselves into the community we were meant to be.

Questions for Individuals or Groups

1. Describe a relationship in which you know you are deeply respected. How is this respect communicated? How does it affect the way you function in the relationship?

2. "Much of the hurt that is present in male-female relationships has disrespect (or lack of understanding about how to communicate respect) at its core." Do you agree or disagree with this statement? What difference would respect make in the male-female relationships with which you are familiar?

3. What aspect of effective communication—acceptance, active listening, empathy, directness—is most challenging for you? What step would you like to take to improve in this area?

4. What would you most like to ask members of the other sex to work on in their communication with you?

5

Beyond Stereotypes
to Partnership

*We often hear the comment that women and men
are the opposite sex. Yet we are more like each other
than anything else in creation.*[1]
ELAINE STORKEY

Do you have a boy or a girl?" Since this was the first time I had been asked this question at a fast-food drive-up window, I was a bit unprepared, but I answered the question the way it was asked. "A girl," I said, not sure why they needed to know. We proceeded to the pick-up window and soon discovered the reason for this line of questioning: in the special meals for children girls received a Barbie and boys received a racecar. My daughter was highly disappointed, for she would have much preferred a racecar, having never had an interest in Barbies. I was more than a little irritated that this fast-food company would make such sweeping generalizations about the nature of boys and girls.

I forgot about the incident until the next time we visited this establishment and I was asked the same question. Though caught off guard again, this time I understood the reason for the question and stammered, "A boy," just to make sure that my daughter did not have to add another unwanted Barbie to her collection.

My dubious methods did solve one problem: my daughter got the toy she wanted. However, it highlighted a more complicated issue which my daughter quickly raised: "Why do they think that just because you are a girl you would want a Barbie rather than a cool car?"

Thus, it became my sad duty as a mother to discuss with my ten-year-old daughter this human tendency to make assumptions about people based on their sex. I explained that it happens to boys too and reminded her of a time when she was much younger and a neighbor boy tried to join in the girls' forays into the world of Barbie and Ken. His mother told him in no uncertain terms that he was not to play with Barbies. Realizing that this was not the first or the last time she would confront her own or someone else's tendency to stereotype, we discussed other situations in which stereotyping might be even more detrimental and brainstormed effective ways of handling it.

This experience was educational for me as well, so the next time we ordered food at this restaurant I was ready. I informed the cashier in no uncertain terms that although I was buying for a girl, she wanted a car. I hoped that perhaps a little education had taken place.

The Trouble with Stereotypes

☐ "All men ever think about is sex."

☐ "Women are so emotional you just can't take them seriously."

☐ "Real men don't cry."

☐ "Give a woman an inch and she'll take a mile."

Most stereotypes are either insulting or are gross generalizations. While stereotyping is a natural process our mind engages in as it tries to sort out reality, stereotypes are damaging to women and men because they lead us to judge others prematurely and even to reject them before we have had a chance to get to know them. When we engage in stereotyping we respond to others based not on their needs and personality but on our expectations.[2]

Some of the prevailing notions about men maintain that they are aggressive, logical, unemotional, independent, dominant, competetive, objective, athletic, active and above all competent. Conversely, women have frequently been viewed as passive, nonassertive, illogical, emotional, dependent, warm and nurturing. Single women in particular wrestle with stereotypes associated with the belief in our culture that a woman is not fully mature as a woman until she has snared a man. In the workplace and in the church, they find that men view them as less credible than married women and that married women view them as a threat.

Women have been understandably offended by the limited scope of images by which they have been understood, and most men have become aware that these female stereotypes are harmful and limiting to women. More recently, however, some are beginning to understand that male stereotypes are harmful as well. Writing to men, Andrew Kimbrell, author of *The Masculine Mystique,* observes, "We treat women as sex objects, but men are treated as success symbols. You and I were taught from the time we were kids that we had one job and one job alone. We're going to be judged by our parents, our spouses, our competitive male peer group by how successful we are."[3] Kimbrell argues further that men have been indoctrinated to believe that they have no problems or that their problems are not worth talking about. Yet men's life expectancy has dropped dramatically over the last several decades, they are suffering from sexual dysfunction in epidemic proportions, and they are the primary victims of crime (63 percent more than women). In addition, the vast majority of those killed or injured on the job are men, American men are far more likely to suffer from substance addiction, men commit suicide four times the rate of women, and fathers have lost meaningful contact with their children as family courts discriminate against men in child custody decisions.[4] In short, he says, "the expectations of popular culture—and of most people—that you be strong, successful, powerful, authoritarian, and efficient—are impossible to fulfill."[5]

Neil Chethik, a frequent writer on men's issues, has this to say about his desire to be released from rigid gender stereotypes: "Biology is not destiny for men. . . . Our world would be a better place if men could break out of the rigid roles we've been taught, if we could be freer to explore different kinds of work and styles of living. . . . For when we get trapped in our work or isolated within ourselves, we risk dying a slow death, and taking others with us."[6]

Broad generalizations about maleness and femaleness are among the most common stereotypes. This is understandable since the two genders are major categories that we have tried to make sense of over the years. But as much as it might comfort us to have categories for things, it is important for us to realize that stereotyping undermines partnership in significant ways.

Stereotypes magnify the differences between men and women. A plethora of writing and research in recent years has emphasized the differences between men and women. Books such as *Men Are from Mars, Women Are from Venus; In a Different Voice; You Just Don't Understand; Talking Nine to Five;* and *The Female Advantage: Women's Ways of Leading* highlight these differences in areas such as communication, sexuality, leadership style and group behavior. These resources have been helpful on some levels and have led many readers to "Aha!" moments as they have seen themselves more clearly and gained understanding about their interactions with the other sex. I do not mean to devalue these authors' contributions when I say that we need to be careful how we interpret and apply their insights; as psychologist Harriet Golder Lerner responded when asked about John Gray's bestselling book *Men Are from Mars, Women Are from Venus,* "It's not useful to treat relationships as interplanetary."[7]

While the practice of making broad generalizations about the sexes may smooth out some rough spots in the short run, there are serious consequences in the long run. For example, painting men and women in such broad strokes makes it easier for us to categorize each other based on the group we are part of, rather than making any real effort to know each other as individuals. We may attribute certain behavior patterns to inherent, physiological differences without understanding the ways cultural influences, socialization, personality and family of origin have influenced and are influencing an individual's way of being in the world. Carol Tavris believes that the paradigm we use to conceptualize the relationship between the sexes has a direct impact on how this relationship is played out.

> Thinking of the sexes as opposites implies that women and men invariably act in opposition to one another. It implies an underlying antagonism or conflict, the pitting of one side against the other, one way (which is right and healthy) versus the other's way (which is wrong and unhealthy). Yet nothing in the nature of women and men requires us to emphasize difference and opposition. We can emphasize similarity and reciprocity. . . .
>
> As long as people think in opposites, they will be prevented from envisioning a future that would combine, for example, "male" access to power and resources with "female" values and skills. They will continue to define problems in a narrow way, instead of expanding the visions of possibility. They will continue to provoke animosities across the gender line, instead of alliances.[8]

Stereotypes lead ultimately to a distortion of the truth. There is usually a grain of truth in every stereotype; this is one reason why we accept them so readily. However, stereotypes overstate and exaggerate the truth in ways that lead ultimately to untruth. For instance, the idea that "all men ever think about is sex" is an exaggeration of the truth that most men are very interested in sex. The stereotype exaggerates this reality to the point that it is untrue because it fails to acknowledge another truth: that men are capable of thinking about other things.

My brother, who enjoys mountain biking, is quick to point out that if he were to start thinking about sex as he races down a mountain, he could end up in a ditch or worse! He wants to be known as capable of concentrating on other things and does not appreciate being reduced to the one-dimensional experience that this stereotype suggests. It is bad enough when women believe this stereotype and act accordingly, but when men start believing it, they sell themselves short as well.

Stereotypes obscure all that men and women share in common. Women often think about sex too. We might not be stimulated to think about sex by the same things as men are; we might not think the same kinds of thoughts about sex as men do. But most women need sexual intimacy, they desire sexual expression, and they spend a significant amount of time thinking about issues related to their sexuality. That men and women share this and most other aspects of human experience is obscured if we fail to confront the stereotypes. We can become convinced that men and women are hopelessly different, that we will never be able to understand each other, that women have their ways, men have their ways and never the twain shall meet.

This is only one of many areas in which we need to resist the urge to think in polarities such as "the opposite sex" when we might be better off to speak of "the neighboring sex"[9] or "the other sex."

Stereotypes oversimplify the complexities of issues and relationships. When we view individuals or groups stereotypically as "the fighting fundies," "a flaming liberal," "an angry feminist," "a male chauvinist," "a blonde bimbo" or "those prolifers who bomb abortion clinics," we see them as conforming to an unvarying pattern, and we forfeit the opportunity to consider their perspective. We have made an early judgment that makes it difficult or impossible to be open to the mystery, potential and the uniqueness of each individual.

This is often a way of avoiding the hard work that is required of us if we are to relate and work together effectively. As Kaye Cooke and Lance Lee have observed, "If men are mysterious and incomprehensible to women and women to men, then maybe we are free. We don't even have to try to understand them, pay attention to their needs, or be hurt by them. We can make jokes about them and dismiss them ('He didn't call me last night when he said he would. What else can you expect from a man?' 'She's always talking on the telephone. Yack, yack, yack. Just like a woman!')."[10] So, convinced that we can never understand each other or contribute meaningfully to each other's lives, we segregate ourselves into women's Bible studies and men's prayer groups, male elders and women's serving groups, all-male boards and women's auxiliary groups, men in management and women as support staff. By trivializing others and their concerns, we avoid having to deal in a substantial way with each other.

Stereotypes create barriers that interfere with mutual trust and interdependence. If I believe that all men ever think about is sex and that they cannot control themselves, I will find it difficult to trust them. If I assume that all men are male chauvinists who do not know how to respect women, I will conclude that it is not worth my time to share ideas with them, to brainstorm and learn together. Similarly, if a man harbors the fear that "if you give women an inch, they'll take a mile," then it will be difficult for him to share with women. If he sees women as overly emotional, easily deceived and not meant to teach men, he will have a hard time listening to his wife, a female coworker or a woman in the pulpit. Without basic trust and a willingness to share, partnership will be impossible.

Without denying that there are some differences between men and women, we can also acknowledge that gender stereotypes hurt us all because they create walls of misunderstanding and disrespect. Cultural myths about gender go far beyond what the Scriptures have to say about the meaning of maleness and femaleness. Indeed, they trap us in small boxes created by our culture rather than freeing us to become all that we are in Christ.

A Biblical Basis for Moving Beyond Stereotypes

We are, of course, not the first culture to fall into stereotyping. There were also deeply entrenched prescriptions for gender roles in ancient Jewish culture, but there were always people who went beyond the stereotypes and experienced God's blessing as they did so. In a culture where wives and daughters were little more than a father's or a husband's possession, God said to Abraham, "Whatever Sarah says to you, do as she tells you" (Gen 21:12).

In a religious system where women and girls were not even taught the Torah, the high priest Hilkiah led a group of men at King Josiah's instruction to the prophetess Huldah for spiritual guidance (2 Kings 22:11-20).

In a patriarchal society in which men sat as elders, priests and kings, Deborah sat under a tree and received God's people, offering them leadership and spiritual direction. In Judges 4 we learn that God had given Deborah a message for Barak, a general in Israel's army. He was to take ten thousand men and march to a certain mountain where God would give him a great victory against his enemy. Barak accepted her instruction without hesitation, but he insisted that Deborah go with him into battle. We are not told why Barak felt so strongly about this, but we do know that Deborah went with him and they won a great battle together.

Deborah and Barak had a highly unconventional relationship, especially for that particular period. One of the keys to their success was Barak's ability to see past Deborah's sex to her God-given strength and calling. He did not care about who got the glory; he cared about effectiveness, which he and Deborah could achieve if they teamed up together. Their example moves us to be more flexible and open in our expectations and vision for maleness and femaleness and what we can accomplish together.

Despite this refreshing example of a man and a woman who were able to move beyond stereotypes to true teamwork for the good of God's people, the Old Testament is weighted more heavily with illustrations of great dysfunction in male-female relations. In fact, by the time Christ came, Jewish men had observed women's lot in life long enough to be thanking God regularly "that I was not born a woman." Women were completely excluded from religious life, they were not taught the Scriptures (Torah), and the community that gathered in the synagogues to teach and learn and make decisions was made up of men and boys. If women were present for worship, they were kept silent behind a wall or in a balcony. Men were the undisputed leaders in the home and religious community, and women were barely even spoken to in public.

Christ, however, regularly and consistently moved people beyond their stereotypes, beyond their preconceived notions of how men and women were to relate, and thus created new norms that reflected more accurately God's heart regarding women and men and their partnership. He moved his disciples beyond stereotypes when they found him talking to an immoral Samaritan woman about theology, worship, the state of her relationships and the state of her soul. He moved self-righteous men beyond the woman-as-temptress stereotype when he came to the defense of the adulterous woman, pointing out that men as well as women were responsible for their sexual choices.

Christ shattered social norms for male-female relations when he allowed Mary to touch him and worship him and then said that her act was much more meaningful than anything that was going on in the synagogues. He pushed the disciples to respond differently to children when he instructed them to let the children come around rather than always relegating their care to the women. He disregarded religious conventions when he allowed (probably even invited) a woman to take the traditional posture of a student with a teacher and sit at his feet and learn. When he chose to appear first to a woman after his resurrection and instructed her to speak prophetically (in the truest sense of the word) to the disciples, it was clear that Christ had done something new among men and women. Christ was untainted by the sexism that characterized the society in which he lived. He consistently turned the gender myths and stereotypes of his day upside down and raised a new standard for men and women in their relationships.

There is no doubt that as we each take steps to move beyond stereotypes in our relationships with the other sex, we will be following in Jesus' footsteps. We too can move beyond the stereotypes of our day if we will work consciously in the areas discussed below.

Understanding Why We Do What We Do

As we have already discussed, stereotypes help us categorize and make sense of the constant variety in our lives. They also provide some measure of security in changing times.

There has probably never been a time in history when change has happened so rapidly. This causes understandable stress and confusion and a certain nostalgia for "simpler times" and old familiar ways. Many of our stereotypes have grown out of these old familiar ways, and we have then enshrined them as reflecting God's order for us. This makes them powerful from an emotional and psychological standpoint but also from a theological standpoint. This is particularly true when it comes to our views about roles within the family, which have far-reaching effects on opportunities for men and women to achieve true teamwork in the church and in the workplace.

It is helpful to admit that sometimes we may long for the times when sex roles were more clearly defined, when men went off to lead and initiate in the world while women stayed home, tended children and had dinner and the newspaper ready when their husbands returned. How much easier it was when no one challenged the belief that men were to be the leaders in church while women organized potluck dinners and staffed the nursery. Sometimes men wish for the kind of pampering their fathers received, and women are often tired from juggling their jobs and their home responsibilities. The movement toward including women more fully in all levels of responsibility in the life of the church and in the workplace has not been without pain and controversy.

However, the fact that change is difficult does not make it wrong, and we need to acknowledge that many of our comfortable ways of functioning are culturally conditioned notions, not prescriptions consistent with Scripture. The Bible demonstrates that women and men alike speak prophetically, teach Scripture to persons of both sexes and all ages, prepare food, discuss theology, get involved in politics, generate income and provide pastoral care. Judging from Christ's attention to children during his earthly ministry, my guess is that if he were involved in one of our churches today, he would spend at least some of his time in the nursery. In many of our homes, churches, ministries and businesses, we have a long way to go before we get back to the flexibility and freedom in gender expectations demonstrated throughout Scripture.

Being Honest About Fears of Loss

Besides the fact that stereotypes are comfortable and help us make sense out of the complexities of life, on some level we realize that we reap benefits when we cling to our stereotypes. These are benefits we stand to lose if we move beyond them. A helpful question to ask regarding stereotypes is "Who benefits from this particular stereotype, and how?"

We can be assured that someone benefits or the stereotypes would not have survived.

For instance, have you ever considered how men and women benefit from the stereotypical view that men are better-suited/called by God to visible leadership and that women are more suited/called to be followers? Men benefit because they retain a certain amount of prestige, power and control—an exhilarating experience for many. If a woman buys into the stereotypes, she avoids the risk and responsibility of leadership. She can sit back and say, "That's not my responsibility." When things are neglected or mistakes are made, she can say, "It's all the president's fault or the board of elders' fault." When a financial decision is made within the family and turns out to be a mistake, she can get herself off the hook by saying, "It's because my husband took an unwise risk."

It is easy to level blame and criticism (even if only in one's private thoughts) from the safety of nonleadership or unresponsibility. This is especially easy if we have never been required to exercise the discipline and study of digging out truth and presenting it in creative ways or sharing the equal responsibility of true partnership.

As we move beyond stereotypes, some of these benefits are lost. Men have to share power, control and the limelight as women begin getting some of the opportunities that had once been reserved for men. Women, on the other hand, have to grapple with issues of calling and personal responsibility that they never had to deal with before. They have to ask, Is God calling me to take more leadership and responsibility within my family, my church or my place of employment? What preparation will this require? Am I willing to take the risks associated with leadership and responsibility rather than sitting back in silence and passivity? For both men and women there are significant losses and responsibilities to weigh.

Even some of the nicer-sounding stereotypes—that women have a natural ability to be connected, attached, loving, peaceful, that they speak in a different voice, have different ways of knowing or different moral values—have a downside. They get men off the hook in family arrangements; they ignore men's affections and attachments and keep us believing that women or men are more suited for some jobs than for others. They also can keep us in a pattern of always looking to men for leadership (whether they are qualified or not) and always looking to women to do the work of relationships (whether it is their strength or not); in so doing, both sexes can remain passive and abdicate their personal responsibility in the areas of life they think belong to the other sex.

When we open ourselves to exploring our stereotypes in this fashion, we can achieve greater insight as to why we hold on to our stereotypes so tenaciously. At some level we know that we have something to lose or that more will be required of us if we let go of our preconceived notions. We need to face these fears of loss but also consider what we have to gain, because the benefits of moving beyond stereotypes do far outweigh the disadvantages.

Envisioning the Benefits

The benefits of moving beyond stereotypes begin as subtle shifts in attitude that move us toward new behaviors. When we see ourselves as made of the same flesh, created in the same image and sharing the spiritual journey together, we become more open to each other. How it changes my stance toward men when, rather than believing that they are invulnerable and hold all the power, I recognize that they are often full of self-doubt and vulnerability just as I am! Such a realization creates within me a desire to be an encourager rather than a critic.

The heart of a man is changed in much the same way as he realizes that the women in his life share basic human longings to have a full range of choices, to reach their potential and to contribute meaningfully in whatever area impassions them. Chances are if he understands that women's hearts beat with many of the same longings as his own, he will be empowering rather than limiting in his dealings with women.

As we open our hearts to each other, we begin to reap the benefits of greater effectiveness in marriage relationships and friendships in which men and women alike are skilled in and committed to emotional and relational work. We begin to discover the freedom that comes in churches where men and women alike take personal responsibility for their contribution to community building, pastoral care and leadership rather than laying it all on one sex or the other. We begin to see that greater diversity in leadership and decision-making increases the effectiveness of teams and committees and boards in the workplace. We discover that there is more for us to learn when we allow both men and women to teach us. We realize a quiet joy when men and women are no longer lonely for each other because we have learned to be in each other's lives in meaningful ways. We experience great relief in knowing that neither men nor women are alone in carrying the responsibility for generating income, nurturing children, solving the problems of the world, caring for the home and leading the church. We discover how much more rich and multidimensional our lives are when we share the worlds of home, work, church and government. We must keep this vision before us as we take further steps toward making this dream a reality.

Observing and Asking Questions

Many of our stereotypes, fears and even our theological beliefs are unspoken or unacknowledged, even to ourselves, and yet they affect how we function together. In order to begin developing a partnership model for men and women we must bring our own "stuff" and the stuff of our religious systems into the light of conscious thought, into the light of Scripture, into the light of the Holy Spirit's leading and teaching, and into the healing of community. We can begin by noticing subtle messages about maleness and femaleness that were sent to us as we were growing up and are still sent to us today.

1. Were girls expected to be quieter and more passive (to "act like a lady") while boys' rambunctiousness was tolerated because "boys will be boys"? How do you feel about that now?

2. Were there some emotions (e.g., anger) that were more acceptable for boys to display and some (e.g., sadness) that were more acceptable for girls?

3. Men, were you ever called a "girl" in an insulting way? When? What did this communicate about yourself as a male and about females?

4. Women, were you ever called a "tomboy"? Did you understand this as a compliment or an insult?

5. What toys did people buy for you as a child? What toys did you want?

6. What activities were you encouraged to participate in as a child? Did you sense any limits due to your sex? What is your experience of that now?

7. Who were the visible leaders of your church? Who was given the opportunity to speak? What did this communicate about maleness and femaleness? What was taught to you in your family, church and school about maleness and femaleness? Were the words consistent with unspoken messages and experiences?

8. What terminology was used in church to refer to people in general?

9. What biblical characters were referred to and taught about most often? How were these choices made?

10. Who were the teachers of children? of adults? What did this communicate?

11. Did you observe healthy male-female friendships and partnerships in your family, church and the professional lives of your parents, or did there seem to be a lot of fear and segregation?

12. Who did the relational and emotional work in your family? Who generated the income? How did this affect your understanding of power issues in your family?

13. What were you encouraged to envision for your life? Was your sex a factor?

This kind of questioning is not for the purpose of judging our past experiences as much as it is for the purpose of raising awareness. Since most stereotypes are held at an unconscious level, questions like this can bring our stereotypical beliefs to the surface so that we can make more conscious choices about our beliefs and behaviors. In the process we will probably uncover some unexpressed fears or fuzzy theology. A man might discover that his hesitancy to work with women as equal partners has little to do with his perception of their competence and lots to do with his fears about the sexual dynamic. A woman might understand that her reticence to work alongside men in a leadership capacity is not really about theological belief but about her deep-seated feelings of inadequacy and intimidation around men. Perhaps she will discover that teaching from her childhood convinced her that there were limits to how she could contribute. We might find that certain long-held beliefs do not hold up well when we ask, Where does the Bible say *that?*

Hopefully, these kinds of questions will help us evaluate our beliefs and behaviors more consciously in light of broad scriptural themes such as those outlined earlier: teamwork in the context of community, the life of Christ, early New Testament teaching about the priesthood of all believers, the interdependence of male and female, and the giving of spiritual gifts without regard to one's sex.

Being Proactive

The rubber begins to meet the road when we evaluate our relationships and structures in light of the clarity we have gained. A new set of questions begins to emerge, intended to encourage a certain proactivity in moving beyond our old familiar ways. We may look around the groups we are a part of and ask why women are under- or unrepresented in the top leadership positions. We may ask why the care of children is assumed to be the responsibility of women. We may ask why young women are not groomed for leadership positions with the same energy expended on grooming young men. Then we need to listen to the excuses, some of which we may have used ourselves, in the face of such questions.

Excuse 1. "We can't find any qualified women." This is similar to the excuse that is used when African-Americans and other minorities ask to be included. Since women are starting their own businesses, rising up through the ranks in corporations and attending seminary in unprecedented numbers, this excuse is not valid. Those who offer it as an explanation for a lack of true teamwork between men and women are not looking hard enough, are not looking in the right places or are not willing to put forth the effort that it will take to mentor women into the qualifications that are needed.

This excuse is most often put forward where women are being evaluated by men according to typically male standards such as academic credentials, lengthy résumés and polished public communication. The problem in this situation is that most women have taken more time away from the workplace and academia than men in order to raise children, put husbands through school by taking entry-level jobs, and do volunteer work. They have often had more opportunities for interpersonal communication than for public speaking. Consequently, their résumés look a little different from their male counterparts' and there may appear to be more gaps.

Until men and women share the responsibilities of childrearing and care of the home more equitably so that our "qualifications" develop at a similar pace, women will often be at a disadvantage in settings where such qualifications are being evaluated. As one woman stated, "Until there is equity in the home, there will never be equity anyplace else. Women will always be measured against the standards of men who have had forty-plus hours a week to build their careers while someone else (their wife usually) raised their children. With that kind of setup at home, the playing field will never be level at work. Women will always be behind and subjected to numbing conversations about the lack of qualified women. The ironic thing is that many of the men who are bemoaning the lack of qualified women are the ones who have wanted their wives to be home taking care of their children. The problem for the woman who dutifully carries out this role is that she takes herself out of the running for top positions in her field. If she takes fifteen to twenty years off, she may never catch up. While some women have accepted this, many women have not."

This catch-22 should encourage us to dig a little deeper than the traditional resume and academic transcript to discover what women can contribute. We can use it as an opportunity to adjust our thinking about what makes someone qualified, and to think of new and creative ways to respond to the excuses that keep us from achieving true teamwork. Perhaps we could learn to value the learning and experience that is gained in the process of raising children, managing a home, handling family finances, overseeing remodeling jobs, and volunteering in the church, school and community as they relate to opportunities in the workplace. Perhaps the personal discipline and interpersonal skill necessary for balancing the lion's share of responsibility for home and children, volunteer work, graduate schooling and a part-time job could be commensurate with the qualifications of a man who has been able to spend forty hours or more a week pursuing his career aspirations. He may have completed more schooling faster or worked full time outside the home longer, but does that necessarily mean that he is more qualified? By the same token, should a man be penalized for jumping off the fast track to focus on the home front, to put his wife through school or to give her the opportunity to focus on her career for a while? Could this not be viewed as a well-rounding experience and one that demonstrates his commitment to empowering others?

These questions point to the serious brainstorming and synergistic thinking that still need to take place among women and men who care about each other and care about partnership. A desire for partnership is not enough; we need to be proactive in our efforts to make it happen.

Excuse 2. "Women aren't 'seasoned' enough for the strategic positions of leadership in our organization." This may be true. When roles have traditionally been assigned based on sex (or race or any other characteristic that has been used to limit someone), those who have been limited to certain roles have been socialized to develop only the characteristics that will fit them for those roles.

When new opportunities open up to people who have previously been excluded, they cannot easily enter into the new roles because they have not developed the characteristics and skills that are needed. Women who have been socialized to fit the traditional role of wife, mother and support person are often unprepared for positions of responsibility in the world of work and governance. However, if we really believe that diversity is needed and that we are not adequately reflecting the image of God when we lack representation by one sex or the other, we need to be proactive. In many cases we will need to identify women with potential, passion and willingness to learn and groom them to move into the roles that have been traditionally reserved for men. Women and men need to work carefully to craft a lifestyle in which both have the opportunity to make contributions in the home and beyond (see chapters eight and nine). At times we may decide not to move ahead on a task until we have a well-balanced team of women and men in place. We may decide not to add someone to the board, the vacant upper-management spot or church staff team until we find persons who will add the diversity that demonstrates our belief in partnership.

Excuse 3. "Well, you know, it's a good ol' boys' club; the men just wouldn't be as comfortable with women around." Although it is becoming increasingly "politically incorrect" to put this excuse into words, the sentiment still exists. Sometimes it is put in kinder, gentler terms such as "We're just not ready to include women." My answer to this excuse is not very charitable, but I usually try to temper it in some way. I generally say something like, "So it's a good ol' boys' club. So what? Just because it would be hard to change and it would make people uncomfortable doesn't mean we should leave things as they are." Someone needs to confront this excuse whether it is expressed in words or not. When any one of us recognizes this insidious excuse, we must find the courage to bring it to light and work for change.

Allowing Ourselves to Be in Process

One woman remembers a time when an opportunity opened up for someone to oversee her church's small group ministry. The pastor who was charged with filling this position chose a man who was already overloaded and not even sure he could give adequate time to it. Meanwhile, this woman had just stepped down from a staff position at the church and had some time available. Since she had already been involved in the small group ministry and had a passion for it, she was curious as to why she had not even been considered for the opportunity.

When she asked her pastor how he had gone about choosing someone to oversee the ministry, he admitted that he had only considered his friends—people with whom he prayed regularly or played basketball. Because these persons all happened to be male, the thought of considering a woman had not even crossed his mind. He was not aware that this is a natural consequence when persons network and develop friendships only with others of the same sex.

Happily, this man's nondefensive attitude and the good working relationship he had with this woman enabled them to talk through the issue. His awareness was raised about how his patterns of thinking and choosing were limiting to women, even though it had been completely unintentional. This woman felt that she had been heard and that there was a good chance things could be different in the future—at least in their little corner of the world. Best of all, their community and their partnership in their desire to build this church had been preserved.

Going beyond stereotypes is not a one-stage process. Moving toward partnership requires as much attention as the actual tasks we are trying to accomplish through our partnership. The way the process is handled— with honesty, time for listening and deepening our understanding, a willingness to see ourselves for who we are, to repent and extend forgiveness—will give us the opportunity to build community and to partner in growing and stretching each other.

There is nothing shameful about being in process, about knowing that we have not arrived and that there are still ways we need to grow and learn. In community we will continually need to confront our tendency to put each other in boxes and to limit each other rather than continuing to unlock the mysteries of our individuality. We will need to work consciously to create the kind of safe environment where we can say to each other, "I don't feel like you really understand me yet. Can we work on this some more?" or "Do you feel like we understand what you are saying, or would you like to add anything?" This safety will be created as we maintain an openhearted stance toward one another rather than a defensive stance.

As we share our concerns, listen more and repent when necessary, partnership will develop—sometimes without us even knowing it. When we are working at these levels, we are doing life together and coming together in ways that are healing and life-giving to ourselves and ultimately to the world.

Questions for Individuals or Groups

1. Describe a time in your life when someone treated you in a stereotypical fashion. How did you feel? How did you respond?

2. What were some of the messages about maleness and femaleness that you picked up as a child? (The questions on pp. 91-92 may help jog your memory.) How were these messages communicated?

3. How might these messages from childhood be affecting the way you regard or respond to members of the other sex today?

4. What stereotypes regarding the other sex are operative in your own life? How will you go about changing these?

6

Improving Male-Female Communication

*Communication between men and women can be
like cross-cultural communication, prey to a clash of
conversational style. Instead of different dialects,
it has been said they speak different genderlects.*[1]
DEBORAH TANNEN

I came across an article recently that illustrated the difficulty of cross-cultural communication by highlighting situations in which something was lost in the translation of marketing slogans from one language to another. For instance, when Kentucky Fried Chicken tried to market their product in China, their "finger-lickin' good" slogan translated into "eat your fingers off." When a Hong Kong dentist tried to communicate to English-speaking folks that he used the latest methods, his advertisement actually read "teeth extracted by the latest Methodists"!

My personal favorite is the story of the elevator company that set up an exhibit at a trade show in Moscow. Those staffing the table were puzzled that rather than expressing interest in the product, the Russians who came by would smile and snicker. They later discovered that a sign that was supposed to say "completion equipment" actually read "equipment for orgasms."[2]

For many of us, communication between men and women seems almost as difficult as that reflected in these advertising snafus. In fact, such widely acknowledged difficulties have led researchers such as linguist Deborah Tannen to conclude that male-female conversation is a kind of crosscultural communication. Whether one agrees with Tannen's assertion or not (her research and that of others is discussed more thoroughly later in this chapter), most men and women seem to agree that if there is any area in which men and women have "dropped the ball" in their efforts to achieve true teamwork, it is the area of communication. In preparing to write this book, I have asked many men and women what they would most like members of the other sex with whom they live, work and worship to know. If they could speak honestly and without fear of negative repercussions, what would they most like to say? Not surprisingly, a vast majority of the answers have related to communication issues.

Women's answers have included the following observations:

☐ "Men like to dominate the conversation, they 'speechify' and interrupt. I wish they would consider being a little quieter and listening more."

☐ "I want men to know that I am not on a hormonal binge—that I do have something valuable to say."

☐ "I would like to tell men that emotion, which has traditionally been perceived as a weakness in women, is really a strength."

☐ "I wish men would pay attention to me in conversation. They assume that I have no interests or input to give beyond the world of home and family, so they don't even ask me about my work or address any thoughtful questions to me."

Men, of course, have their own concerns:

☐ "I would like women to know that sometimes I do come to them for compassion, but there are other times when I just want to get the job done."

☐ "Don't take the position of 'You guys have a lot to learn; we're the teachers, you're the learners.' The general perception is 'There's not a whole lot wrong with women; we're pretty infallible creatures, and if you guys could fix yourselves it would really help everybody.' That message continues to come out, and guys get defensive."

☐ "I would like my wife to appreciate the fact that even though our communication is frustrating at times, I do want to be helpful and I am trying."

☐ "I'm not very good at reading between the lines and digging around for hidden meanings. I like women to be direct in offering their input and letting me know what's bothering them. I don't have time to play games."

Gender Differences—Real or Imagined?

When I was elected president of a community group and a male colleague was elected vice president, my first thought was about gender differences. I wondered how we would work together and what difference our genders would make.

Having read extensively on the subject, my concerns were specific: What would I do if he always tried to stay ahead of me in our conversations by interrupting, aggressively putting forth his own views, refusing to acknowledge any doubts or questions? When I expressed doubt or uncertainty and asked for his input, would he view it as a sign of weakness? If I led meetings by actively seeking dialogue and building consensus (a major value of mine), would he view it as a lack of strong leadership? If I took time at the beginning of a phone call to ask him about his family or how his day was going, would he be frustrated by my "lack of efficiency"? What would happen the first time we experienced conflict? Would my desire to work it out seem like women's relationship stuff? Would I be able to negotiate the minefield between being a strong leader and coming across as the kind of woman men experience as being overly aggressive? What would happen if I ever got emotional or—heaven forbid!—cried?

I can laugh now at these concerns because my relationship with Mark turned out to be remarkably effective and uncharacteristically free of the difficulties that often plague men and women when they work together. Over time our relationship began to move easily between friendship and working relationship, and we were blessed at times by the participation of our spouses as well. When we decided later to unpack the secrets of our success, we agreed that they included mutual respect and genuine affection, a free flow of power and influence, and a give-and-take system of sharing feedback and information.

We also noted that Mark is very comfortable in the realms of relationship and emotion, which are comfortable for me as a woman, and, being the Type A personality that I am, I am very comfortable with the task orientation that is often associated with a more masculine way of being in the world. Rather than experiencing deep gender differences, we found it almost effortless to move between what is sometimes referred to as "feminine" and "masculine" conversation and working styles. Both styles were comfortable for both us. This did not mean we were unaware of each other's sex; in fact, part of the joy of the whole thing was the awareness that we were male and female and yet our relationship worked.

It may seem strange that I would begin a chapter on gender differences in communication with an example of a male-female relationship that seemed to transcend those differences. I have chosen to begin this way as a caution against stereotyping and placing each other in simplistic categories. My partnership with Mark reminds me not to view all differences as the result of a gender gap. It has cautioned me to hold my understanding of these differences with an openness to the individual. When I asked myself about moving into a partnership with Mark, my questions were just that—questions. I honestly did not know if we would fall into some of the typical male-female difficulties, for he is a unique individual and so am I. However, it helped to be familiar with the issues because I knew what to watch for.

The first time we asked questions of each other, listened to each other and experienced a free flow of ideas that ended in a mutually agreed-upon decision, we learned that we use conversation basically in the same way. As I saw Mark stay calm, engaged and supportive in the face of someone else's emotional outburst, I knew that he was comfortable and competent in handling emotion. As I saw him skillfully draw others out in a meeting, I knew we shared a similar understanding about the purpose of meetings. I saw these early indicators as evidence that I could relax a bit because gender differences in communication were not going to be a major issue for us.

Obviously, if I had observed any of the typical gender differences, it would have made our communication a bit more challenging. But knowing about those differences would have made the territory more familiar and would have helped us work through our differences rather than allowing them to become a wall between us. Tannen believes that such knowledge can make the difference between a relationship that works and one that does not:

> Learning about style differences won't make them go away, but it can banish mutual mystification and blame. Being able to understand why

our partners, friends, and even strangers behave the way they do is a comfort, even if we still don't see things the same way. . . . And having others understand why we talk and act as we do protects us from the pain of their puzzlement and criticism.[3]

The Research: Hitting the High Points

One of the earliest works on the difference between male and female conversational styles was *In a Different Voice* (1982) by Carol Gilligan, a researcher who highlighted differences in men's and women's life experience and how that affects their communication patterns. She wrote her book in part to highlight the repeated exclusion of women from critical theory-building studies of psychological research, which has resulted in the development of theories about human development in which the voices of women are never heard. The resulting disparity between women's experience and prevailing theories of human development has generally been understood to signify a problem in women's development rather than a flaw in research methodology.

For instance, the repeated findings of one study on sex-role stereotypes found that

> the qualities deemed necessary for adulthood—the capacity for autonomous thinking, clear decision-making and responsible action— are those associated with masculinity and considered undesirable for the feminine self. The stereotypes suggest a splitting of love and work that relegates expressive capacities to women while placing instrumental abilities in the masculine domain. Yet looked at from a different perspective, these stereotypes reflect a conception of adulthood that is itself out of balance, favoring the separateness of the individual over connection to others, and leaning more toward an autonomous life of work than toward the interdependence of love and care.[4]

To rectify this imbalance, Gilligan embarked on significant research that compared adolescent boys' and girls' experiences of themselves in relationships and how that affects their communication styles and moral development. She discovered that the girls' experience of themselves in a web of interdependent relationships characterized by nurture and care was quite distinct from the boys' experience of the world as a place of hierarchy and achievement that call at times for acts of violence and aggression.

Gilligan also noted that because mothers are the ones who, for the most part, are the primary caretakers of young children, issues of identity formation are different for boys than they are for girls. Female identity formation takes place in the context of an ongoing relationship in which a girl can continue to think of herself as like her mother. Boys, on the other hand, recognize from early on that they must separate or differentiate from their primary caretaker if they are to define themselves as masculine. Their father, the person with whom they could identify strongly while continuing to develop their gender identity, is usually not as accessible to them. Thus, separation and individuation are critically tied to gender identity for boys, while for girls and women, issues of feminine identity do not depend on the achievement of separation from the mother or on the process of individuation. "Since masculinity is defined through separation while femininity is defined through attachment," Gilligan concludes, "male gender identity is threatened by intimacy while female gender identity is threatened by separation."[5]

It is not difficult to imagine the impact that these findings would have on male-female relationships and communication. They do, in fact, help us understand how certain stereotypes—such as the woman who is wanting greater intimacy and the strong, silent man who continually thwarts her efforts—have developed. Gilligan summarizes her study this way: "Men and women may speak different languages that they assume are the same, using similar words to encode disparate experiences of self and social relationships. Because these languages share an overlapping moral vocabulary, they contain a propensity for systemic mistranslation, creating misunderstandings which impede communication and limit the potential for cooperation and care relationships."[6]

Deborah Tannen's book *You Just Don't Understand* (1990) provided further observation and research about the different worlds in which boys and girls grow up. Girls, she observes, grow up in a world of small groups and pairs that emphasize intimacy and connectedness, while boys grow up in a world of larger groups that are hierarchically structured with constant competition for status. One result of this, she points out, is that men and women are often at cross-purposes in conversation. While women are concerned with establishing intimacy and connection, men are often more concerned with building status, preventing themselves from losing their place in the hierarchy, or solving a problem and moving on to the next item of business.

It is not difficult, then, to understand the disappointment that a woman might feel when she shares a problem with a man only to have him step into the role of problem-solver before she is even finished going over the details. Likewise, it is not difficult to understand why a man might experience some frustration when he approaches conversation as a means to an end and it seems like all his female companion wants to do is talk and express emotion.

One of the most helpful insights Tannen offers is the importance of learning to distinguish between the *message* and the *metamessage* in conversation. The message is the obvious meaning of an act such as sharing a problem or giving advice. However, the metamessage—the underlying message about the relations among the people involved, their attitudes about what they are saying and the person to whom they are saying it—is what really counts. The metamessage is relayed by the words in combination with nonverbal signals, such as how comments are worded and in what context, the relationship between the speaker and the listener, tone of voice, gestures and inflections. The metamessage is like the frame for the conversation, and it is on this level that problems usually occur.

For instance, many women complain that when they share a problem with a man, he is too quick to offer a solution rather than empathy or comfort. According to Tannen, when a woman shares a problem, her underlying message is a bid for an expression of understanding ("That must have been awful for you") or a similar complaint ("I know what you mean"). When she receives advice instead of this kind of reinforcement, she is likely to hear the underlying message "We're not the same. You have the problem; I have the solution." Of course this is not the meaningful connection she seeks.

Men, on the other hand, tend to be more utilitarian in their approach at conversation. They are not looking for connection; they want to get the job done. Consequently, it is easy for them to feel frustrated when, as one man put it, "women want to wallow in their problems rather than taking our advice and getting on with it." In addition, men have been socialized to be the problem-solvers for women—the knight in shining armor who comes galloping to the rescue of the damsel in distress. Consequently, when a woman shares a struggle or a complaint, men will likely offer a solution because they assume that this is what is being asked of them. Most often they do this out of a sincere desire to be helpful, but when that help is rejected, it can be painful.[7]

Once we understand that these two levels of conversation exist and begin noticing them in our conversations, we can tell each other more directly what we want and need. A woman can preface her conversation with a man about a problem by telling him what she needs. If she wants to share a problem but is not ready to brainstorm solutions, she can say, "I need to talk to you about something, and I would really like to be able to just emote for a while before we start discussing solutions." If this approach frustrates the man, he might say at some point, "I'm really frustrated because I feel like there is nothing I can do to help." The woman can then assure him that being able to sort through her thoughts and emotions with someone who is willing to listen is a great help indeed. Conversation does not have to be completely one way or another.

Chris and I often engage in conversation in this fashion, and there usually does come a time when he will say, "Can I offer a suggestion?" I find that I am usually more ready for this if he has taken some time to listen rather than quickly offering solutions. By the same token, there will be times when he will begin a conversation by saying, "I need to tell you something, but I don't really want to talk about it much right now." As both of us are more clear about what we want and need in conversation, we find that both of us are getting it more often.

The man who wanted to tell women not to take the position that "men have a lot to learn and women are pretty infallible creatures" was wishing that women would pay attention to the metamessage as they communicate with men. He was not saying, "Don't talk to us about what's bothering you." He was saying, "Don't frame it in such a way that it is insulting. We want to be respected as having something to offer in the process."

Ironically, that is what women are saying too. I remember one committee meeting where the topic was (and had been for several meetings) the lack of visible women leaders in the organization and how important it was for the men to "mentor women into leadership." After a while I began to feel that the tone of our interaction was a bit condescending. As a woman sitting there with some commendable qualifications, I was hearing the metamessage that there is not much that women can offer men, but the men have plenty of wisdom they would like to bestow on women. When I spoke up to say that I would like to see us frame our discussion more positively, perhaps by talking about what men and women could offer to each other, I was relieved to find that several in the group agreed that my impression was valid. The man who had broached the subject was able to use this as an opportunity to clarify what he meant by the word *mentor.* He was referring to the fact that the men in this organization were still the gatekeepers of power and would need to be willing to open those gates to women. I had assumed that he meant the traditional mentor-protégé relationship between a junior and a senior person in a business setting. Although the language is still a bit bothersome for me and we did not take time at that point to brainstorm a better way of framing this issue, it felt like an important moment to me because it was the beginning of dealing with both the message and metamessage in our communication.

Different Planets?

Psychiatrist John Gray entered the dialogue about gender differences in 1992 with the publication of his provocatively titled book *Men Are from Mars, Women Are from Venus.* Subtitled *A Practical Guide for Improving Communication and Getting What You Want in Your Relationships,* it is a self-proclaimed "manual for loving relationships in the 1990s" revealing "how men and women differ in all areas of their lives. Not only do men and women communicate differently but they think, feel, perceive, react, respond, love, need and appreciate differently. They almost seem to be from different planets, speaking different languages and needing different nourishment."[8]

One of the biggest challenges for a man, Gray points out, is "correctly to interpret and support a woman when she is talking about her feelings."[9] For example, women tend to use speech to express feelings and they often use various superlatives, metaphors and generalizations. Men, on the other hand, tend to use speech to convey facts and information, taking words more literally than perhaps women intend them to be taken. So when a woman says, "I feel like you never listen to me," and the man begins to argue with her about the accuracy of her use of the word *never* ("What do you mean I never listen to you? I'm listening now, aren't I?"), the sparks begin to fly. The woman may be trying to communicate that she does not feel listened to in that moment or that generally she does not feel understood; she is expecting him to respond to her *feelings* about their relationship, not to argue with her about semantics.

If one of the greatest challenges for a man is to correctly interpret and support a woman when she is talking about her feelings, the biggest challenge for a woman, says Gray, is "correctly to interpret and support a man when he isn't talking."[10] Whereas women tend to process life by talking things over with an interested listener, men tend to mull things over quietly before they respond. "Internally and silently they figure out the most correct or useful response. They first formulate it inside and then express it. This process could take from minutes to hours. And to make matters even more confusing for women, if he does not have enough information to process an answer, a man may not respond at all."[11] As difficult as it may be for women, Gray suggests that they need to fight their impulse to become scared or to feel abandoned and instead allow men to go into their caves (so to speak). After a while they will come out and everything will be fine.

In this and many other areas, Gray encourages men and women to "stop offering the method of caring that they would prefer and start learning the different ways their partners think, feel, and react."[12] This advice can prove helpful at times, but we must be careful about totally releasing ourselves to such stereotypical behaviors. Women can benefit from learning the value of silence and careful thought before speaking so that they are more effective and accurate in their communication. Men need to experience the support and clarity that can come from processing thoughts and ideas with others. They need to be careful not to use their retreat to "the cave" as a way of avoiding issues that really need to be discussed in their relationships.

Communication in the Public Arena

So far we have explored the more private conversations that take place among family and friends. But what happens when men and women communicate in the more public settings of work and governance? Deborah Tannen followed up her previously mentioned book on private speaking with a fascinating study of private speaking in the public context, *Talking from Nine to Five: How Women's and Men's Conversational Styles Affect Who Gets Heard, Who Gets Credit and What Gets Done at Work.* In this book Tannen suggests that perhaps our differing conversational styles make more of a difference than we realize.

Conversational rituals common among men often involve using opposition such as banter, joking, teasing, and playful put-downs, and expending effort to avoid the one-down position in the interaction. Conversational rituals common among women are often ways of maintaining an appearance of equality, taking into account the effect of the exchange on the other person and expending effort to downplay the speaker's authority so they can get the job done without flexing their muscles in an obvious way.

When everyone present is familiar with these conventions, they work well. But when ways of speaking are not recognized as conventions, they are taken literally, with negative results on both sides. Men whose opposition strategies are interpreted literally may be seen as hostile when they are not, and their efforts to avoid appearing one-down may be taken as arrogance. When women use conversational strategies designed to avoid appearing boastful and to take the other person's feelings into account, they may be seen as less confident and competent than they really are. As a result, both men and women often feel that they are not getting sufficient credit for what they have done, are not being listened to, are not getting ahead as fast as they should.[13]

Tannen is not advocating that men and women take on each other's styles; rather she urges everyone to be aware of and to learn from other conversational styles. She is also quick to point out that the differences she enumerates are in likelihood and degree; they are not hard and fast rules. For instance, there are women who come across as being self-assured and men who come across as tentative, but such women and men will pay the price for communicating in ways that others see as uncharacteristic of their sex. The tentative man will in some cases be viewed as a wimp, and the confident woman may be viewed as being too much like a man. We will return to Tannen's book when we discuss men and women together at work.

Is It Gender or Something Else?

Carol Tavris's book *The Mismeasure of Woman: Why Women Are Not the Better Sex, the Inferior Sex or the Opposite Sex,* urges care in how we frame our discussions of gender differences and the conclusions we draw. For instance, we have all heard and perhaps used the phrase "women's intuition" to refer to a woman's alleged special ability to "read" men and interpret male behavior. This is an interesting and widely acknowledged dynamic in male-female communication. But Tavris locates its origin in fear: "Most women learn for their own safety and security they had better try to understand and predict the behavior of men. But this is not a *female* skill; it is a *self-protective* skill, and the sex gap fades when the men and women in question are equal in power."[14]

To demonstrate the veracity of this observation, Tavris cites an experiment in which psychologist Sara Snodgrass paired men and women in work teams, variously assigning women and men to be the leaders. She discovered that

> the person in the subordinate (follower) position was more sensitive to the leader's nonverbal signals than the leader to the follower's cues. This difference occurred whether a man or woman was the leader or the follower, leading Snodgrass to conclude that "women's intuition" should properly be called "subordinate's intuition." Men, like women, manage to develop empathic skills when they need to read a boss's temper and intentions for their own security or advantage. . . . Much of the stereotype of women's innate advantage in empathy derives from the different jobs that women and men do and their different average levels of power.[15]

Here again it becomes clear that many of the differences between men and women that we have accepted as inherent are really more about the ways we have structured our society and about men's and women's experiences in that society. With that in mind, I would like to suggest that we begin to ask a new question: Are we functioning optimally if only one sex has developed skills such as intuition and empathy? According to Peter Senge, author of *The Fifth Discipline,* effective managers and people with high levels of personal mastery use all resources at their disposal—including an integration of reason and intuition.[16] So why settle for "women's intuition" when intuition is something we all need to use effectively? Rather than focusing on men and women being from different planets or speaking different languages, why not ask how we can structure our world so that both men and women have the opportunities to develop the skills associated with leading *and* following?

☐ What would happen if we broadened our thinking in this way regarding many aspects of male-female relationships?

☐ What insight would we gain if we refrained from reducing everything to gender differences and asked questions about how differences in power and life experience impact the way we relate?

☐ How might men's conversational style change if they spent as much time with children and aging parents as women do?

☐ How might women's conversational style change if they spent as much time in the public arena as men do?

☐ How might the whole tone of communication in the business community and the church change if there were as many women in charge as men?

☐ How might the cultivation of true community create new experiences that will replace the inequities that have brought about many of our differences?

☐ In what areas do we as individuals and communities and systems need to grow so that our experiences and resulting communication styles will cease to be so disparate?

☐ Is it possible that men and women could honor each other and improve communication by becoming more well-versed in each other's conversational styles?

The possibilities raised by these kinds of questions, rather than the ones that reduce everything to gender differences, is what gives me the greatest hope.

What Difference Does All This Talk About Differences Make?

In the third inning of game five of the 1996 World Series, third baseman Charlie Hayes of the New York Yankees hit the ball deep into right-center field. Outfielders Marquis Grissom and Jermaine Dye of the Atlanta Braves ran after the ball, but as they converged on it they miscommunicated, and the ball fell from Grissom's glove. The error enabled the Yankees to score later in the inning for a 1-0 win, and they went on to win the series.

Few scenarios offer a clearer example of the costly nature of ineffective communication patterns than the outcome of a game such as this. For those of us who spend time on the sidelines of athletic competitions, it can be eye-opening to observe the cost when players do not communicate effectively. I have seen many a point given up in volleyball games when two players failed to call the ball, allowing it to drop to the floor between them, or when they called it too late, leaving little time for the rest of the team to get in position. I have lost count of the number of soccer games I have attended where parents and coaches chant to the players on the field, "Talk to each other!" I have witnessed the embarrassment of the player who, in rushing to help a teammate, actually got in the way or somehow thwarted her teammate's progress.

Observing enough of these situations, one can begin to get the idea that communication is a significant issue for other kinds of teams as well. As management consultant Maureen O'Brien analyzed the 1996 World Series for the purpose of gleaning management tips: "In an organization using work or project teams, team members must learn to listen and talk to one another, because miscommunications can prove very costly."[17]

Men's and women's difficulties in communicating with each other is still proving to be costly. In many cases we have still not achieved the partnership and teamwork that would make us great. I have summarized the research on gender differences so carefully because it holds much of the insight that will help us communicate more effectively. We do not want to be like Grissom and Dye, bumping into each other in the outfield and dropping the ball. So how can we apply the knowledge we have gained and avoid such mistakes?

Resist the urge to think of one conversational style as better than the other. Both the female and the male conversational styles are equally valid; the benefit comes from being able to recognize them and use whichever style fits the occasion. A man who is part of a meeting being led by a woman may observe that she is more tentative than he would be and asks more questions than he would. Rather than assuming that she is doing so because she lacks confidence or expertise (and looking down on her for it), he can remind himself that she is communicating according to her value of caring and consensus, that there are benefits to her style and that he can probably learn something by observing her. Likewise, a woman interacting with men who rarely ask questions or request feedback can resist the urge to view this as arrogance and insensitivity and can look for ways to offer input anyway. She may have to be a little more forward than she is used to being, but that is part of the process of learning from each other and becoming better versed in each other's styles.

Gilligan's research on masculinity defined by separation and femininity defined by attachment could encourage men to explore the possibility of allowing themselves to be more meaningfully attached to others, while women might consider pushing themselves to become more independent.

We might, then, meet somewhere in the middle.

In considering Tannen's research, men might become more aware of their own tendencies to use conversation as a means of competition. Perhaps they could become more willing to voice questions, ask for feedback and listen more. Women might need to moderate (but not do away with completely) their tendency to do relational work every time they get together with men. They might need to be more assertive in conversation, putting forward their own views (whether anybody asks for them or not), speaking up when they feel that the conversational style is leaving them unsatisfied and mentioning their achievements at times so that people at least know what they are doing. To move in conversation in new ways will be hard for both men and women, but it is necessary if we want to find middle ground.

Watch for metamessages in your own and others' communication. Be willing to verbalize them and clarify them.

Be sensitive to each other's needs or wants in conversation. Feel free to ask for what you need, and then respect each other's requests in a spirit of mutuality and willingness to grow.

Resist the urge to reduce everything to gender. Instead, ask questions about power, opportunity and life experience that might contribute to the way someone communicates.

Acknowledge the difficulties and learn to laugh about them. I have another male friend with whom communication has been more challenging than it is with Mark. Part of the challenge has to do with the transitional nature of our relationship. We met when he was my seminary professor, then we became colleagues and then friends. Part of the challenge had to do with gender, and part of it had to do with our personalities and just not knowing each other that well.

At one point, after several incidents where our communication simply did not work (even though we had tried everything from phone conversations and putting things in writing to leaving long, clarifying messages on voicemail), we finally acknowledged the difficulty and laughed about it. What a moment of freedom that was! We talked for a few minutes about what some of the dynamics might be, explained our conversational styles a bit, took a deep breath and said, "Let's start at the beginning and go a little slower." He was even gracious enough to mention that he had experienced similar communication difficulties in another relationship.

This was a great relief to me, because even though I knew that these kinds of difficulties are normal, I still wondered if it was all me (a typical female response) and if he was convinced yet that I was an idiot. What a gift it was to acknowledge the difficulty, to laugh, to share responsibility and to know that we would go on.

These are the gifts of grace that we must extend to one another in our humanness as we learn to pull together in more effective relationships. We can be aware of gender differences while at the same time being surprised by the joy of relationships that are easier than we ever thought they could be. We can let the experience of being challenged and stretched be as joyful as the experience of finding comfort and ease. With one kind of relationship I receive the gift of comfort, growing in my awareness that men and women share so much of the human experience in common—a knowledge that continues to bless me and engender great love within. With the other I receive the gift of growth, of being stretched by diversity in the context of remarkable respect. It is a gift that gives me courage and faith that unity in the context of diversity is truly possible.

Questions for Individuals or Groups

1. Do you think gender differences in communication are real or imagined? Why or why not?

2. Describe a situation in which you experienced a communication challenge that seemed to be related to gender. How did you handle it? What new insights have you gained that would be helpful in similar situations?

3. Read through the questions on pages 109-10. Which question most interests you at this time? Why? With whom would you like to discuss it?

4. This chapter proposes that women and men become more well-versed in each other's communication styles. What aspect of the other sex's style would you like to incorporate into your own style?

7

Teaming Up
to Get Things Done

Creating a successful team . . . is essentially a spiritual act.
It requires the individuals involved to surrender their
self-interest for the greater good so that the whole
adds up to more than the sum of its parts.[1]
PHIL JACKSON

Since *teamwork* has become a buzzword in business circles today, many of us have at least a cursory understanding of the value of teams and the skills that make them effective. However, in their extensive interviewing for their book *The Wisdom of Teams,* Jon Katzenbach and Douglas Smith discovered a common problem: many people simply do not apply what they already know about teams in any kind of a disciplined way and thereby miss the team performance potential before them.[2] Men and women are still missing the potential inherent in a world that is rich with the diversity of male and female because they are not disciplined in applying what they know about teamwork in their relationships with each other. In this chapter we will explore the disciplines associated with teamwork that will help us pull together effectively to accomplish specific tasks.

Commit to a Common Purpose and Performance Goals
Several years ago I had the opportunity to talk with Joy, a young woman excited about starting to lead a small group Bible study with her husband,

Rick. She could hardly contain her enthusiasm as she told me, "I have so many goals and expectations for this group!" After discussing these with her, I asked if her husband shared the same goals and expectations, to which she replied, "I don't know; we haven't talked about that yet."

Joy's comment highlighted two potential problems that could occur as her work with Rick unfolded. First of all, their failure to commit themselves to a common purpose set them up for a tug of war between two sets of aspirations. Of course, there are only two possible results in a tug of war: either the opposing sides pull against each other so hard that no one moves very far in either direction, or one side is constantly pulled in the other one's direction but is not happy to be there. Either way, members of the team spend so much time and energy pulling against each other that they are unable to put their combined energies toward their common goals.

In fact, Rick and Joy experienced this dynamic in their teamworking relationship. They began to feel that they were constantly at cross-purposes, and because they had not clearly verbalized their expectations beforehand, it became difficult for them to decide on a method that would fit their purposes. They generally understood that they wanted a group characterized by practical Bible study, deep sharing and accountability. They did not state clearly enough that Joy wanted the emphasis to be on the practical nature of the discussion and on personal sharing, while Rick expected a more intellectual Bible study experience. For Rick, leadership of the group took the form of gathering little-known facts about the material they were studying, leading to the proverbial "cognitive dump." Not only did this greatly inhibit discussion and sharing within the group, it did little to help the group apply Scripture on a practical level.

Because Rick and Joy had not carefully worked out a common purpose, it became difficult for them to envision their roles in the group. If the purpose for the group was to engage in a primarily cognitive approach to Bible study, Rick's role of careful student turned teacher might have been appropriate. If the purpose was more on practical sharing, Joy was the obvious choice for leading their discussions. She had more skill and training in facilitation than Rick, but their traditional understanding regarding sex roles had caused them to fall into a pattern in which Rick did all the leading. Consequently, much of the benefit of Joy's experience was lost to the group. Joy could see that group members were growing frustrated, but she was not sure what to do about it.

Rick and Joy's difficulties are not unique. Often when we team up to get a job done, we assume—without actually clarifying—that everyone's purpose is the same. Especially when husbands and wives or other individuals who know each other well team up together, it is easy to assume that we do not need to discuss purposes and the short-term objectives that will help us accomplish them. We may think that we all share the same purpose, but these assumptions, left unstated, are usually too general to be useful, and they may or may not be an accurate reflection of people's true motivations. In addition, if we fail to thoroughly identify our mission, we may focus on one aspect of it to the exclusion of other aspects that also need our attention. For instance, in a business situation we may all be in agreement about the need to increase sales in the company; however, there may be other important aspects of our vision— such as maintaining excellent service for the customers we already have or having fun while we do it—that also need to be stated.

If Rick and Joy had taken time at the outset of their work together to clarify their purpose, many things would have been clearer: their choice of method, how they would use the gifts that each one brought to the task and how they would evaluate success and failure. With a clearly stated common purpose, it would have been natural for one to say to the other, "You know, in the beginning we said we wanted to accomplish thus and so. How do you think we are doing with that?" In the context of such a discussion, both would be free to give their input regarding their effectiveness as individuals and as a team.

Each of us brings our own expectations to our involvement in meaningful tasks. We can envision what we would like to see happen and how we hope to be a part of making it happen. Taking the time to put our vision into words and brainstorming together ways that that vision can become reality gives each member of the team a greater sense of ownership in the task. This way, each individual knows that his or her goals and ideas have become part of the foundation for planning and the standard by which success will be evaluated.

Part of the problem with the traditional pattern (intentional or unintentional) of excluding women and other minorities from groups such as boards, task forces or pastor/elder teams is that they are removed from the very process that would give them ownership of the tasks in which they are being asked to participate. We expect them to buy into the outcome of a process without being included in the process itself. But as Paul points out, there is greater joy and effectiveness when we as men and women create for ourselves opportunities to truly be "united in spirit, intent on one purpose" (Phil 2:2 NASB).

Women and men will never achieve true teamwork until they are in the same room together consciously honing purposes that reflect the values and dreams of both. As Katzenbach and Smith have discovered in their research,

> The best teams invest a tremendous amount of time and effort exploring, shaping, and agreeing on a purpose that belongs to them both collectively and individually. In fact, real teams never stop this "purposing" activity because of its value in clarifying implications for members. With enough time and sincere attention, one or more broad, meaningful aspirations arise that motivate teams and provide a fundamental reason for their extra effort.[3]

Cultivate a Mix of Complementary Skills

The challenge of valuing and utilizing a diversity of strengths and giftedness increases exponentially with each individual who is added to a team. But just as the greatest challenges of true teamwork are often related to managing diversity, so is the greatest power and effectiveness. It is crucial, then, that we form teams with a view to the diversity of skill and perspective that is needed to get the job done.

Almost any team would be served well with both sexes fairly represented, for women and men often bring complementary skills and emphases to whatever it is they work on together. We must be cautious, however, in discussing these differences. First of all, we need to remember that there are always exceptions to any generalization we might make; none of us wants to be shoved into categories that leave little room for individuality.

Second, there is always the fear that if we make generalizations about gender differences, they might be used against us. We are afraid that people might make judgments like "She's too concerned about relationships to make tough decisions; maybe she doesn't have what it takes to lead the team in this project" or "He is so task-oriented it won't do any good to talk about how the process feels. I'll just gut it out." We need to recognize that many women and men are finding that as they move away from stereotypes, they are able to uncover both the masculine and the feminine characteristics within themselves and access the ones that are most helpful in the moment. We do not want to hinder this kind of balance by holding too tightly to generalizations.

A third reason to be careful is that we really do not know how much the differences we observe are culturally conditioned. We do not know if, for example, women are more relational and men are more task-oriented because those are the characteristics that have been expected of them. We do not know who we will become as we give ourselves more freedom to function on the basis of personality, giftedness and passion rather than gender stereotypes, so any generalizations made here could very well change over time.

As long as we realize, then, the dangers of overgeneralization, we can take the risk of identifying several gifts that women and men bring to each other in a teamworking situation so that we can grasp the importance of having good representation from both sexes on the teams that we form. We have already mentioned that women seem to be more process-oriented than men, choosing to focus not only on the task to be accomplished but also on how to get there and how the process feels to everyone. They will often bring concern and skills related to interpersonal issues into their participation on a team because they have generally been brought up to take care of relationships.

My husband recalls a time in his banking career when a female teller supervisor who worked for him mentioned that he was too task-oriented and that the tellers needed him, as president of the office, to take more of an interest in them. In response, he made a greater effort to stop and chat, to ask how they were doing and to bring in doughnuts periodically on those early Saturday mornings. He was amazed at the way these small gestures lifted morale and contributed to the team effort. His task orientation was good for the office, but so was the supervisor's attention to the way the job was done and how relationships were faring. Since balancing task and relationship is such an important aspect of successful teamwork (as we will explore later), a team with an equal representation of males and females can bring wonderful balance.

Women's concern for relationships fosters an intimacy and an informality that is different from the atmosphere created when team members simply deal with the task and then go their separate ways. Women tend to be willing to take more relational risks and communicate more freely than men, which can significantly change the dynamics of team interactions. A man confessed to me that he finds this refreshing and easier to work with than the way some of his male coworkers "hold their cards so close to the vest." This comfort and increasing intimacy can, over the long haul, make us more effective in our work together because it keeps the wheels of teamwork humming. The downside of women's emphasis on relationships is that they can get caught up in petty issues that take time and energy away from the task. If women are open to their input, men can balance this tendency by helping them learn when to let certain things "just roll off."

Another set of complementary gifts is the male orientation toward a more authoritative leadership style and the female preference for collaboration and consensus building. Since collaboration—the willingness to share power, information and vision—is a hallmark of true teamwork, women have a strong contribution to make. They realize that with this model power must not be viewed as finite. In an empowerment model, if persons share power, everyone has more. If men are willing to share the wisdom and perspective they have gained from holding power in more traditional ways while at the same time being open to women's perspectives on new ways of sharing it, this will enhance our teamworking capabilities.

Of course, these differences can cause tension at times and make teamwork seem less comfortable than when we are working with those who approach tasks in ways more similar to our own. When we select people to join us for projects, mentoring, boards and committees, our tendency to gravitate toward our own kind limits the scope of our success. We must be proactive in including those whose gifts complement our own rather than only choosing those who make us feel comfortable.

In addition to the technical or functional expertise needed to get the job done, every team needs men and women who are skilled in troubleshooting, who understand the team-building process and have demonstrated interpersonal skills such as communication, risk-taking, conflict management, consensus building and vision casting.

Cultivate Rather Than Compete
The word *cultivate* conveys intentionality, which is required if we are to

draw out the giftedness of each member of a team. Unfortunately, we often feel threatened or competitive regarding each other's gifts. Some of us have a hard time believing that there is enough opportunity for everyone, and we experience someone else's giftedness as a diminishment of our own. At other times we might feel that we have less to offer than others on the team and choose to distance ourselves, thereby failing to offer the gifts and insights we have. Neither of these attitudes promotes true teamwork. We can instead hold before us Paul's instructions to Timothy about developing his gifts so that his progress would be evident to all (1 Tim 4:14-15).

We would do well to incorporate into our teamwork approach an ongoing process for identifying the strengths that each individual brings to the task and using them to the full in accomplishing our goals and purposes. This may be as simple as encouraging team members to set realistic goals for their own character development and spiritual growth as they set out to work together. By sharing these goals with each other we can offer each other our support, encouragement and sufficient opportunity for the development each one is seeking.

Closely linked to the idea of fully utilizing each other's gifts is a mutual commitment to shoring up areas of weakness or lack of experience. It is probably safe to say that no team will have every skill they need right from the beginning. And as they move forward in accomplishing their task, they will make new discoveries about what is needed or ways that they as individuals and as a group need to grow. This points to another great thing about teams—according to Carol Becker, they are a wonderful means toward personal learning and development.

> Their performance focus helps teams quickly identify skill gaps and the specific development needs of team members to fill them.... Once harnessed to a purpose and set of goals, natural individualism motivates learning within teams. And individualism drives the majority of us to find some way to make our own distinctive and individual contribution to the team. Accordingly, as long as the skill *potential* exists, the dynamics of a team cause that skill to develop.[4]

Sharing strengths and weaknesses and planning ways to help each other grow levels the playing field and paves the way for true teamwork. Competitiveness and pride melt away when a person is able to say, "You know, I realize that I tend to be dogmatic and a bit overbearing when we discuss things. I know I could improve my contribution to the team if I would listen more. Would you give me the high sign when I need to do less talking and more listening?" Our openness to giving and receiving observations and input regarding our participation in the team's work together contributes not only to the effectiveness of the team but also to our own individual growth through the fine-tuning of our gifts.

Develop a Common Approach

In any situation where a given task requires a team approach, team members need to agree on the specifics of how they will accomplish the goal. Such specifics include practical decisions about who will do what (e.g., call the team together, keep minutes, handle finances, communicate with the powers that be), how schedules will be set and adhered to, how the group will make and modify decisions, and what skills are still needed and how the group will go about developing those.

Of course, there is always the potential for fireworks when individuals who are very different work to achieve the right blend of personalities and gifts. However, as Carol Becker explains,

> only through the mutual discovery and understanding of how to apply all its human resources to a common purpose can a group really develop and agree on the best team approach to achieve its goal. At the heart of such long and, at times, difficult interactions lies a commitment-building process in which the whole team candidly explores who is best suited to each task as well as how all the individual roles will come together.[5]

Another piece of the team-building process is to agree on the specifics of how we want to relate to each other as we work together. Here we invite members of the team to share the relational values that will help them function optimally on a team. These can be framed as rules or as a code of conduct that governs the team's functioning. While some of our methods for working together emerge as we go along, some rules are best put out on the table at the outset. Those that pertain to attendance at meetings, freedom to express different opinions (no sacred cows), confidentiality (what stays within the group, what can be shared outside the group), everyone's doing "real work" and how we will deal with conflict within the group are especially important because initial impressions and experiences set the tone for the group as it begins the process of becoming a team. Expression of these ground rules early in the team's life together and a conscientious adherence to them will promote openness, trust and commitment, which are hallmarks of effective teamwork.

Whenever I lead teams through the process of developing a common approach, I am always delighted by how much of themselves people are willing to share when they know that their input is valued. Here we learn about what is really important to people, and we give the opportunity for each person's values to influence the values and working approach of a team. The significance of the sense of ownership and power that each person derives from this process and the safety net that it creates for our work together cannot be overestimated.

For instance, in working through this process recently with a team of which I am a part, I remember sharing that one of my highest values in a team is communicating directly with each other. I mentioned that if I had to fear that people would talk behind my back instead of coming to me directly with their input, it would be harder for me to carry out my role as team leader with confidence. I was also concerned that everyone commit themselves to doing "real work" rather than allowing a few people to do it all. Someone else expressed her belief that it is important that people follow through on their commitments; otherwise she could get left holding the bag, and she could not really afford that kind of crisis management at the current stage in her life. Another man who carried a lot of responsibility in other areas of his life said that he valued efficiency because time was so limited for him. Others shared desires that we would be able to gracefully give and receive constructive criticism, that our team would be safe enough so that we could take risks and try new things, and that there would be mutual care for each other beyond the tasks we were undertaking.

Looking back on it now, I realize that these were beautiful moments of sharing some of the values and concerns that lie closest to our hearts. After these values had been shared and written out, we had the opportunity to look at them carefully and decide if we could commit ourselves to them. When everyone was ready we made the commitment not only within our own hearts but out loud to the group. This helped to form such a strong foundation for our work together that it is hard to imagine functioning without it. When this kind of process is not carried out early in the life of a team, members set themselves up for more uncertainty, confusion and even pain as they try to figure out how to relate to each other and work together effectively. This is especially important when women and men work together because their expectations and patterns of relating can be so different.

It should never be assumed that a team's common approach is cast in stone. In fact, periodic checks to see how people are experiencing and responding to the team's way of functioning can offer opportunities for fine-tuning or even for major shifts. It is each person's responsibility to give input in a timely fashion so that patterns that are not working do not have the opportunity to become entrenched. This mutual accountability is about staying true to the commitments we have made to each other in the areas of purposes, goals and working approaches. Having committed ourselves to each other in these areas, we then have a context for evaluating successes as well as areas in which we as a team are falling short. In this context it is entirely appropriate to raise questions such as "When we began this project, we all agreed to be present at our meetings, and yet we are rarely all in attendance. This creates an extra burden for those who do show up. What do we need to do to solve this?" or "We all agreed that we would each do equivalent amounts of real work, and yet we have fallen into a pattern of two or three of us doing the lion's share of the work. We're getting burned out. How can we distribute the work more fairly?"

Teams also hold themselves mutually accountable for their success or failure at accomplishing their purposes and goals. All are responsible at different times for asking themselves, Are we accomplishing what we set out to accomplish? When we find that we are not accomplishing our goals and purposes, each of us takes responsibility for our own role in this failure. When we grow lax in following the code of conduct that governs our work together, anyone in the group can call us to account. When in the process of holding ourselves accountable we discover that we are accomplishing what we set out to do in the way we set out to do it, then the whole team deserves to celebrate!

Use Conflict Constructively

We have all experienced it. Things seem to be going along just fine as our team works on accomplishing tasks together. In our meetings we proceed placidly from one report to the next, make the decisions that need to be made and disperse to carry out our respective tasks. Then it hits. Someone is unhappy with a decision arrived at by the group, someone is frustrated regarding group process, there is an interpersonal flare-up, and all of a sudden the atmosphere is tense. For those who are directly involved in the conflict, emotions run high and it begins to feel threatening. Those who are not directly involved start to squirm, but they are also secretly relieved that they are not the ones on the hot seat. If this is the first conflict the team has experienced, people might wonder how they are going to deal with it and whether or not they will make it through.

Welcome to the real world of teamwork! As Gareth Icenogle has adapted a familiar verse, "Where two or three are gathered together—there will be conflict."[6] It is difficult enough to know what to do with conflict in the context of a culture that routinely resorts to denial, avoidance, acquiescence, aggression or abuse. Most of us simply have not been given the tools required to make conflict *constructive* rather than *destructive*. To make matters worse, women and men have different levels of tolerance and different patterns for dealing with conflict, which makes the situation even more complex. While men seem to be more willing to deal with conflict that relates to tasks and opinions, women are much more likely to express their displeasure around process and relationship issues. Once into a conflict, men generally feel more comfortable dealing with conflict on a rational level, sharing facts and perhaps some opinions that might contribute to solving the problem. If the women feel confident they may share some opinions too, but they will probably also include information about how they feel. To the men this can seem uncomfortable or irrelevant.

If both men and women in the group remain at these different levels, their communication will run on parallel tracks that never intersect in meaningful resolution. If, however, women and men are willing to stick with each other and work through their differences, they will achieve balance in dealing with conflict by paying equal attention to task and relationships, fact and feeling, the obvious and the hidden. But how can men and women respond to each other in such a way that conflict does not destroy our ability to achieve true teamwork but rather enhances it?

Affirm the value of conflict. This should happen *before* the team's first conflict by including it as one aspect of the common approach. When it is understood that conflict offers an opportunity to work through differences and adjust the team's approach in order to honor each member, some of the tension and fear associated with conflict can be relieved. It is important to affirm those who behave responsibly in helping the team to live out of this value. When someone raises a difficult issue, we can thank them for their courage. When members of the team listen to us in a nondefensive, respectful way, we can acknowledge that. When someone expresses a value that is important to them, we can receive that as a significant issue for the team. When an issue is resolved in a way that shows respect for everyone involved, we can give ourselves a few moments to celebrate it as a significant accomplishment.

Be sensitive to other's sensitivities. Simply knowing that men are not as comfortable with sharing on a "feeling" level and women are hesitant to get involved in a battle of facts and statistics can give us the opportunity to support each other in the process of using conflict constructively. If a woman recognizes that her communication is fairly passionate, she might acknowledge it by saying, "I know I'm coming across strongly on this point. It's just that this is really important to me." If an interaction becomes more personal between her and a particular man in the group and she senses that it is a bit hard for him to take, she might check in at some point and ask, "Are you okay? Are we okay?" In so doing, she acknowledges the difficulty of the situation and expresses care in the midst of conflict. Knowing that going head-to-head with a man in a conflictual situation can be intimidating for women, men can encourage women's contributions to conflict resolution by asking for their opinions, giving serious consideration to data they have gathered (even when it comes from different sources than they are used to) and listening respectfully to their interpretations.

Move beyond facts to feelings and values. Facts are an important tool for resolving conflict, but resolution cannot come from facts alone. Conflicts are fueled by our emotions, passions and pains, and run much deeper than facts.[7] Men and women will never be able to use conflict constructively until they are willing to deal on three levels: fact, feeling and values.

One woman recalls being part of a team in which the men would sometimes get together in their off hours to play golf or basketball, and in those contexts their conversation would often turn to issues facing their team. When they were all in meetings together, private jokes and information that the men had already shared would surface, making her feel like an outsider. At the time she declined to broach the subject, because she feared they would respond by saying that they had the right to get together socially and talk about whatever they wanted. She was not at all certain that her *feelings* would stand up to their *facts* or that they would even care how she felt. Since she was not yet at the point where she could move beyond her feelings to express clearly the deeply held values that motivated them, she knew that it would be hard to reach a resolution. That she was the only woman on the team and had never seen the team move constructively through a conflict only made the situation more intimidating. She never did talk about how she felt.

Today she is in a much better position to see conflict as a manageable and even helpful phenomenon. When conflicts arise within her current team, the members are relatively comfortable in allowing profitable interaction between facts, feelings and values. In a situation similar to the one she faced on the previous team, they would acknowledge the facts (the men's right to play a game of basketball together), respect the feelings (her feelings of being left out, their enjoyment of being together as guys) and work to understand the values that are represented by the conflict (the desire for everyone to feel that he or she is equally part of the team). With all of these factors clearly on the table, they would be in a position to work in a synergistic way for resolutions that honor everyone's deepest values.

Stay open to learning, to growing and to changing. Stephen Covey tells the story of David Lilenthal, the man commissioned by the United States to head the Atomic Energy Commission after World War II. Lilenthal brought together a group of highly influential people who were all accomplished in their fields and very busy. The magnitude of the task that had been assigned to them weighed heavily, and they were anxious to get on with it. The world waited, right outside their door it seemed, to see what they would accomplish.

But Lilenthal devoted several weeks to the process of allowing the team members to get to know each other. He took the time to facilitate the kind of human interaction that bonds people together, and he was heavily criticized for not doing things more "efficiently." One of the results of this "inefficient" beginning, however, was that the respect among the members of the commission was so high that if there was disagreement, instead of opposition and defense, there was a genuine effort to understand. The attitude was, "If a person of your intelligence and competence and commitment disagrees with me, then there must be something to your disagreement that I don't understand, and I need to understand it. You have a perspective, a frame of reference I need to look at." Nonprotective interaction developed, and an unusual culture was born.[8]

When men and women listen to each other and inquire of each other from this kind of open, nondefensive, respectful stance, they are able to use conflict to work through differences to greater understanding. This is difficult. It is no small thing to rein in our human tendencies to defend ourselves and our point of view at all costs. But as Peter Senge points out in his book *The Fifth Discipline,* trying to "fix" someone else's defensive routine is almost guaranteed to backfire. The only person we can really fix is ourselves, and sometimes even that seems difficult. A place to start, though, is to make the undiscussable discussable. In other words, we can learn to recognize defensiveness in ourselves or defensive routines in our teams, so that we can at least name the reality and everyone can work on it together.

When someone has the courage to name what is going on inside themselves ("I'm feeling a bit threatened by our discussion; maybe you could help me figure out where my uneasiness is coming from") or within the group ("It seems like we've made so-and-so the problem rather than looking at the problem she has raised"), the tension and negative energy in the group is shifted so that everyone can open up to more helpful ways of communicating. Someone might respond by saying, "I can see how there might have been a sharp edge to what I was saying. Let me try again," or "Thanks for saying something; I thought I was only one who was feeling uncomfortable," or "Can you remember the point in our discussion when you started to feel uncomfortable?" It is here that the possibilities for new learning and understanding begin to unfold and transform our work together. Senge advocates such honesty:

Teams stay stuck in their defensive routines only when they pretend that they don't have any. . . . It is not the absence of defensive routines that characterizes learning teams but the way defensiveness is faced. A team committed to learning must be committed not only to telling the truth about what's going on "out there" in their business reality, but

also what's going on "in here," within the team itself.[9]
The ability to work through conflict constructively is a means and also a sign of our growth in partnership. However, many of us have had such negative experiences with conflict that we are deeply afraid of it and will do almost anything to avoid it. Men have deep fears about not knowing how to cope with angry, emotional women. Women are deathly afraid of sharing how they feel for fear that they will no longer be liked or respected. All of us wonder, *If it goes badly, will we ever get past it?* We are so afraid of getting hurt or looking foolish or failing to do everything perfectly that we miss potential learning opportunities.

In moments when conflict is unfolding we can keep our perspective by opening our hearts to God and asking,

☐ What do you have for me in this?

☐ What am I supposed to notice about myself and my own patterns?

☐ What am I supposed to learn about others?

☐ How can I show love and respect to my fellow team members throughout this interaction?

☐ If I am not directly involved in the conflict, are there still ways in which I can support the process?

☐ What of my true self am I supposed to offer in this situation?

If we want to become truly effective in our partnerships, we will have to face our fears. We may need to ask ourselves, *What is the worst thing that can happen if I enter a conflict that may help us as women and men work through our differences?* As we consider this question, we may decide that the possibility of never learning what we were meant to learn and never achieving the teamwork that God intends is more frightening than conflict. We may discover with Katzenbach and Smith that taking such risks can lead a group forward: "Real teams do not emerge unless the individuals on them take risks involving conflict, trust, interdependence, and hard work. . . . Yet only when someone opens up conflict—and one or more other people respond constructively—can individual differences and concerns be discussed and molded into common goals."[10]

Keep Teamwork in the Context of Community

Katzenbach and Smith point out that high-performance teams are the ones that combine commitment to a shared mission with a commitment to one another's personal growth, well-being and success. The result, these authors found, is that the high performance team significantly outper-forms all other similar teams and outperforms all reasonable expectations for the team's success.[11]

A particularly poignant example of teamwork in the context of such committed relationships is the U.S. Navy SEALS, whose "sense of identifi-cation with the group is all but total. One great source of unit pride is that no dead SEAL has ever been left behind on the battlefield."[12] This amazing feat speaks volumes about the power of teamwork in its truest sense. It is teamwork at a rarefied level because the individuals involved have gone beyond mere commitment to a task. Their commitment to the task is inextricably interwoven with their commitment to each other—a covenant relationship, if you will—that makes for an unbeatable combination.

The U.S. Navy SEALS illustrate what is perhaps the greatest challenge facing teams, that of holding community relationships in creative tension with purpose, mission or task. It is a challenge that is built into the creation account as well. Adam and Eve were created to *be* in community with God and each other and also to *do* the tasks that God had set before them. Community without task can make us satisfied with the comfort of warm relationships to the exclusion of other callings in life. We can lose sight of our responsibility to continue partnering with God in the work of creation and in acting as agents of reconciliation and redemption. The creation mandates remind us of the continuing privilege we have of joining God and each other in work that has meaning for eternity.

On the other hand, it is also our tendency as human beings to allow physical things and tasks to rob us of the opportunity to be fully present in relationship with God and with each other. Too much task orientation can cause us to value each other only in relation to the work we are accomplishing together. When this kind of imbalance exists, people begin to suspect that once the task is completed or they cease to contribute to the task, their value lessens. Using people in this way is a dangerous pitfall that can result in great disillusionment for tender souls.

By placing work in the context of a community life that values people as image bearers regardless of their relationship to any task, we are spared such excesses. We are reminded that "the things and jobs of creation are servants to the redemption of human community. To gain the whole world but lose one's soul is the continuing tragedy of human community."[13] It is a tragic tendency that can be avoided as women and men determine to build community as they work together.

The hardest thing about balancing commitment to the task with commitment to relationships is that relationships take time and time is the commodity that we all seem to have the least of these days. Katzenbach and Smith describe how teams typically deal with their shortage of time:

Busy executives and managers too often intentionally minimize the time they spend together. In fact, even when physically together they often limit their interactions by design. Meetings get scheduled for the shortest possible time to cause the least disruption to other tasks. Agendas are strictly adhered to as the group pushes to get on with it. Too often . . . people find reasons to step out for a phone call, or they avoid attending at all. All of this yields poor results: the potential team never gives itself time to *learn* to be a team.[14]

I do not believe that every time men and women decide to work on something together it is necessary for them to become a high-performance team with the kind of commitment that characterizes the U.S. Navy SEALS. However, I am suggesting that the higher the stakes, or the more important the task, the more we should consider the kind of partnership that yields significant results. Visionary leadership of the church, pastoral care of God's people, the training of children, evangelizing the world, and leadership of our country and our world belong in the high-stakes category. Accomplishments (or the lack thereof) in these areas count for eternity, and they will require high-performance teams that utilize all that is best in men and women.

Any efforts we make in balancing our commitment to the task with our commitment to each other honors God, for it keeps us moving and responding to the creative tension that is built into our life as a community. When I, as a team leader who tends to be task-oriented, decide that our team will have dinner before a meeting, or I take time to ask a coworker about a decision he is facing or a crisis he is navigating (even though everything in me screams to get to the point and then end the conversation), I am participating in this challenge of balancing my commitment to accomplishing tasks with my commitment to realizing community.

The same is true for the person who tends to be so relationship-oriented that he is not accomplishing the tasks to which he has been called. He may choose not to get involved in a lengthy phone conversation or to cut back the time he spends networking over lunches so he can keep his nose to the grindstone until he achieves a better balance. Not only will these efforts at balancing help us become more effective, but we will find ourselves experiencing the true teamwork that is the fulfillment of our own desire to be part of something that is larger than ourselves.

Questions for Individuals or Groups

Becoming an effective team does not happen by accident; it takes careful planning and hard work. Here are several key questions that men and women working together in a variety of settings can ask and answer together as a way of increasing their effectiveness:

1. What are our goals regarding the task we are working on together, and what is our plan for accomplishing them?

2. What are the strengths that each of us brings to this task, and how can we best utilize these in accomplishing our goals?

3. What are some areas in which I would like to grow and change through our experience of working together? How might our different strengths and life experiences contribute to each other's growth process?

4. What are the relational values and working approach for which we hold ourselves mutually accountable (e.g., commitment, everyone doing an equitable amount of real work, honest and direct communication, balancing task and relationship, confidentiality, valuing diversity, promoting true dialogue)?

5. How will we deal with the issues that working together will raise in our relationship?

8

Together at Work

*The latent fears of cultural bigotry will never be purged until
men and women learn to work together and share all arenas
of human responsibility—as God has always intended.*[1]
GARETH ICENOGLE

A manager in a large insurance company hired an African-American
woman from another division of the company for a leadership position;
however, after three months he was disappointed with her performance
and considered demoting her. He explained to one of the vice presidents
of the company that when he hired her he was certain that she had
tremendous leadership skills. He was sure that her open and empowering
management style would have a great impact on the rest of the management team, but it had not panned out that way.

The vice president, puzzled that someone would contemplate demoting a fifteen-year veteran of the company—and a minority woman at
that—probed further. In the course of her conversation with this manager,
she found that he had observed his new employee in the less formal
settings of church and community and knew her to be an effective,
sensitive and influential leader. She then asked the manager, "If that's
what you know about her, why can't she bring those skills to work here?"

In a meeting between the three of them, the African-American woman
explained, "I didn't think I would last long if I acted that way here. My
personal style of leadership—that particular style—works well if you
have permission to do it fully; then you can just do it and not have to look

over your shoulder." Pointing to the manager who had planned to fire her, she added, "He's right. The style of leadership I use outside this company can definitely be effective. But I've been in this company for 15 years. I know this organization, and I know if I brought that piece of myself—if I became that authentic—I just wouldn't survive here."[2]

A lack of understanding about how to fully tap into the benefits of a diverse workplace caused this company, for a time, to miss out on the best that this woman had to offer. In fact, it almost resulted in the permanent loss of a fine leader with unique assets and perspectives to share. We can only imagine the additional stress for the woman herself as she tried to do her job while attempting to keep the most authentic and effective parts of herself hidden.

Tapping into the Benefits of Gender Diversity

Diversity is the word we use to refer to the distinctive contributions that different identity groups bring to a given situation. Honoring diversity means respecting and valuing people for who they are and what they bring. Increasingly the business community is realizing the broad ramifications involved: "Diversity is not just a human resource issue. It is a moral issue, a management issue, and a business issue."[3]

It is widely accepted that women and men often bring different leadership styles, values, strengths and perspectives to the workplace. Some business leaders are more aware than others that the best of what both sexes have to offer is needed in order for organizations to compete and succeed amid the complexities of today's marketplace. Not only is acknowledging and respecting diversity the "politically correct" thing to do, it increases an organization's effectiveness in providing goods and services, which in turn increases profitability. A business that views diversity as a strength is able to recruit and promote the best talent (rather than drawing from only part of the labor pool), creating a synergy that keeps organizations in touch with the complexities of a diverse marketplace, offering management-style options instead of the dominant style traditionally offered by white males, reducing the stress that is inevitable in a workplace where people who are different have not learned how to work together, developing professionals who are more tolerant and well-rounded, and creating a workforce that more accurately reflects the customer base.[4]

Many organizations make the mistake of measuring gender diversity by how well a company or organization recruits and retains women. If a number of women have made it into the ranks of middle management, many organizations feel that they are doing well, even if senior management and the board of directors are almost exclusively male. If they are able to place one or two women on their board or upper-management team, they may feel that they can rest on their laurels. Getting people who are different (in this case, men and women) into the organization or invited to the table where discussion and policymaking is taking place, however, is only the beginning. As the situation described at the beginning of this chapter illustrates, the greater challenge is creating an atmosphere in which people who differ from each other and/or from the established environment can feel free to bring the best of who they are to the workplace.

In an article in *Harvard Business Review,* David A. Thomas and Robin J. Ely explain that those who are outside the mainstream of a particular workplace environment (this often includes women) bring more than just "insider information" about their own people.

> They bring different, important, and competitively relevant knowledge and perspectives about how they actually *do work*—how to design process, reach goals, frame tasks, create effective teams, communicate ideas, and lead. When allowed to, members of these groups can help companies grow and improve by challenging basic assumptions about an organization's functions, strategies, operations, practices, and procedures. And in doing so, they are able to bring more of their whole selves to the workplace and identify more fully with the work they do, setting in motion a virtuous cycle.[5]

Some of the most significant questions that arise in discussions about men and women in the workplace have to do with how to reap the full benefits of all that both women and men have to offer and how to grow through the challenges that our different approaches to work and relationships present. Although the answers are complex and multifaceted, any group of men and women who are working together can tap into the benefits of the diversity represented among them by creating an atmosphere of safety and taking the necessary practical steps as an organization.

Creating an Atmosphere of Safety

Human beings seem to have a built-in mechanism for sensing when we are safe and when we are not. This applies not only to physical safety, but also to emotional and psychological safety. In relationships, professional or otherwise, if we feel that there is any risk of being hurt, ridiculed, dismissed or judged to be stupid or incompetent, our immediate reaction is to become defensive or to run and hide. On the other hand, if we know that we are respected and valued for who we are and that others want to understand us, we can take the risk of revealing our true selves and bring the best of who we are to the workplace. Several attitudes and actions will go a long way in creating this kind of safety.

Challenge our own biases. Chapter five discussed the problem of stereotyping and how our stereotypes often function on an unconscious level. Stereotyping and the sexism that results causes the most damage when it is unacknowledged. While it is impossible for us to eliminate completely all of our prejudices and biases, we can examine our attitudes toward the other sex to determine if our reactions to specific individuals are more related to our assumptions about their sex than to our actual experiences with them. As we become more aware of these hidden assumptions, we can challenge their validity.

We may ask ourselves some of these questions:

1. What biases and generalizations do I make about the other sex? For example, do I assume that men do not have feelings or that women are so relational that they cannot make tough decisions?

2. What "buzzwords" or emotional reactions are associated with these generalizations? How might these generalizations affect decisions I make about working with, interacting with, promoting or including a member of the other sex?

3. Is there anything in my behavior or in the culture of my organization that would make members of the other sex feel uncomfortable, unwelcome or discriminated against?

4. Do I ever use labels, make jokes, or display cartoons or pictures that might offend members of the other sex?

5. Do I ever schedule work-related events that exclude members of the other sex, such as all-male golf outings and sporting events or women-only lunches?

6. When I have asked for input only from members of my own sex, do I assume that I have gotten all the input I need, or do I actively seek contributions from both men and women?

7. Am I significantly more comfortable with members of my own sex than with members of the other sex? Why? Am I willing to push beyond my discomfort so that I can be more at ease?

Obviously, asking and answering these kinds of questions requires courage and at times a willingness to be brutally honest. However, individuals and groups who are willing to engage in the process of uncovering their own biases will go a long way toward creating an atmosphere in which both men and women are free to flourish and offer the best of themselves to the workplace.

Engage in dialogue. At present there is no way for men to fully know what women's experiences in a male-dominated workplace have been like or what it is like to be on the cutting edge of change. Even if they did understand it all, there is no way that men can generate all the ideas and plans that will establish workplace environments that are more equitable and comfortable for everyone. Much dialogue is still needed. *Dialogue* means literally "to speak across." When we speak across the space that divides one from another through sharing what each has to give, the dividing space is reduced. Not only do we speak across the space of our differences, we need to listen across that space as well.

One of the most consistent messages I hear from women is that they want men to listen. Even though a man's first inclination when faced with a problem might be to rush right in and fix it, for most women that is the wrong approach. Patient listening is the first step toward significant change. One administrator had this to say about the role of listening in his own change process: "I had no idea how much [sexism] hurt women. I had no idea how much pain is there. I just never thought about it. I decided, well, I'm not going to contribute more of that [pain]. If I can, I am going to do something about it."[6]

Women need to listen too, not so much to the words that men say as to the spirit behind the words. Certainly there are still men around who are condescending and discriminatory in their actions and attitudes toward women. With these men, we can feel free to challenge them in a spirit of love and power and move on if no progress is made. A principle in Christ's instruction to the disciples when he commissioned them has application for women today as they move into the workplace: "As you enter the house [or anyplace where you have come to offer what God has given you], greet it. If the house is worthy, let your peace come upon it;

but if it is not worthy, let your peace return to you. If anyone will not welcome you or listen to your words, shake off the dust from your feet as you leave that house or town" (Mt 10:12-14). However, there is a growing number of men who value and respect women and see the benefits of full partnership. They are beginning to understand the issues, but they still have questions and sincerely want to work for solutions. There is nothing more disheartening for these men than to try their best to listen and understand, only to be ridiculed or scorned. It is no wonder that some have adopted a permanent defensive posture.

On the other hand, when men and women are willing to listen and speak truly, dialogue is possible. In his book *The Fifth Discipline: The Art and Practice of the Learning Organization,* Peter Senge describes dialogue as one of the important disciplines of team learning.

> The purpose of dialogue is to go beyond any one individual's understanding. . . . In dialogue, individuals gain insights which simply could not be achieved individually. . . . In dialogue a group explores complex difficult issues from many points of view. Individuals suspend their assumptions but they communicate their assumptions freely. The result is a free exploration that brings to the surface the full depth of people's experience and thought, and yet can move beyond their individual views.[7]

Dialogue may find its beginnings among members of a task force or committee formed specifically to explore gender issues in a particular organization. This group can lead the way in raising issues related to gender diversity and in so doing free individual men and women and members of departmental teams to engage in dialogue in the context of their working relationships. Hopefully, in their own relationships and in the way they present themselves, they will become a model for how dialogue can create deeper understanding that results in more satisfying solutions.

Acknowledge the reality of the "white male system." Anne Wilson Schaef is among those who have described the prevailing paradigm of our culture as a hierarchical system in which power and influence are held by white males.[8] Practically speaking, this means that in existing systems men still hold most of the power to decide which communication styles are acceptable in the workplace, which leadership traits are most highly valued, which women will fit into the existing system, how much information is shared, to what extent others are empowered and how to "work the system" to one's advantage.

One corporate executive who spent thirty years in such a system before joining an organization run primarily by women corroborates Schaef's position:

> Corporate culture is really a white male culture. Men had the power, so we made the rules to suit ourselves. . . . Men have noticed that women don't seem to conform to all of our rules. But until very recently, most men never stopped to consider why. In fact we really didn't care much why. The corporate structure worked for men. If women wanted in, let them figure out how to make it work for them. Most men in corporate America still don't know how to deal with women.[9]

Not surprisingly, then, women often experience the workplace as a foreign land where foreign rules govern. One woman described the resultant double bind this way: "Men are graded on how well they do [work] the masculine way, and women are graded on how well they do it in a masculine way *as long as they also remain feminine.*"[10]

These are hard realities for men and women to acknowledge, and yet it is tremendously important that we do so in a spirit of truth and love. If we do not recognize where we are, we will not be able to figure out where we want to go and how we will get there. On the other hand, if we are able to acknowledge that the system within which we are functioning right now is only one paradigm among many, we might be able to open ourselves up to other ways of doing things that incorporate women's values, strengths and experiences as well.

When men acknowledge the power that they hold in the present system, they can choose to use it intentionally to include and empower women and also to challenge the system from within when it is appropriate. It is widely acknowledged among men and women alike that men have a primary responsibility to advocate for and nurture the success of women at this time. "From everyone to whom much has been given, much will be required" (Lk 12:48).

Be sensitive to gender differences in communicating and emoting. Deborah Tannen's book *Talking from Nine to Five: How Women's and Men's Conversational Styles Affect Who Gets Heard, Who Gets Credit and What Gets Done at Work* is fascinating just for the title alone!

Conversational style really does affect who gets heard, who gets credit and what gets done at work. Being careful again not to fall into stereotyping, we need to acknowledge that men are often the ones who run the meetings, which gives them an advantage right from the beginning. In addition, men tend to be more direct, they feel freer to interrupt, they are more comfortable expressing their opinions strongly and talking about their accomplishments and expertise. Aside from the tendency to interrupt, most of this is positive as long as everyone else in the group has the same freedoms.

The problem is that many women do not feel this freedom; their socialization process and their life experiences have produced a different conversational style. They tend to be more deferential and polite, they are often not comfortable talking about their accomplishments for fear of coming across as prideful, and they try to tone down their thoughts and opinions because they realize that there is serious ambivalence in our culture about strong women. In her book *When You Need to Take a Stand,* Carolyn Stahl Bohler explains why it is so difficult for women to exercise power in organizations:

> Females in our culture are reinforced in their avoidance of their own power. Not openly expressing dissent is seen as being cooperative, and not risking hurting others is seen as being sacrificial. Some men, too, may remain silent, fearing that if they speak they will hurt someone, but in general men are not as incapacitated in speaking for this reason. Neither do they have quite the same fear of ostracism for having spoken. For men, being seen as outspoken is not felt pejoratively, as it is for many women.[11]

These differences in communication style can place women at a disadvantage in workplace settings and can create tension between them and their male counterparts. For a solution to be found, two things must happen: men must pull back a little in conversation so that women can speak, and women must be more courageous and confident in expressing themselves. Men need to be aware that when a woman has spoken out strongly or expressed a dissenting view, it probably took a lot of courage, and she may have temporary feelings of misgiving once she has done so. If men can support women in this process of finding their voice, express appreciation for the different perspectives that they bring and consider whether their own conversational style invites the full participation of all persons, women will become more comfortable holding their own in the communication process. If women can believe in themselves enough to take risks in communication, if they are open to giving and receiving feedback about their communication style and fine-tuning it when necessary, gender differences in communication will not be such a significant issue.

Encourage a balanced view of emotions. In both the religious and secular aspects of our culture we tend to have a deep distrust of emotion. This puts women at a disadvantage because, in general, women are more emotionally expressive than men. This can be an area of discomfort for men as they partner with women, and women often fear losing respect and credibility if they allow the emotional side of themselves to come through.

The uneasiness that we experience in the face of deep emotion is not consistent with what we see in the Scriptures. From the Scriptures we learn that you can be angry and not sin (as Jesus did), that you can weep over the loss of a friend (as David did), that you can be beastly with jealousy and by admitting it take the first step to getting free of it (as the psalmist did), that you can sing and dance with joy (as Moses and the Israelites did), that you can weep with passion for ministry (as Paul did). Throughout the Scriptures emotions are signs of life and authentic relationship with God and others.

Our uneasiness in the face of deep emotion can result in significant losses to the team. When an organization refuses to accept emotional responses as valid or values only certain emotions, managers are forced to deny their own emotional sides, thus rendering them incapable of accepting many of the contributions that other members of the team can make.[12]

The information systems department of a company that was undergoing a complex computer conversion acknowledged and even utilized both positive and negative emotion. Rather than denying the huge demands placed on the department and the enormous stress everyone was under, the project director had T-shirts made that said on the front, "Yes, it's hard," and on the back, "But we can do it." In addition, during biweekly meetings the team used the first fifteen minutes to "visit Pity City" and talk about their gripes and struggles. However, they were told up-front that "you can visit Pity City, but you aren't allowed to move there." So for the second fifteen minutes the meeting became a brag session in which people would showcase their victories. Everyone was required to participate at least once a week in the griping and the bragging.

The team discovered that these sessions created a remarkable degree of camaraderie among the team members, making it easier for them to ask each other for help and give each other ideas for handling tough situations. As they told each other about little victories, they began to feel that they were part of a winning team. When the pressure period was over, they felt better about themselves and their organization than they had at the beginning. Denying or disallowing "negative emotions" such as anger and frustration would have robbed them of these benefits.[13]

Because women are typically more in touch with feelings and more comfortable expressing them than men, women may well be the ones to lead the way toward a healthier view of emotions. But here, as in many areas, there is a need for balance. In their book *Getting Together,* Roger Fisher and Scott Brown suggest some ways to balance emotion and reason. One is to develop an awareness of your own emotions and those of others, because "insecurity, frustration, fear, or anger can take hold and begin to affect our actions without our realizing what is happening. [If we fail to] recognize our own feelings or the feelings of others, it will be difficult indeed to control how we express them. And if we cannot control how we express our emotions, we are unlikely to deal well with substantive issues."[14] Once we are more practiced at recognizing our emotions, we are in a better position to take charge of our behavior instead of reacting emotionally.

While we may try to hide our emotions in the workplace for fear of the consequences of showing them, this only compounds the problem: "Unless we reveal our emotions at least to ourselves, potentially destructive feelings like anger and resentment can fester until they flare into an outburst that causes long-term damage to a relationship. Furthermore, when we hide our feelings we may be ignoring underlying substantive problems [in the relationship] that need attention."[15]

One way to deal with emotions is to talk about them. Talking about our emotions rather than displaying them or denying them actually demonstrates self-confidence, honesty and self-control—character qualities that engender trust. The purpose of acknowledging our emotion is not to blame another person; in fact, it is important that we accept responsibility for our own emotions and behavior. But we do want to explain them to the other person so that negative feelings will not stand in the way of a good working relationship.

It is also helpful to prepare for emotions before they arrive. Whenever our emotions catch us off guard, we are more likely to react than to make a rational choice about how we want to respond. Any work we can do to anticipate our emotions and plan our response in a given situation will take us a step further toward balance.

Emotions are nothing to be afraid of; rather, they give us important clues and real information about what is important to us as we work together. The more we practice recognizing emotions such as anger or disappointment, acknowledge them to ourselves and those with whom we are working, give ourselves enough space to analyze them and choose a constructive response, the more confident and effective we will be in our team relationships. It is the process of learning to be angry (or sad or frustrated or disappointed) without sinning (Eph 4:26). Every time we are able to work through this process with a coworker, we gain confidence in each other and prevent unresolved issues from detracting from the work we are trying to accomplish together.[16]

Value differences. It is tempting for us as human beings to view the differences we observe in others as weaknesses or as problems to be overcome. At times, we find the differences between us to be so threatening that we avoid all but the most superficial encounters. We have even resorted to placing our gender differences in a hierarchy, with men's ways considered inherently better than women's ways. In a reaction against that, some women have developed a mindset and a body of research that has attempted to point out the ways in which women are superior to men. Neither of these approaches is helpful to men and women who want to work together effectively.

In organizations and relationships where differences are valued, diversity is seen less as a legal requirement than as a deeply held value and a key to growth and success. In this kind of environment there is a concerted effort to acknowledge the need for different perspectives, to seek them out and to express gratitude when differences are perceived rather than feeling frustrated or threatened when they are received. We can say, "This is helpful because it means that we will be more effective and well-rounded as a group, and the work that we do will be of a higher quality because of our differences."

This kind of attitude is a wonderful antidote to the "people-like-me" syndrome characteristic of so many boards and working groups in which people seek those who are mirror images of themselves to join them. When an organization is committed to the idea that differences are a good thing, great value is placed on those managerial qualities that make it possible for a diversity of leadership and work styles to flourish: interpersonal sensitivity, flexibility, communication skills, conflict resolution and inclusion of both men and women in all important aspects of the organization's efforts. Success in these areas becomes part of any evaluation process for managers and may even be tied to their incentives.

Honor sexuality. With the influx of women into the workplace, it has become necessary to deal more openly with the issue of sexuality in the workplace. Women feel vulnerable to physical attack or coercion to give sexual favors in order to keep their jobs or get ahead. Men feel vulnerable to false accusations that could derail their careers or to misunderstandings that might arise from a simple compliment or an act of human kindness.

Awareness of sexual harassment has been on the increase, and even well-intentioned souls who would never think of harassing someone wonder where to draw the line between ordinary friendliness and improper sexual advances. Sexual harassment can take many subtle and overt forms, all of which are personally offensive and none of which contribute positively to bottom-line goals. At this time sexual harassment is understood to include sexist jokes, sexual innuendo, touching that makes the recipient feel uncomfortable, the display of suggestive or pornographic magazines or pictures, and requests for romantic or sexual activity from a manager who has the right to hire, fire or promote.

Respect is the most powerful antidote to the problem of sexual harassment. A man who respects a woman as a multidimensional human being who bears the image of God and is greatly loved by him would never think of reducing her to the single dimension of her physical appearance and sexuality. He would never ask her to choose between career advancement and her sexual purity; he would never violate her personal boundaries. Sexual harassment is always a question of respect or the lack of it.

Women also need to respect men and the power of the male sex drive by finding a line between behaving in a friendly manner and being flirtatious, dressing attractively and dressing seductively. Many men would like to say to women, "If you want a professional relationship, don't dress for something else." While a man's behavior is always his own responsibility, there are ways that women can show their care and respect.

Since some aspects of the description of sexual harassment are a bit subjective,[17] it is important that men and women clarify and communicate when there are misunderstandings and mixed messages. In a relationship characterized by respect and care, a man should never have to fear that a woman would accuse him to others without coming to him and talking to him directly. If she is bothered by his conversation or behavior, she must acknowledge her discomfort and seek to clarify what is happening in the relationship. As friendships develop at work, the lines get even more fuzzy between what is professional behavior and what is appropriate between friends. It is appropriate in such moments of discomfort to ask, "Where are you going with this line of conversation/questioning/behavior?" Although such conversations may be awkward, we actually show respect when we acknowledge that we do not always know everything about the meaning of someone else's behavior, and when we make the effort to clarify rather than assume. A woman can give a man the chance to tell her about himself, and she can give him feedback about how his behavior is affecting her. When relationships are characterized by respect, such honest questions are well-received and things are clarified. In fact, such interactions can result in a deeper level of understanding and trust.

In the same way, a man should feel free to ask a woman what is going on if her behavior is confusing or misleading to him. If she is too familiar with him through touch, or if she dresses in ways that are problematic to him or to others, he may want to speak with her. Simply put, respect and care for each other will lead us to a place of comfort and ease with each other in the area of sexuality.

Share power. Power is right up there with sex as a subject that many religious people do not know how to talk about and would rather not acknowledge. Men, who hold most of the institutional power in many organizations, are not comfortable acknowledging that they have it. They may even deny that they have more power than others, and yet feel threatened when they sense they are losing it. Women are ambivalent about power. They know that they do not have it, they know that they need it, but they are not sure how they feel about having it or what to do with it once they get it.

An earlier chapter identified power as the capacity to act or the ability to have influence. Carol Becker expands this definition:

Power can also be understood *as a commodity* or *as a relationship.* Power *as commodity* is "power over," the authoritative power that is so often maligned by women. It is external to the leader, and accumulates or diminishes. In this interpretation, power is played like a zero-sum game. The more one has, the less there is for others. Power *as relationship* is "power with." It is based on the interaction of people and organizations to accomplish its ends. *Each of these forms of power is legitimate and useful. The abuse of any one of them is illegitimate and not useful for effective leadership.*[18]

If men and women are to enter into full partnerships, we must move together toward a new understanding of power as one of God's unlimited resources available to us for the purpose of carrying out his purposes in the world. We need to be influenced by Jesus' use of power: It was always his intent to establish power in others so that they could accomplish great things. A fresh understanding of power will challenge our human tendency to hoard power and create in us a willingness to share. This will be challenging particularly for men as it relates to the sharing of institutional or external power (i.e., power bestowed by systems through title, money, proximity to "the powers that be," ordination, election to public office). At first blush, the thought of sharing power may seem to entail loss, but men who have made the conscious choice to share power with women have experienced it as full of gain. Gareth Icenogle is one who has been intentional about sharing power with women on the church staff team where he serves as copastor. When I asked him about the benfits of this choice in his own life, he replied,

Women have a different framework and perspective; I benefit from the different ways they deal with problems and the way they see the world. When we partner together, our sense of balance is elongated, our wisdom is broadened and deepened, our justice carries more universal equity, and our righteousness acts more holistically. In the growing partnership of shared feminine and masculine power, there is a synergy of multiplied motivation—an exponential expansion—to accomplish a task or solve a problem. In fact, I believe it is only when women and men share their power that they will help one another grow, mature and be transformed into the full stature of Jesus Christ.

Because women have so often been victims of the abuse of power or have been excluded from positions of institutional power, the challenge for them is to stop fearing power and learn to welcome their own power as an ally and as a force for good. Women's power is an inner authority that comes out of the essence of who they are. As Becker describes, it includes "their ability to focus on the whole, their comfort with relationships, a process orientation, a willingness to share information and thereby empower others, the intimacy they bring to the workplace, and their risk taking."[19] When women enter the workplace confident in the power that comes from within and offering the best of themselves, they will have an impact. When they are met by men who are willing to acknowledge them and share institutional power with them, the possibilities for effective partnership are unlimited.

Organizational Steps

A concerted effort among individuals and work groups throughout a company in order to create an atmosphere of safety would go a long way toward helping us tap into the full benefits of gender diversity. Each of us can commit ourselves to these initiatives, regardless of what anyone else is doing. We can be sure that when we make the effort to change our own attitudes and receive others in the ways described here, we have made an impact on our own little corner of the world. But we must not stop there. There are also systemic changes that need to be made, action steps that can be taken by an organization as a whole that will become key components in the process of moving men and women into full partnership.

We can incorporate valuing and managing gender diversity into our vision statement. Such a statement should take us beyond diversity as a "feel-good" human resources issue and articulate it as an integral part of our organization's goals and strategies. This initiative should come not only from those in upper management who have jumped on the diversity bandwagon but also from a felt need within the organization. For instance, the large Midwestern bank for which my husband works has established valuing diversity as one of its primary corporate goals through an initiative called LEAD:

Leadership in our human resource practices
Equal opportunity for all employees
Affirmative action as a tool for diversity
Development of a diverse workforce

Their commitment to these goals is demonstrated by the establishment of LEAD-related performance objectives throughout the company, annual awards for those who champion LEAD principles in the workplace, ongoing discussion of LEAD-related topics at senior management council meetings, and consistent application of work-and-family wellness policies and programs across the organization.[20] Most recently, senior management has developed policies that support employee participation in diversity networks formed throughout the corporation for the purpose of sharing common interests and experiences and supporting personal and professional growth.[21]

Although many companies are not large enough to commit themselves to such a sophisticated program, they can still learn from what other companies are doing and perhaps implement a few of the ideas that could work for them.

We can be more intentional in our recruitment. Many companies now recognize that unless they actively recruit more women, they will never see their goals met for gender diversity. When they recognize that women are underrepresented throughout the ranks of their workforce, they might increase recruiting efforts at women's colleges, advertise in women-oriented magazines, attract women to their company by using female interviewers, make conscious efforts to include pictures of women in their marketing and recruiting literature, and emphasize family-friendly policies. The strategy should be to go where the qualified women are and do what needs to be done to get them into the organization.

We can conduct periodic surveys. Surveys should look at every aspect of an organization where bias or discrimination could exist, such as the interviewing and selection process, opportunities for development and training, coaching and mentoring, performance appraisals and succession planning. It is important that top management express its support of the survey process and that specific steps are recommended and implemented as a result.

We can set up a task force. Setting up a task force within a company to study gender relations, make recommendations and implement strategies is one way that management can express its commitment to partnership between men and women in the workplace. The task force may begin without a clear sense of its mission, since it has not yet determined the exact nature of the problems. Different problems will surface in different organizations, and it should not be expected that the task force will be able to solve or even identify every problem. However, if a task force makes progress on the issues it does identify, this will demonstrate the sincerity of a company's efforts to help men and women value their differences and work together more equitably. It also gives people a place to go with their concerns as they surface.

We can participate in mutual mentoring and networking programs. Many companies have found that hiring women in sufficient numbers is often not enough to ensure that they will stay in the company and be developed fully. Since women still perceive most workplaces as dominated by men, they find that it takes extra effort to achieve full inclusion. Men can help women find their way by sharing with them what they know from having been in the system longer: how to use power, how to be direct and ambitious, how to work the system, introducing them to people they need to know, giving helpful feedback on how they come across to others.

Women have much to offer men as well: relational insight, input on process issues, different perspectives on leadership, ideas about how to better service customers and concern for overall quality of life. Although it might be a stretch for some to network and mentor across lines of gender, we cannot exclude anyone from such opportunities due to their sex without commiting discrimination.

We can offer periodic diversity training. Learning to value and relate effectively with those who are different from us is not something that we learn once and for all. Increased awareness of our own biases happens over time, and companies who want the benefits of gender diversity to be a part of the fabric of their organizational life will periodically offer training that will keep people's personal awareness and relational skills sharp.

We can plan ahead for succession. With women making up only 10 percent of the corporate officers at the five hundred largest U.S. companies, and with about one hundred Fortune 500 companies having no women corporate officers at all, it is clear that women still need to be intentionally identified and groomed for particular positions.[22]

Achieving a balance of men and women in upper levels of management does not happen by accident; it usually happens due to good planning. One company planned ahead by identifying a number of "pivotal" jobs that would lead to positions of leadership within the organization. Upper management then set goals for ratios of women and minorities in each division and at each level for these jobs. To ensure that these goals were met, they set up a system of rewards and made the achievement of these goals part of the managers' performance reviews.

We can address family issues as "people issues" instead of "women's issues." In a Canadian study on gender issues in the workplace, Carlton University business professor Linda Duxbury found that men and women held widely different views on what their organizations were doing to promote gender equality, what problems remained to be solved and what order of priority should be given to the problems. But there was one point of agreement: men and women alike said that issues related to balancing work, family and outside life were the issues they wanted most to see addressed.

It is insulting to both men and women when we do not recognize that both desire to be meaningfully involved with family, to be involved in meaningful work and to slow the pace of their lives so that they can be healthy. These issues are of such huge concern that some companies have established task forces just to deal with them. When we understand that family issues affect both men and women, when both sexes can acknowledge love and responsibility for children and aging parents, when both can express their need for flextime or job sharing, men and women in the workplace can enter into the dialogue and partnership that will result in creative solutions.

We can reward success. Unfortunately, lectures about morality are rarely sufficient in motivating us to do what is right. Some people will not change until change is tied to the bottom line of incentives and performance evaluation. At the very least, there should be a section in a manager's yearly performance review in which issues related to recruiting and managing diversity are addressed. This is an excellent built-in opportunity for experienced managers to give praise and encouragement and to share ideas about how to tap into the benefits of diversity. If there is a piece of the compensation package that is tied to this issue, so much the better. It might be just the extra push that someone needs.

Work: God's Gift to Women and Men
Although there are great challenges associated with a more equal partnership between men and women at work, there are many benefits to be

counted as well. For one thing, more equal participation gives both men and women the opportunity to fulfill the creation mandate of exercising responsible dominion in the world. In so doing, men and women reflect the image of a God who creates and works to accomplish his purposes in the world. When we are involved in caring for our world and opening up the possibilities in it, we actually become coworkers with God, whose desire it is to bless and prosper his creation.

A tremendous sense of satisfaction comes from being involved in work that we enjoy and that fulfills a sense of calling. While we tend to think more of men as those intended to derive satisfaction from meaningful work, a recent Gallup poll indicated that "working mothers in America view their work as an extremely important part of their lives. . . . In fact, three-quarters say that they like or love the job they have right now; only 4 percent say that they hate their work."[23] Surprisingly enough, Miriam Neff's 1996 survey of 1,200 Christian women resulted in the same kind of discovery: "Christian women *are* working—and not just to make ends meet. With 73 percent of our respondents employed, a higher percentage of Christian women are working than the general national average. . . . When asked to rank the rewards of their employment, the number one reward was 'fulfilling my spiritual calling.' "[24]

While there are some high-profile Christians today who advocate a theological position that limits a woman's primary "calling" to motherhood, the writer of Ecclesiastes notes that

it is God's gift that *all* should eat and drink and take pleasure in all their toil. . . . *All* to whom God gives wealth and possessions and whom he enables to enjoy them, and to accept their lot and find enjoyment in their toil—this is the gift of God. For they will scarcely brood over the days of their lives, because God keeps them occupied with the joy of their hearts. (Eccles 3:13; 5:19-20)

The woman described in Proverbs 31 experiences a great deal of fulfillment through her work inside and outside the home: "She considers a field and buys it; with the fruit of her hands she plants a vineyard. She girds herself with strength, and makes her arms strong. She perceives that her merchandise is profitable. Her lamp does not go out at night. . . . Give her a share in the fruit of her hands, and let her works praise her in the city gates" (vv. 16-18, 31). Her involvement in the marketplace does not in any way diminish her husband's contribution but rather seems to enhance his life ("the heart of her husband trusts in her, and he will have no lack of gain" [v. 11]) and his good standing in the community ("her husband is known in the city gates, taking his seat among the elders of the land" [v. 23]).

In addition, we must not underestimate the value and legitimate power of being able to care for oneself and one's family that comes from engaging in work for which we receive financial compensation ("the laborer deserves to be paid" [1 Tim 5:18]). Men often take for granted the opportunity to engage in paid work because they were prepared from childhood to do so. For such a man, an experience with unemployment or marriage to a woman who makes more money than he does can be revealing as he realizes how much of his self-esteem relies on his ability to generate income.

Women, in contrast, have not been as widely encouraged to plan on generating income. Even with the changes that have taken place in our society, many women still assume they will spend a good part of their lives performing unpaid domestic labor or volunteer tasks. For some women this is fine. Others, though, want to receive some financial rewards for the skills, talent and hard work they bring to the world. The ability to provide for themselves is an important component of their self-esteem. As Paul points out in 1 Timothy 5:8, providing for the physical and financial needs of our families is honorable and integral to the life of faith. Whether we are male or female, working to provide for our own needs or the needs of our family is something that God wants done in the world. It thus brings value to our lives.

Questions for Individuals or Groups

1. What are some of the benefits of gender diversity in your particular line of work? What are some of the stress points?

2. Does your work setting seem to offer an atmosphere of safety so that it is comfortable for both men and women to offer the best of themselves to the tasks at hand? If your answer is yes, what makes it safe? If no, what is the most important thing that would need to change in order for both women and men to flourish?

3. What steps has your organization taken in order to tap into the benefits of gender diversity? Have these steps been effective?

4. If you could choose one or two of the ideas in this chapter to recommend to those in management at your workplace, which would you choose? Why?

9

Mutually Empowering Marriage

We know that the first gift of God and the [unavoidable] challenge
of a marital spirituality are that we must not possess one another.
We are called to give back to the Creator the gift of equality, respect,
and thoughtful mutuality with which human life began.[1]
PATRICK J. MCDONALD AND CLAUDETTE M. MCDONALD

When Greg and Julie married, they were regarded by their conservative community as the epitome of what a Christian couple should be. They were committed to Christ, bright, attractive and willing to get involved. As an Olympic-level athlete and natural leader, Greg had aspirations to do great things: "If you had asked me what my dreams were, I would have told you 'I want to do something great.' I didn't know if that meant being president of a company or going to the Olympic games and winning a gold medal or what, but it felt like the list would have had those kinds of things on it."

What role would a wife play in such a plan? "I assumed that a Christian wife's fulfillment would come from being a 'helpmate' to her husband," says Greg. "I understood my role as husband to be a benevolent spiritual leader who would set the overall tone for the family, establish direction and clarify roles within the marriage. While I felt it was my responsibility to make bottom-line decisions on major issues, I always intended to consult Julie and take her input seriously. I was sure that Julie would thrive in this kind of arrangement just as my own mother had."

This arrangement proved fine for Julie, who had been raised with the understanding that a woman should be quieter and more introverted and exercise gifts such as helping others and demonstrating hospitality and mercy—the type of gifts that would assist her husband in achieving his goals. Even though she had been a leader in her school and church as a young person, she now says, "If you had asked me about my goals and aspirations, I would have said, 'My job is to help Greg!' There was this image of the ideal woman that was held so high. I desperately wanted to do what pleased God, so it became my goal to do just that—by becoming this ideal woman."

So Greg and Julie entered marriage with a mutual understanding that theirs would be a relationship between a leader and a helpmate. Greg was not abusive or domineering: "I did think that the Bible clearly taught that the man was to be the leader—a good leader who leads in such a way that the people want to follow. I was trying to be that kind of benign leader. Unfortunately, I was completely unaware of the subtle assumed superiority inherent in this way of thinking."

What's Wrong with This Picture?
In order to become the ideal, supportive, submissive woman that Greg prized and the church system applauded, Julie began to repress her spiritual gift of leadership and to moderate her naturally extroverted personality. A few observant souls noticed that as Greg and Julie's relationship progressed toward marriage, Julie started changing: she was no longer as fun and outgoing, she took on a more serious demeanor, and she began dressing more conservatively. Despite all her efforts to be "the ideal woman," Julie recalls, "My leadership stuff would ooze out and we would get caught. Greg would think that I was trying to do a power move or something."

As early as their honeymoon they had arguments in which Julie would express a differing opinion and Greg would perceive it as a trust issue: "I thought, *Why can't you just trust me to lead here? Why do you have to throw your two cents in the mix? The decision has been made; just go with it.*" At times Greg's "benign leadership" might even lead to kicks under the table and looks that were meant to communicate that Julie needed to be quiet. Often through Greg's silence and withdrawal Julie would pick up the general feeling that she had stepped over a line. Greg, however, thought that he was providing leadership by letting her know when she was out of line.

If you had asked Greg and Julie about the quality of their marriage during this time, they would have said it was good; however, they also began to sense a cloud hanging over their relationship. As Greg puts it, "I felt that our marriage was heading in the direction of quiet desperation with a huge amount of denial that said 'It ain't so; we're good Christians, we're a great Christian couple, we're in Christian leadership.'"

One of the earliest hints that all was not well in their marriage was the way they organized their whole lives around Greg's desire to compete in the Olympic decathlon. Almost as a condition of their marriage Greg had said, "I have to give the Olympics my best shot, or I will not be acting responsibly with the life that God gave me." So for two years Julie's life was consumed with Greg's drive for achievement: picking him up from work, taking him to the track, timing him or just waiting in the car. When they got home, they would eat late, go to bed and get up to repeat the process the next day. At this point Julie did take a job teaching in a high school, but it was only for the purpose of making it possible for Greg to fulfill his Olympic dream. They did not even consider that maybe this job or some other way of carving out time and resources might help her to realize her dreams in life. She consoled herself with the fact that this was supposedly a temporary situation; Greg had promised that he would only train for these two years and stop, no matter which way things turned out.

The Wake-Up Call

As it turned out, Greg's Olympic performance was respectable, especially since he had not been able to prepare properly due to a previous injury. But when it was all over, he could not help playing the game of "what if?" He had had his leg rehabilitated and had gotten through the decathlon without reinjuring it. What if he trained for another four years? Just imagine!

But one day, as he wondered out loud with his father about this very thing, Greg got his first glimpse of the unwellness in his marriage. Julie overheard what they were talking about. Greg describes the moment: "I remember looking over at her, and I felt that I was looking at a shell of a person. Hollow. It was almost a look of despair—very scary."

That glimpse into the emptiness of Julie's soul became a moment of awareness for Greg. Even though he did not know fully what to do with this awareness, it changed him so profoundly that he put an end to additional Olympic aspirations: "For me it was a matter of integrity. I had said it was only going to be for two years, and that was the deal." Four months later Greg was notified that he had been accepted at a prestigious business school, but he and Julie had made no deals about that. So they packed up and moved to another state and into campus housing, in essence hopping off one fast track and onto another.

There the quiet desperation deepened into a full-blown crisis. Greg worked on his M.B.A. while Julie kept their tiny apartment and took care of their baby. Here for the first time Julie was exposed to many women who had clear aspirations for their lives and were actively pursuing them. Having been raised a Southern Baptist in a conservative southern town, she had never considered any other calling for her life than being a stay-at-home mother and submitting to her husband's leadership. Now seeing so many women who had made a different kind of choice caused her to remember with a certain amount of wistfulness the leader she had been when she was younger. She had to admit that she too could have followed her own aspirations but instead chose "to hang all my expectations on someone else's goal and dreams."

"That realization," she recalls, "coupled with the fact that Greg spent most of his time studying and I was left alone in this tiny apartment with a baby, made me feel like my life was a prison. I remember looking in the mirror and saying, 'I have no idea who I am. I have no idea what I like to do. I don't have the first clue.' I honestly thought that this was what God had for me, and yet I didn't have anything to show for it.

"After we had our second child, I remember sitting on the floor by the window just sobbing, but I didn't know why. Greg would try to talk to me about it and ask me what I wanted, and I would say, 'I don't know.' I honestly thought that what I was doing in giving myself up for Greg was what God had for me. But if that were true, I began to wish that he would take me in my sleep. I thought, *God, if this is what you have, I can't do it. For whatever reason—I don't know if it's the fact that I'm not strong enough or what—I just can't do it anymore.*"

At this point Julie almost stopped functioning. Until then she had been typing papers and taking care of administrative details within their family, but now she stopped everything except for taking care of their two children. There was a part of both Greg and Julie that thought she was being rebellious. Greg, in particular, found himself completely at a loss. "I had no language for what we were going through other than 'My wife is screwed up.' But I didn't want anyone to know it. If you had seen us at church during that time, you would never have been able to guess that there were any kinds of issues going on. But basically I had given up, except for trying to do some image management. We weren't purposely trying to cover anything up; we were just trying to survive."

Can This Marriage Be Saved?
Sometimes it takes a wake-up call as frightening as the one described here—a young wife reduced to debilitating depression and a young husband who has given up all hope for meaningful marriage—to force us to look at the configuration of our marriage to evaluate whether or not it is truly life-giving to both partners.

As is true with most crises, there were many factors that precipitated the one in Greg and Julie's relationship. Her parents' divorce after twenty-nine years of marriage and the death of two of her grandparents caused Julie to look to Greg almost as a savior who would take her away from the trauma of her life. Greg's self-centeredness made it difficult for him to value the dreams she had for her life as much as his own.

Each marriage is a complex and continuing process of merging two personalities, and unpacking and sorting through the baggage, blessings and expectations that each spouse brings. Greg and Julie's relationship is a poignant example of a marriage that crashed and almost shattered on the craggy rocks of faulty theology and teaching that often lurk beneath the surface of our idealization of traditional Christian marriage. Theirs was a marriage built for one: one person's dreams, one person's goals, the development and exercise of one person's gifts and calling.

Greg and Julie realize now that their marriage was not set up to accommodate two fully developed human beings. It was not an equal partnership marked by mutual commitment to help each other grow, develop and respond to God's call in their lives. For all practical purposes, Julie's life was subsumed into Greg's.

As Greg describes it, "She joined my essence in terms of goals and priorities, education, time, spending and resources. Clearly my life had the edge when it came to making those kinds of decisions. That she would love me and want to help me achieve my goals—all that was good stuff. What was wrong was that it wasn't reciprocal. In the early days of our dating and marriage, I don't recall having even one significant conversation about her life dreams, her aspirations and God-given passions. Because she didn't really have any goals I basically said, 'Well, good. I know what my goals are, so let's do mine.'"

This lack of a clear understanding that marriage is about merging two individuals' lives and callings led them to make the choice over and over again to place the highest priority on Greg's aspirations while Julie's identity and calling remained in embryonic form. Their marriage became a powerful example of the danger that psychologist James Olthuis describes:

> Although at times it may seem easier to let one partner take over, a husband and wife can jeopardize their entire relationship by establishing a male-dominated marriage. When a woman virtually surrenders her personality to her husband, she has less to give to the relationship as the years pass. Outwardly she may seem rather content, but inwardly grows more and more dependent until she is only an adjunct. Often powerful feelings of hostility well up inside her, against herself for succumbing and against her husband (and God) for demanding such subservience. She feels her marriage is a "trap" with four walls and a husband as keeper.[2]

New Beginnings

With the completion of Greg's M.B.A. in sight, Greg and Julie moved back to Julie's hometown so that Julie could be near her family. She says, "I had never known anybody as bad off as I was, and I knew I needed healing. But still no one knew what was going on, and we couldn't talk about it with anyone. Everyone in and around the church had so much respect for Greg that they couldn't imagine anything was wrong."

In the meantime, Greg visited a new and thriving church that was different from any he had ever experienced. While visiting, he picked up some materials from a course on spiritual gifts and shared them with Julie. As she read through the materials she noticed that there was no reference to gender as it related to spiritual gifts. Throughout her spiritual development, there had always been a subtle teaching that some gifts were meant for men and some for women. Now she realized that all the gifts can be given to both men and women! She began to wonder, *If all this is open and available to me, then what is it that has held me back from living out of my giftedness as a leader, from knowing who I am and what I am called to do?*

This was a powerful question for a woman who had spent her entire married life supporting her husband's calling. It was a disturbing question for a man who had received that support with little awareness of the inequity of their arrangement. But it was a question that they were both brave enough to pursue until they got an answer.

A joint trip to this new church marked the beginning of a new era in Greg and Julie's marriage. Julie attended a seminar conducted by the pastor's wife that gave her words and concepts for the struggle in which she was embroiled. The message, titled "I Died to Self and My Self Almost Died," paralleled Julie's own experience of having given up so much of her own life and calling for someone else's that there was little of her own self left. Over the next few months, she worked through the reading list that the pastor's wife had recommended and was freed up to take a more honest look at the "junk" that surfaces in marriages—even Christian ones. She learned that her willingness to give up her identity in service of Greg's was more about long-standing psychological patterns than it was about God's definition of the ideal woman. She was able to understand that her view of God and what she had perceived to be God's plan for her life were not all that accurate.

When Greg was asked to join the staff of the church they had visited, Julie knew deep in her heart that this, finally, would be a good move for both of them. In this church they were already finding the support of a community of faith in their quest for a more equitable marriage. They began to conceive of a marriage in which individuals love and give to each other in such a way that both souls are nourished and provided with whatever is necessary for growth into full personhood.

While this new understanding was life-giving for Julie, for Greg it was more like having scales torn painfully from his eyes. The questions with which he had to wrestle were deep and penetrating: *Do I have the right to follow my own life's calling at someone else's expense? If we had had a marriage of equality and mutuality, our decision about my pursuing an M.B.A. might have been different. How do I feel about that? How could I have said no to the opportunity of a lifetime?*

When he felt threatened by Julie's new insight and understanding he had to ask, *What is preventing me from looking into this and allowing Julie to look into this? After all, I know in my heart of hearts that she wants to know God, so what am I afraid of?*

It is a tribute to Greg's insight and openness to the Holy Spirit that he was able to perceive the answer to those questions: "I knew that what was preventing me was insecurity. I would have to admit that I was insecure or I would have to give Julie the freedom to explore these issues, and I wasn't about to let my insecurity be the reason to stop Julie's development!" Not only did he give Julie his blessing in her explorations, he also started looking more critically at the explanations for hierarchical marriage that, for so many years, he had assumed was the biblical pattern. He was surprised to find them intellectually weak and unsatisfying, and he began to consider that perhaps for centuries men and women had been misguided in their views on marriage.

In Search of a Better Way

It is painful to think that in many ways the Christian community, with its emphasis on gender roles and structures, has failed to capture the beauty and meaning of Christ's life-giving presence within the church. Yet to model Christ's loving relationship with his people is one of the great purposes of marriage in the first place.

Greg is still moved to tears as he remembers the emptiness in Julie's eyes when he mused out loud about another Olympic run, the sacrifices that she made so that he could go to graduate school and the realization that he had perhaps taken more than he had given. Her emptiness was a far cry from the splendor of the well-nourished bride in Ephesians 5:25-33 who has been loved into greatness.

Part of the agony of looking back is that Greg and Julie did not set out to craft a marriage that would be destructive to either of them. As Greg observes now with great poignancy, "I didn't mean to do anything wrong or bad. In fact, I meant to do right, so how could I have ended up being so destructive to the person I loved most—my wife?" As we have seen, some of Greg and Julie's difficulty in figuring out how to craft a marriage in which both husband and wife are mutually supported and empowered sprang from a narrow understanding of the marriage relationship as God intended it.

As noted in earlier chapters, God's original and best plan for the marriage relationship was a partnership model in which a man and a woman function together as a team of equals. Both the man and the woman were created equally in God's image, and both were given the responsibility for carrying out God's purposes on earth. This male-female team was not characterized by hierarchy or top-down authority structures but by an equal sharing of power, strength and helpfulness to the task at hand. Neither the man nor the woman was given the option of standing on the sidelines cheering while the other one did all the work. Neither was given the option of reneging on responsibilities that had been given to the two of them together. Rather, they would both bear equal responsibility for being fruitful and nurturing life, for being wise stewards of the earth's resources and for exercising appropriate leadership and dominion. Any configuration for marriage in which one partner or the other is prevented from being involved in each of these creation mandates robs that individual of the full human experience for which he or she was created.

From Genesis 2 we know that God observed that it was not good for Adam to be alone. As a loving solution to this situation, God created Eve, a helper suitable for him. Traditionally (as was the case in Greg's and Julie's circle of influence) theologians have interpreted this passage to mean that woman was somehow subordinate to man because she was created to be his helper *(ezer)*. However, as noted in chapter one, in the Bible the word *ezer* is never used to refer to a subordinate. Of its twenty other appearances in the Old Testament, seventeen are references to God as our strength or power. (The other three refer to a military ally.)[3]

It is no wonder that Adam was completely overjoyed when God brought Eve to him after his deep sleep. Here, finally, was one who was more like him than anything he had yet seen: "This at last is bone of my bones and flesh of my flesh" (2:23). When we read this verse with our hearts, we can almost feel this man relax as he realizes that here is one who will rescue him from his aloneness by being a companion for his body and soul, one who will bring additional strength when he was weak, and one whose power in combination with his own will be more than adequate for the tasks God has assigned to them.

Adam recognizes their shared humanity and their sexual diversity when he identifies Eve by a different form of the descriptive word used to identify himself: "This one shall be called Woman *[ishshah],* for out of Man *[ish]* this one was taken" (2:23). Because of their fundamental unity the man is instructed to leave his own family and cling to his wife. Rather than pull her into the authority structure of his family (as in the patriarchal system that developed later), Genesis teaches that the man is the one who should move away from his family toward his wife in a new relationship that is characterized by interdependence. Their unity and oneness is captured in the image of becoming "one flesh." There is nothing here to suggest that one is "over" the other in any way; rather the man and the woman come together in the way cells cluster together and form skin. Any introduction of hierarchy seems completely contradictory to the oneness and interdependence pictured here.

Learning from a Great Marriage Team

When I envision a marriage in which a woman is a power or strength equal to her husband, I am reminded of Catherine Booth, powerful evangelist and cofounder of the Salvation Army. She answered God's call to preach one Sunday morning as her husband William, a Methodist minister, finished his sermon at Bethesda Chapel. Moved by the Spirit, she stood in front of the congregation of more than a thousand and announced, "I want to say a word." William was as surprised as anyone when Catherine made her unexpected announcement, but he allowed her to speak. When she finished, he announced that she would preach that evening. This marked the beginning of thirty years of a preaching ministry that some feel was perhaps more significant than her work with the Salvation Army.

Shortly after her rather unorthodox pulpit debut, William became ill. Because of his slow recovery, Catherine took over his entire preaching circuit, and her dynamic and forceful preaching style drew crowds of thousands. Apparently William was not threatened that, in the opinion of some, "no man exceeded her in popularity or spiritual results, including her husband."[4] When he recovered, they worked together again in a revivalistic ministry that involved preaching, rescue mission work (especially with teenage prostitutes), founding the Salvation Army and training their own children into the ministry.[5]

The Booths' marriage is a testimony to the power that is unleashed when marriage is configured in such a way that both the wife and the husband are fully supported to answer the call of God in their lives. If Catherine had not followed the Holy Spirit's promptings to launch her preaching ministry, she would have been ill-prepared when it came time for her to "help" her husband by bringing her strength to the ministry he had begun. If William had been at all threatened or uncomfortable with his wife's calling to minister in the home and beyond, he might have refused to open his pulpit to her or in some other way unwittingly thwarted her development. In either case, their preaching ministry and the work of the Salvation Army might have come to a grinding halt during William's illness rather than continuing with anointing and power under Catherine's able leadership. Not only were they empowered as individuals to reach their fullest potential, but as a team they became a whole that added up to more than the sum of its parts.

At Catherine's funeral, William delivered a deeply moving eulogy that described their marriage partnership and Catherine's role as *ezer* in all the best senses of the word. He described her as a tree that had been his shadow from the burning sun, whose fruit had been the very stay of his existence; a servant who had lovingly ministered to his health and comfort; a counselor whose advice he had followed without regret through the intricate mazes of his existence; the most pleasant of friends who understood the rise and fall of his feelings, the bent of his thoughts, the purpose of his existence; the mother of his children who had cradled, nursed and trained them into the service of the Lord; a wife who had stood by his side on the battle's front. She had been a comrade willing to place herself between him and the enemy and was ever the strongest when the battle was the fiercest. At a loss to describe her with just one image, he said, "Well, my comrades, you can roll all these qualities into one personality and what would be lost in each I have lost in all. There has been taken away from me the delight of my eyes, the inspiration of my soul. . . . And yet . . . my heart is full of gratitude, too . . . because God lent me for so long a season such a treasure."[6]

As far as I can tell from the biblical understanding of *ezer,* not only is it possible but it is *preferable* that a woman be all that God created her to be—in strength, in power, in nurturing, in servanthood, in giftedness, in calling to work and ministry. As she follows the call of God in the home and beyond, she will be more of a blessing to her husband, her marriage and the kingdom of God than anyone ever thought possible.

Learning from Christ's Relationship with the Church

Just as Greg and Julie experienced some confusion regarding the wife's responsibility in marriage, they also had a limited understanding of the husband's responsibility. Greg recalls, "When we got married, no one encouraged me to ask about Julie's goals and aspirations. When it became clear that she didn't really have an adequate vision for her life, I should have said, 'I think every person should have a calling for their life, and if you don't have a handle on that, I want you to know that I am here as a resource. I am going to walk with you until we find your gifts and calling, because they are there. They may be buried under a lot of things, but they are there. And I will work as hard at helping you discover your calling as you will at helping me realize mine.' But I didn't even know it was an issue. And so she lost herself in my life."

Greg is not alone in his desire to craft a marriage that works for both him and his wife. As David Mains, executive director of Chapel of the Air Ministries, acknowledged to me, "On some level men know that it's not enough for all the woman's effort to go into the man's life. We want to be fair, and we know that *life is better* when you have a fully developed human being as a partner."

When I asked David how he experienced life getting better as his wife, Karen, developed into the gifted author and communicator that she is today, he replied, "I take great pride in my wife and the person she has become. It sure makes for a much livelier marriage. Deep down you know that you want to be married to an equal—not just a beautiful face and body. There is something deeply attractive about a mature, complete woman."

This is what the biblical concept of headship is about. Just as the concept of the helper relates to a wife's commitment to bring her strength, power and nurturance to the challenges of her husband's life, so the biblical concept of headship is about a man's partnership with his wife in her process of becoming a mature and complete woman. Their relationship is modeled on the one-of-a-kind relationship between Christ and the church—not the hierarchy of corporate America with its presidents and vice presidents.

According to Ephesians 5:22-33, Christ's role as head of the church involves being its Savior (giver of life), Lover (to the point of laying down his life) and Nourisher (caring for her as his own body). Staying with this passage, we find that headship has nothing to do with demanding obedience, being the one who makes final decisions or being the one who pursues his calling while the wife tries desperately to be supportive and fit in. Rather, the word *head* has to do with being the one who initiates and leads the way in loving and is virtually synonymous with *beginning* or *origin*.[7] The wife responds (as the church does) to this kind of love with a heartfelt desire to please her husband. Paul admits that the way headship works itself out in a loving relationship is somewhat mysterious. Gilbert Bilezikian offers this moving description that captures the beauty and the mystery that is marriage:

> The concept of headship in the New Testament refers to the function of Christ as the fountainhead of life and growth and to his servant role of provider and sustainer. . . . Because Christ is the wellspring of the church's life and provides it with existence and sustenance, in return the church serves him in loving dependency and in recognition of him as the source of its life. Because man as the fountainhead of the woman's existence was originally used to supply her with her very life, and because he continues to love her sacrificially as his own body in marriage, in return a Christian wife binds herself to her husband in a similar relationship of servant submission that expresses their oneness. The imposition of authority structure upon this exquisite balance of reciprocity would paganize the marriage relationship and make the Christ/church paradigm irrelevant to it.[8]

Of course, we cannot ignore the kind of dysfunction in which a husband is not loved into full personhood. Wives can also become dominant while their husbands become more and more distant from their families. Most of us know of at least one family in which the husband spends most of his free time puttering in the garage or basement, sitting at a bar with people who give him a sense of importance and belonging, or glued to the television in numb silence. Meanwhile the wife runs the household, brings up the children, keeps the social calendar and frequently verbalizes what she sees to be her husband's weaknesses. Certainly the male-dominated marriage is the more common one, but imbalance in either direction is unhealthy and does not reflect the reciprocity and shared responsibility that God intended for marriage.

Learning from the New Community

Scriptural instruction regarding Christian marriage is most often given in the context of mutual submission in the community of faith. Before, during and after marriage, we are first and foremost brothers and sisters in Christ who are to love each other, bear with one another, forgive each other, tell each other the truth and teach and admonish each other (Eph 5; Col 3:12-16).

In the context of mutual submission Paul emphasized respect and submission as issues that the women to whom he was writing needed to focus on in relation to their husbands. He emphasized love and consideration as character qualities and behaviors that the men to whom he was writing needed to practice in relationship to their wives. Obviously, this does not mean that women are absolved from the responsibility of loving their husbands and showing consideration for them or that men are absolved from the responsibility of respecting and submitting to their wives. Respect, love, submission and consideration are required of all of us in the body of Christ. In fact, ultimate submission and servanthood to the point of laying down one's life is required of men in this passage.

"But," I hear so often, "what about those times when we as husband and wife just can't agree? Shouldn't the husband be the one to make the decision?" There is nothing in Scripture to support this idea. Rather, the Bible sets forth unity as the goal for relationships among those in the community of faith, married or not: "Be of the same mind, having the same love, being in full accord and of one mind. Do nothing from selfish ambition or conceit, but in humility regard others as better than yourselves. Let each of you look not to your own interests, but to the interests of others" (Phil 2:2-5). This is the norm for Christian marriage.

To help us keep things in perspective we need to ask ourselves, How many decisions come along in life that are truly worth sacrificing the powerful unity that we are speaking of here? How many are so important that we cannot wait for each other and listen and work lovingly to achieve the one mind that Paul describes? Chris and I have not come across a decision yet that was worth such a sacrifice.

The rush to designate the husband as the one who makes the final decisions is rooted in fear and unbelief: fear that if we do not give more power to one or the other, we will never be able to make decisions. Some hold deeply rooted doubts about the possibility for unity and consensus; others have long-held beliefs that if you do not keep women under men's authority, they will lead their men and families down the path to destruction. While some of these fears may be understandable, they are woefully inadequate as a foundation for marital relations. They totally discount the efficacy of the one Spirit whose job it is to create unity among us and the power of Christlike love.

In the conclusion to his book *Beyond Sex Roles,* Gilbert Bilezikian cautions against designating the husband as the family decision-maker:

> Consistently placing responsibility for the final word on the husband is the least God-honoring method for resolving . . . the decision-making impasses that occur when opinions differ. This puts an unrealistic burden on the husband to make always the right decision, and it promotes a cop-out mentality for the wife, who then resigns herself to the status of permanent loser or of devious manipulator of the power-wielding male.
> . . . Under the guidance of the Holy Spirit, other creative methods can be found to resolve differences without resorting to the repulsive pagan practice whereby one spouse exercises control over the other.[9]

Bilezikian then outlines ten biblical approaches to decision-making that support a partnership model for marriage rather than relying on the chain-of-command approach many have tried and found wanting. I mention them here briefly in summary form:

1. Defer to each other. Take turns in giving each other preference (Phil 2:3-4). Deliberate stalemates cannot persist between two spouses who are bound together in a shared desire to please one another, to give each other the advantage, to be servants to each other and to anticipate and yield to each other's needs, desires and pleasure.

2. Divide responsibilities for decision-making on the basis of spiritual gifts, competency, experience and expertise (Rom 12:3-6; 1 Cor 12:4-7). Each spouse is designated to render final decisions in specific (predetermined) areas of proficiency.

3. Compromise. Seeking middle ground is a biblically sound procedure (Acts 6:1-6).

4. Define the biblical principles involved in the debated issue and make

decisions on the basis of such evaluations.

5. Pray together for guidance and then wait for it. God uses both prayer and the perspective of time to resolve differences and conflicts.

6. Allow God to provide guidance through circumstances.

7. Whenever a decision affects one spouse more than the other, the spouse who has more at stake should have the greater say in it.

8. Initiate joint research projects on the debated issue. Read, attend conferences or take courses to develop a basis for sound judgment (Eph 5:17; Jas 1:5-6).

9. Decide to refer the matter to a trusted and objective third party (1 Cor 6:5; Prov 13:10).

10. Engage in parts reversal. After partners articulate their respective positions, they each assume the position of the other partner for a period of time. The empathy generated by this exchange will generally break the deadlock.[10]

There is a world of difference between a marriage in which love, deference and submission flow voluntarily back and forth and the marriage in which the husband always holds the trump card in decision-making. It is a testimony to the strength of our fears that we would cling to a power imbalance to solve our problems with decision-making in marriage when there are so many other God-honoring options available to us. When we are living out of faith rather than fear, however, we hold out for God's ideal of unity and oneness. In the midst of our decision-making we can hear faith whisper, "I believe that unity is God's will for us, and he can bring our hearts and minds together."

Today Greg and Julie will admit that their shift from a marriage made up of a leader and a follower to a marriage that is a partnership of equals has made a world of difference in their heart stance toward each other. They have found that tenacious faith in the possibilities for unity and the use of creative, biblical decision-making processes have helped them to share power and influence as they have built a new life together over the last five years. They admit that they are still working to unpack the baggage from their past, but they also recognize that they are not making nearly as many mistakes—a great benefit of true teamwork.

When a couple begins their married life with the traditional configuration such as the one that characterized Greg and Julie's marriage, the shift to an arrangement that is satisfying for both husband and wife is a process that must be worked out over time. In their book *Shattering Our Assumptions,* Miriam Neff and Debra Klingsporn outline eight key areas of decision-making for couples who desire greater mutuality. The questions they raise are also excellent for couples who are contemplating marriage and want to function from the very beginning as a partnership of equals. It is good for both individuals to review this list independently and then compare their responses. Even if these questions open up emotional discussions, it is important not to back away or table the discussion indefinitely. Rather, acknowledge that you have hit a nerve, and agree to a method of talking through the difficulty.

1. Where do we live and how do we decide?

2. What criteria do we use to choose where we live?

3. What about family (having children or choosing not to, deciding when our family is complete, who does most of the "active" parenting)?

4. Tasks of family living

   a. Home (Who is in charge of the inside and outside tasks? of maintenance and repair of household items? of establishing cleaning routines?)

   b. Vehicles (Who decides what kind of car to buy, how much to spend and when to buy a new one? Who takes care of maintenance?)

   c. Meals and eating (Who does the shopping and cooking?)

5. Employment

   a. Who is able to do what?

   b. Whose abilities are used in the marketplace?

   c. Are the choices mutually satisfying to both spouses?

6. Children

   a. Whose schedule offers more flexibility to care for the children?

   b. Who visits the school and attends conferences?

   c. Who volunteers in the school?

   d. Who does what tasks related to raising children?

7. Vacations

   a. Whose hobbies and activities influence where to go and what to do?

   b. What portion of income goes for vacations?

8. Holidays

   a. How will we decide which family of origin to spend holidays with?

   b. What new traditions would we like for our marriage?[11]

Realities and Rewards

Julie and Greg continue to grapple with the differences between the ideal and the realities of their own situation. Even if Greg wanted to stay home for the next five years so that Julie could finish her education and get established in a job, she does not have the earning power to sustain the family. That is one of the harsh realities that must be faced when women and men have not seen themselves as partners in generating income.

In addition, Greg's decision to go to graduate school and the student debt that went along with it still looms like a patch of gray clouds over their financial horizon. It has meant that Julie has had to postpone some of her own plans for further education and training or find creative ways to generate income to cover these costs. They have been able to navigate through the pain of this situation by committing themselves to thinking creatively. The beauty of their situation now, as Julie puts it, "is that I no longer feel that if he can't make the money it just won't happen. My mentality now is that I need to find creative ways to earn the money so that I can accomplish my dreams. I am not feeling like he has to do everything, and that is a good shift." To some this may reflect merely a subtle change, but for a woman who had been accustomed to looking to her husband as a savior, it is a very important shift away from unilateral dependency to a shared responsibility that, in the long run, will bring greater freedom to both of them.

In addition, they are now being more proactive about Julie's development. As Julie has identified work and ministry opportunities that she is passionate about, they have worked creatively together to make it possible for her to participate. Since Greg cannot make up for all of the hours that Julie is out of the house, they have learned to accept a messy house, refusing to lose any emotional energy over it or resent it. As Greg says, "If giving Julie the freedom to get involved in other things means that people come over to the house and find it messy and think less of me, I am prepared for them to think less of me. But I had to make a formal decision in my mind; otherwise I think it would have bothered me."

Greg admits that on occasion he wrestles with the feeling that he works all the time. "When I go home, it's not like I go home to rest; I start working. I'm always working! Sometimes I do wish we could go back to the way it used to be. It was so clean!" It is important for him to express these feelings and to have them validated. For a man who is used to putting his best energies into his job and then using his time at home to regroup (rather than participating fully in the responsibilities of family life), there are going to be losses to grieve when things change. The wise woman is able to give space for this part of the process—and even some comfort—without belittling her husband or losing her own conviction that this is what is needed if both women and men are to have the opportunity to become all that God intends for us to be.

Most couples find that working through this change process is well worth any sacrifice they have to make. Julie has discovered that when she becomes passionate about something and feels a strong call, she has more energy and needs less sleep. "Taking care of kids and cleaning house are responsibilities that need to be done, but in and of themselves they are not a complete expression of who I am."

Greg has found that working through this process of change has been an invitation to his own spiritual journey—a journey toward more self-awareness, a greater capacity to love, a deeper faith in God's presence on the journey and more opportunities to discover what it means to be like Christ. When he decided not to fight Julie's questions and struggles, he embarked on a new leg of his own spiritual journey that gave him the opportunity to confront his own character issues, especially his insatiable drive for achievement. He is a better man today for having opened himself to the questions that Julie's struggle raised.

Greg also derives a great deal of satisfaction from knowing that he is participating in his marriage in ways that express greater mutuality. They are realistic about the inequity of Greg having fifty-plus child-free hours a week to pursue his calling while Julie has to fit her dreams into much smaller and more interrupted blocks of time. But they accept this as one of the ramifications of earlier decisions made in a marriage configuration in which they both willingly participated. This helps them not to resort to blaming or fault-finding. As Julie observes, "At least now Greg is aware of the inequity in educational opportunity and time, and he's willing to help where he can. It's something we work back and forth on."

In addition, Greg and Julie are enjoying an increasing number of authentic moments together, moments when two whole people come together to express love to each other through physical intimacy, verbal communication or simply the tone of their daily interactions. Even though the process of change has been painful and difficult, they both agree that their relationship now is far more satisfying than before. As Greg says, "The moments of authentic love exchange—when you know that it is a whole person returning love rather than a shell of a person—those are the moments that make it all worthwhile."

Questions for Individuals or Groups

(If you are not yet married, answer these questions from your perspective now.)

1. What was your understanding of the marriage relationship as you prepared for marriage? How did you and your spouse plan to organize roles and responsibilities?

2. How have your perceptions about the marriage relationship changed? Have you had any experiences that have forced you to rethink previous ideas?

3. How do you make decisions, both large and small? Is there anything about your process that you would like to change?

4. Which issues raised by the questions on page 168 need further discussion between you and your spouse or the person you are planning to marry?

5. Does your marriage/dating relationship feel like it is big enough for two fully developed human beings, or does it seem like it is weighted more toward the development of the gifts and calling of one person? What adjustments need to be made?

10

Partners in Parenting

*I have been known to say to my students that the real test of their commit-
ment to healed gender relations will come not after
graduation, not even upon marriage, but when they start to have children.
Because then, of all times, it is seductively easy
to decide that men were "really" designed for dominion and women were
"really" designed for the maintenance of relationships.
In the process, we often turn fathers into absentee landlords who barely
know their children—a denial of their creational call to intimacy;
at the same time, we isolate mothers in nuclear-family households,
denying them the exercise of the cultural mandate that
is just as much a part of their creational call. And then we wonder
why middle-class men often become ulcerous workaholics
and middle-class women often suffer depression.[1]*
MARY STEWART VAN LEEUWEN

It was not one of our prettier moments as a married couple. I was complaining about the difficulty of juggling graduate work, writing, speaking, mothering and taking care of a home. When Chris responded by suggesting that that was my job, I exploded: "Motherhood is not a job; it is a biological fact just like fatherhood is! Your job is banking and mine is writing and speaking!"

I realize, of course, that motherhood (and fatherhood too) is more than just a biological fact, but this moment was an epiphany of sorts. It was a moment of clarity in which I finally found words for my frustration about motherhood in our society being so much more defining and consuming for women than fatherhood is for men.

Not too long after that I sat among a small group of men and women in a hotel lobby during a conference discussing issues related to men and women at work. After listening to some of the women's frustrations about being overlooked and stereotyped at work, one man shared, "Really the whole thing about work stinks." Pulling out pictures of his five children, he said, "I would really like to be home with my kids. I try to work out of the home as much as I can, and right now my wife and I are trying to figure out how we can be more of a team in our marriage and in our parenting."

His sadness over not being able to be more present with his children was palpable. We all sat for a moment contemplating what it means for a man to want so much to be a father—not just biologically but in actual participation—and to find that the way we have traditionally structured the family within the larger society does not support the fulfillment of that desire. Rather than having his life defined and consumed by his work, he was struggling to find ways to understand and experience his fatherhood as a more meaningful part of his identity than the culture has allowed. It was really the flip side of the frustration I had expressed a few weeks earlier.

These snapshots from the real lives of real couples illustrate twin frustrations that are two sides of the same coin: Many men today feel stuck in society's expectation that they do whatever it takes to be success-ful on the job, even if it means sacrificing the opportunity to be meaning-fully involved with their families. At the same time, many women are frustrated with the expectation that they are to be the primary caretakers of the home and children.

In some ways shared decision-making (as discussed in the previous chapter) is the easy part of mutually empowering marriage. The greater challenge comes when children arrive and we seek to somehow configure our lives so that both the man and the woman are empowered to be meaningfully involved with nurturing life, exercising responsible dominion in the world and using our gifts to further the kingdom of God. Before children arrive, this can be almost a nonissue because it is relatively easy for husband and wife to devote forty or more hours a week to the worlds of work and ministry and still share the responsibilities of caring for a home during the time remaining. With the arrival of children, it is no longer that simple.

Grappling with the Issue of Fairness

"Until there is justice within the family, women will not be able to gain equality in politics, at work, or in any other sphere."[2] So says Susan Moller Okin in her book *Justice, Gender and the Family.* While I do not agree with all of Okin's solutions, her analysis of the problem is compelling:

> An equal sharing between the sexes of family responsibilities is the great revolution that has not happened. . . . Employed wives still do by far the greatest proportion of unpaid family work, such as childcare and housework. Women are far more likely to take time out of the workplace or to work part-time because of family responsibilities than their husbands or male partners. And they are much more likely to move because of their husband's employment needs or opportunities than their own.
>
> All these tendencies . . . tend to be cyclical in their effects: wives advance more slowly than their husbands at work and thus gain less seniority, and the discrepancy between their wages increases over time. Then, because both the power structure of the family and what is regarded as consensual "rational" family decision-making reflect the fact that the husband usually earns more, it becomes even less likely as time goes on that the unpaid work of the family will be shared between the spouses. Thus the cycle of inequality is perpetuated.[3]

Although these realities are difficult to acknowledge, this is the point at which issues of true teamwork among men and women in the church and in the workplace intersect with the issue of partnership within the home. When we decide on a rational level that women should be included more fully in all spheres of work and ministry and even commit ourselves to be proactive about it, we have only just begun. Then we must acknowledge that women often lack the same qualifications as men in terms of education, experience and number of years in the workforce because they have taken time off to raise children, they have cut back to part-time work, or they have not had as many of the family resources committed to their education and career goals.

In the meantime their husbands and other male peers have, in most cases, taken a much more direct and uninterrupted route to the fulfillment of their career dreams. While the arrival of children creates just a blip on the screen of most men's careers (requiring them to take a few days off at the most), for many women it means a major detour. Then when a woman reenters the workforce, she learns that the men who were her peers have bypassed her. She may even be subjected to conversations about the shortage of qualified women available to fill the very positions that would result in greater teamwork among men and women. Even if she had decided not to leave her career altogether, to work out of the home or on a part-time basis, she soon realizes how hard it is to keep up in a workplace atmosphere where more and more is expected. In the religious subculture in particular, a woman can feel betrayed when she realizes that she fulfilled the strong expectation that she be at home raising her children only to find that when the children are gone and she is more available, she is considered unqualified for the same kinds of leadership and opportunities as the men.

Likewise, men who want to be more involved in the lives of their children also face the possibility of being penalized at work. They know the truth of the matter, as summed up in a recent article in *Fortune* magazine: "Corporate America harbors a dirty little secret. People in human resources know it. So do a lot of CEOs, although they don't dare discuss it. Families are no longer a big plus for a corporation; they are a big problem. . . . It's fine to have the kids' pictures on the desk—just don't let them cut into your billable hours."[4]

It takes a great deal of love and patience to begin to unravel all the issues involved in crafting a life that is equitable for both a man and a woman, one that incorporates the deeply held values and life callings of both. It takes a willingness from both spouses to give and take, and it is almost certain that the husband or the wife or both will have to slow their mad rush for success, money or power in order to give equal opportunity to the other while at the same time making sure that their children are loved and cared for. Mary Stewart Van Leeuwen cautions that no particular family structure is absolute:

> The root issue is not some historically fixed way of structuring family economic, domestic, and childrearing tasks. The root question is one of priorities. How can a given Christian family, with its particular

constellation of talents, limitations, and needs so structure itself that it contributes to the advancement of God's kingdom here on earth? Perhaps the best environment for children is not the one in which mother stays home, but one in which the whole family, as part of the larger family of God, reaches out to meet the needs of others. Just how an individual family accomplishes this at various stages is a matter of responsible Christian freedom.[5]

The answers to questions such as the ones raised here are not simple, nor are they arrived at quickly in most cases. Chris and I still spend significant time and energy discussing how to balance family and other life callings. Although it is not easy and there is sometimes anger and frustration, more and more we are both satisfied with the life we are creating. We realize now that the issue is not only one of fairness to women, but it is also an issue of fairness to men. When we cut men off from their children, we cut them off from a significant source of health and vitality.

There is no question that there have been significant benefits for Chris and for the children as we have worked through the process of crafting a lifestyle that accomodates the call on both of our lives to parent and to work and do ministry beyond the home. Chris has needed to be more connected with his children, to sometimes let go of the business persona in favor of his own "child within"—the one who rides bikes, enjoys wrestling, tickling and pillow fights, makes pancakes for dinner and cuddles before bed.

Both he and our daughters have needed me to get out of the way so that they can forge their own relationships without Mother in the middle. As hard as I try to give them space, I still find myself meddling sometimes, convinced at some level that I need to orchestrate their relationships. My work and my traveling give them the space they need. Knowing that they can get along fine without me for limited periods has helped me to let go even when I am close by, so that Chris can bring more of himself to the raising of our children and the management of our home. When a woman is around the home and the children much more than her husband, she can begin to see herself as being more fully vested there. She can become convinced that it is her domain in which she always knows what is best. If she believes this (and this can be unconscious) she can, without realizing it, undermine her husband's unique contribution. When this happens, the children do not receive the best of both of them.

Chris has also benefited from knowing and loving and listening to a woman who is a mother and more. The insight, understanding and gentleness that he has gained from working through issues with his wife and daughters has helped him to become more down-to-earth, approachable and sensitive to the many different kinds of people he interacts with at work. When his female colleagues tell me how much they enjoy working with him and how insightful and respectful he is regarding gender issues, I know that a great deal of what they experience in him flows from the work that we have done around these issues in our own relationship.

This Is Not a Job for Supermom

The other side of the issue of fairness has to do with the well-being of our children. Probably every parent reading this book has wrestled with grave concerns about their children. In an article in *Time* magazine, one author describes our culture's legacy to the young as bad schools, poor health care, deadly addictions, crushing debts and utter indifference.

Mothers and fathers worry about the toxic residue left from too much television, too many ghastly movies, too many violent videos, too little discipline. They wonder how to raise children who are strong and imaginative and loving. They worry about the possibility that their children will grow wild and distant and angry. Perhaps they fear most that they will get the children they deserve.

"Children who go unheeded," warns Harvard psychiatrist Robert Coles, "are children who are going to turn on the world that has neglected them." And that anger will come when today's children are old enough to realize how relentlessly their needs have been ignored.[6]
It can be tempting for us as Christian parents in particular to believe that the greatest dangers for our children are "out there" in the big, bad world. We labor under the weighty realization that, to a certain extent, the future of our children depends on our ability to counter the culture in which they live and breathe. We must also realize, however, that our children are in danger because as a generation they have suffered our neglect, our indifference and our inability to do what it takes to keep our families together. The March 1994 issue of *Parents* magazine cites recent studies showing that during unsupervised hours, latchkey children of all social and economic groups are twice as likely to abuse drugs, engage in sexual

intercourse (one psychologist mentions that usually a girl has her first sexual experience in her or her boyfriend's empty house), join gangs or contribute to the astonishing 48 percent increase in the juvenile violent crime arrest rate in the last five years. In addition, these children may be extraordinarily isolated and lose out on valuable life-shaping experiences with friends and role models during the critical period of adolescent development.

Another study highlights the "negative long-term consequences of interparent conflict and divorce for preadolescents and adolescents." Of 170 children of divorced parents interviewed, one-fourth blamed themselves for the divorce and suffered low self-concepts; more than one-fourth harbored illusory hopes that "once my parents realize how much I want them to, they'll live together again"; and approximately one-third lived in fear of being abandoned by their parents.[7]

In the face of such harsh realities we must realize that the job of raising children today is not for Supermom or Superdad alone. It is for mothers and fathers who feel equally responsible for nurturing the physical, spiritual and emotional well-being of their children. It is for fathers and mothers who realize that they cannot delegate their responsibilities as parents to anyone else—not to their spouse, not to the nanny or the daycare workers, not to the church, not to the school system.

The answer to our concerns for our children is for men and women together to fall on our faces before God and confess our selfishness and upside-down values where they exist. Both men and women need to believe God when he says children are a blessing and to translate that belief into the obedience of making them a priority in our lives. Both need to slow down the frantic rush for success, money and power so that we can adequately supervise our children all the way through their teenage years. Both need to share parenting responsibilities so that women and men alike can nurture other parts of themselves even as they nurture children. Together we must cast ourselves upon God daily for wisdom and strength, asking, What will it require of me to nurture the emotional, physical and spiritual well-being of my children? In this area, more than any other, women and men in partnership can accomplish anything.

The High Call of Parenting

I must admit to being somewhat cynical that ministries and support groups for young mothers have become such a popular church and community offering. That women feel so overwhelmed and isolated in their parenting duties that they need support groups indicates that men and women are still not partnering adequately in the area of parenting.

The most encouraging thing that has happened for me as a mother is that Chris and I have begun to see ourselves more completely and clearly as a team in this challenge of a lifetime called parenting. I do not need a support group; I need my husband, the father of these children, to participate fully with me in this great call of God upon our lives. I need to hear him say with words and with action, "You are not alone. These children are just as much my responsibility as they are yours. Yes, I have my own vocational calling and you have yours, but together we have received the high call of parenting." I need to know and experience in relationship with him that raising children is not "women's work"; it is kingdom work that is worthy of the best we both have to offer. In this process, I have been freed to function in other areas of passion and giftedness that have in turn given me love, wisdom and strength to bring back to my family.

Many couples today are rewriting the scripts that tell the story of their lives, especially their growing understanding that God calls both men and women to parent their children and to participate with him in his great purposes in the church and in the world. We are recognizing that meaningful involvement with children *and* work that allows us to offer something of ourselves to the larger world are gifts of God that do not have to be mutually exclusive.

There is little biblical precedent or biological necessity for the pattern of almost exclusive mothering and marginal fathering into which we have fallen. Even though our culture has tended to view motherhood as more defining for women than fatherhood is for men, the biblical truth is that becoming a parent is a defining moment for both men and women. It is moment when a man and a woman receive a new life calling, a calling to become partners in nurturing the new life that God has entrusted to them.

We have already noted that at creation both women and men were given the responsibility to nurture life. The pattern in the Jewish culture of Bible times was for mothers to take responsibility for the first three years (probably until weaning), but that after that religious education of the sons became the fathers' responsibility. During this time the father also taught them the family trade. In addition, extended families lived together so that grandparents, aunts, uncles and older children participated in caring for the younger ones. In this community context the most powerful instruction regarding childrearing was given to the entire congregation of Israel—men and women alike: "Keep these words that I am commanding you today in your heart. Recite them to your children and talk about them when you are at home and when you are away, when you lie down and when you rise. Bind them as a sign on your hand, fix them as an emblem on your forehead, and write them on the doorposts of your house and on your gates" (Deut 6:6-9). These verses presuppose the involvement of men and women in the childrearing process in a way that would seem almost radical by today's standards.[8]

In the New Testament, Christ invited children into his circle of disciples, teaching them by his example and words that blessing, caring for and learning from children was for men as well as women. The disciples, who thought that they were above such mundane matters as childcare, needed to be retrained by Jesus' insistence that they not send the children away but allow them to be in their midst. What a refreshing scene to imagine: a group of men discussing theology while children play and tussle and climb all over them. Jesus then seized this teaching opportunity by saying, "Hey, stop talking for a while and watch these children. Their faith and simplicity is what the kingdom of God is all about" (Mk 10:14-15, my paraphrase).

While challenging men to include children as a priority in their lives, Christ's challenge to women in the New Testament was to clarify that their identity did not revolve around housekeeping and childbearing. Rather, the deepest core of their identity had to do with their obedience in following God's call in their lives and their devotion to Christ. When Mary took the posture of a rabbinical student and sat at Christ's feet to learn from him rather than helping her sister with housekeeping and cooking, Christ affirmed her choice. He told her that her desire to learn from him and get to know him better was the core of her identity that could not be taken away (Lk 10:38-42). When a woman in a Jerusalem crowd shouted out to him, "Blessed is the womb that bore you and the breasts that nursed you!" (Lk 11:27), Jesus corrected her perspective regarding woman's identity: "What makes a woman blessed—what really defines her—is her attention to the will of God in her life and her obedience to it" (11:28, my paraphrase).

It is also interesting that within New Testament descriptions of those qualified for leadership, men as well as women were instructed to be involved responsibly in caring for the household, including children. First Timothy 3:4 states that a bishop "must manage his own household well." Most often we have taken this verse to indicate a kind of supervisory function in which a man delegates the care of the home and the children to his wife, checking in every so often. However, a closer look at Paul's word choice reveals a rich meaning that includes "to go before," "to care for," "to assist," "to apply oneself to." The biblical use of this word involves a combination of the concepts of leading and caring for.[9] Attending to the needs of their households is also a qualification for deacons (1 Tim 3:12). Likewise, female elders are instructed in Titus 2:4-5 to teach younger women by word and personal example to be conscientious about their responsibility to their families. The reason for this emphasis on one's faithfulness in caring for the needs of one's family is obvious: "If someone does not know how to manage [lead and care for] his own household, how can he take care of God's church?" (1 Tim 3:5).

As Rodney Clapp states so beautifully in his book *Families at the Crossroads,* parenthood is wonderful preparation for other kinds of caring and leading in which we are called to participate. He describes children as strangers who come to us as aliens needing to learn to live in our world. They help us see ourselves more clearly and unashamedly confess their need of us:

Christian parenthood, then, is a practice in hospitality, in the welcoming and support of strangers. Welcoming the strangers who are our children, we learn a little about being out of control, about the possibility of surprise (and so of hope), about how strange we ourselves are. Moment by mundane moment—dealing with rebellion, hosting birthday parties, struggling to understand exactly what a toddler has dreamed and been so frightened by in the night—we pick up skills in patience, empathy, generosity, forgiveness. And all of these are transferable skills, skills we can and must use to welcome other strangers beside our children. We become better equipped to open ourselves to strangers, especially to those strangers who are not our children but our brothers and sisters in Christ.[10]

Men and women alike need the lessons in spirituality and leadership that spring from the opportunity to welcome and nurture children. But how do we follow a true partnership model for parenting within a culture and a religious subculture that are not set up for it? That is the question to which we now turn.

Rejecting the Scarcity Mentality

In order to keep working toward a lifestyle that is satisfying and supportive to men, women and children, we must confront belief patterns that do not serve us well. One of these is the scarcity mentality that Stephen Covey describes in his book *Principle-Centered Leadership*. Covey observes that "most people are deeply scripted in the scarcity mentality. They see life as a finite pie: if someone gets a big slice of the pie it means less for everyone else."[11]

Several years ago when Chris and I were struggling with the issues of spousal roles and responsibilities, a friend pointed out how trapped we were in a scarcity mentality. She said, "You two really believe that there isn't enough, don't you? You believe that if one of you gets what you need, there won't be enough for the other one!" She reminded us of the widow of Zarephath (1 Kings 17:8-16), whose resources, a jar of meal and a jug of oil, were continually replenished as she acted in faith when the prophet Elijah asked her to share with him. She challenged us to consider the meaning of that story as it related to our struggles with limited resources. The narrative of Jesus' feeding of the five thousand came to mind as well as we contemplated the truth that we serve a God of unlimited resources. Not only does he have unlimited power, energy and material resources, but he is also not limited by time and space.

The scarcity mentality plays itself out in many ways in human relationships, and chances are each one of us lives out of it in some area of life or another. If a man believes that power is a limited commodity, it will be hard for him to allow his wife to have as much influence in the family as he does. It will be hard for him to give her values and concerns as much weight as he gives his own. If a woman believes that there is only enough time and space in the marriage and family for her husband's opinion, her husband's calling, her husband's power, she may conclude that there is not enough of any of these things to enable her to follow the call of God in her life.

The Christian, however, must reject the scarcity mentality in favor of the truth that in God there will always be enough of whatever we need to live as whole persons and do his will. No one outside a particular family can say how God will replenish its resources from his unfathomable riches or multiply what seems like so little into enough nourishment for everyone. However, when we face the decisions of each day with an abundance mentality at the core of our belief system, it gives us creative energy to come up with more and better solutions, to find more ways to give and take, and to accept the fact that if the resources are not there for something, perhaps it is not part of God's plan at the moment. Our interactions are not about the two of us vying for limited resources; they are about learning to live into God's will. In this way of doing life together, we are both empowered.

Single parents may wrestle harder than anyone with a scarcity mentality. In the face of a discussion about partnership, it may be tempting to believe that there will not be enough of anything for parent or child. But God is a God of abundance who provides in ways that surprise us. If parents are single due to divorce, partnership is still possible, although more difficult logistically. Our culture's growing awareness of the grief that fathers experience when separated from their children is a reminder that even when a marriage falls apart, a great deal of effort should be expended in making sure that the children have as much contact as possible with both parents. In this case it is essential that the mother and the father have help in crafting a relationship in which they are able to respect each other's rights and responsibilities for being meaningfully involved in their children's lives. Neither parent should be expected to handle things alone.

When one parent cannot be fully involved in the parenting process or has died, it is helpful for the parent who is raising the children to accept his or her limitations and ask for help. A single mother might seek out the assistance of an older man or couple in her church so that her children can have a male influence in their lives. A single father might make it a priority for his daughters to be enrolled in club programs where women can nurture and mentor them. Realizing that children need both a motherly and a fatherly influence in their lives, we can ask God to provide for this in ways that will leave us as amazed as the widow of Zarephath was when her jar of oil continued to be replenished.

Shared Parenting: One Man's Perspective

I wish the man at the conference I mentioned at the beginning of this chapter could meet Steve Williams, senior pastor of a United Methodist church in a Chicago suburb. His wife, Jamie Hanna Williams, serves as senior pastor at another church closer to their home. Together they have three children who have had the privilege of being raised by two parents who are fully vested in parenting while remaining faithful to God's call in their lives to serve as pastors. I include their story, told from Steve's perspective, not because theirs is the solution for everyone but because the building blocks of a partnering approach to parenting—love, a concern for mutual empowerment, a commitment to children, a willingness to grapple with the issue of fairness, creative decision-making, and a can-do attitude—are all present in it.[12]

The parenting chapter of Steve's story began in October 1977. He still remembers the way the world seemed to stand still in those moments when he and his baby son, Nathan, first fixed their eyes on each other in the delivery room. Steve says, "In that moment I felt a special claim being laid upon me. It didn't matter that my wife had carried him for nine months, had just gone through labor or would nurse him throughout the year. There was a bond between us too, a bond far stronger than biological necessity."

Although men do not seem to talk about it much, Steve is convinced that there is a fierce parental instinct deep inside men as well as women, an instinct that says *You have a responsibility.* He continues, "As surely as mothers feel warmth, love and a desire to nurture and protect, fathers do too; only with men the feeling is one we handle a bit more awkwardly. There is little in our lives that prepares us for that moment when a nurse says, 'Do you want to hold your son or your daughter?' and then places that brand-new baby in your arms."

In the early months of Nathan's life, Steve contemplated the meaning of nurturance and recognized that this concept was wrapped up in the bond of acceptance and responsibility that he felt the first time he viewed his new son; however, he had deep doubts about his ability to nurture, as many men do. But even in the face of his doubts, he could not help but wonder, "Since few fathers lack affection for their children, why can't men, as well as women, be attentive to their newborn's need?"

During those early months of Nathan's life, Jamie was finishing a graduate program while Steve worked part time and helped with child-care. Like other fathers, Steve found out how much fun simple tasks can be, such as taking his infant son for walks in his stroller. The sky seemed bluer, the leaves greener, and life was filled with fresh new purpose. Hoisted on Dad's shoulders, Nathan responded to his bird's-eye view of things with sounds of delight. Of course, there were endless nonsense games to be played outdoors in the park or at home on the rug. It seemed as if they played morning, noon and night with whatever was close at hand; in the process Nathan felt loved and Steve felt affirmed.

It was no surprise to Steve, then, when he first was introduced to research indicating that play is where fathers excel. Studies show that when fathers hold their babies, it is often for the purpose of playing with them. While fathers are perhaps less verbal, they are typically more physical than mothers. One study showed that fathers "touched their infants with rhythmic tapping patterns" and that play shifted "to peaks of high infant attention and excitement."[13]

Almost in answer to Steve's questions about whether a father's nurturing activity must take a back seat to a mother's early in life, he came across this interesting bit of information: "Amazingly enough, an infant by two or three weeks displays an entirely different attitude (more wide-eyed, playful and bright-faced) toward his father than his mother. The cycle might be characterized as higher, deeper and even a bit more jagged."[14] The study concluded that the physical games fathers most naturally play with their infants have a direct and beneficial impact on later social and cognitive development. It has even been suggested that the ideal combination for building a healthy self-concept in a child is a talkative mother and a playful father.

Dr. Kyle Pruett of Yale University found that children with fathers as their primary caretakers suffered no negative effect on their identity: "They are all very comfortably masculine or feminine. . . . [Their] play is relatively free of sexual stereotypes. The boys are nurturing. The girls are very feminine but also competitive and curious."[15]

Looking back, Steve muses that "babies may be the perfect playmates for men. They will put up with activity no matter how mindless or silly, and in the process Dad feels wonderfully affirmed. When Nathan could crawl, I would race along beside him on my knees. We would have contests to see who could reach the top of the stairs. Invariably, he won.

We played in sand, in mud, with blocks and rocks. As I played with my firstborn I came to understand that there was a special relationship between us. It wasn't better than or more important than the relationship between mother and child. The bond between father and son or father and daughter is, however, different from and as important as the maternal relationship. When Nathan pulled my hair, chewed on my ears or spat up on my favorite coat, he was learning that this big, strong, strange-looking fellow, so different from Mommy, was also someone he could trust."

Child development experts have learned that children who have been adequately nurtured during their preschool years exhibit healthy self-concepts. They believe that a child's self-concept is related closely to his or her social interaction with others and that "children with high self-esteem are likely to be expressive, happy and relatively free of anxiety."[16] One need not look far to see the legions of people who do not relate well with others, especially other men. The roots of the problem may extend all the way back to childhood. Fathers who take time out to play with their children are making a far greater contribution than they realize.

Where the Rubber Meets the Road

The problem with this idyllic scene was that at the time of Nathan's birth Steve and Jamie were not yet finished with graduate school, and like everyone else, they wanted to be an upwardly mobile couple, living in the fast lane with the prospect of bigger and better rewards. But how could this happen if Steve or Jamie took five years off to raise a child? Of course, additional children could extend this period beyond five years. The implications for sacrifice seemed enormous.

This question brought Steve to a crossroads. He began to wonder, "What would give me greater satisfaction: a career that landed me at the top of my profession or raising a healthy, self-confident child? Maybe I should settle for landing at the middle of my profession, learn to be friends with all the other guys in two-career families and still have time to be a real dad.

"But what exactly did a real dad—a good dad—have to do, especially during those important early years? The old rules used to be pretty simple: keep the wife happy while she stayed home and watched the kids, and show up once in a while for a Little League ball game. But no one was playing by the old rules anymore. My wife wanted a career. We both wanted kids. Either one of us stayed home and deferred his or her career, or we both went straight to work to catch our rising stars and hope all the good things we heard about daycare were true.

"Faced with the dilemma of starting our careers and/or starting our families, we decided to do both. I would start my career, Jamie would start our family, and at a given point we would switch. In a world of tradeoffs and new rules, it seemed a logical enough solution."

On June 15, 1983, the moment of truth arrived. By then Nathan was five years old and had a sister named Carey, two and a half years of age. Steve recalls that after he and Jamie had breakfast together, "she blew me a good luck kiss and walked out the door to do battle. I turned, walked into the bathroom, shut and locked the door, then looked in the mirror to confirm reality: *I was a househusband.* I unlocked the bathroom door, stepped back into the hallway and bravely faced my new world. I made beds, got Nathan and Carey dressed, cleared the table, loaded the dishwasher, hauled out the vacuum cleaner, dusted and cleaned. Here I was, thirty-one years old, four years of successful career work behind me, and I had traded it all for a three-year tour of duty at home. Was I crazy or what? What self-respecting, red-blooded male would fork over his independence and do such a thing?"

That question appeared and reappeared for Steve during the three years that he stayed home with his childen. Real men did battle in the real world. Culture defined the real world as "out there," apart from wife and kids. A man's job was to make his mark on the world, obviously of greater importance than making his mark on his kids. This was the mental universe in which Steve (and most men) had grown up and lived. It was a world and life view that he had unconsciously accepted, and now it seemed to rise up against him and call him a traitor. He felt marked forever as a wimp.

More questions arose for Steve when he thought of his own father, a platoon sergeant who fought bravely in World War II and was disabled while traveling behind enemy lines to protect his company. It seemed ironic to Steve that he would have sired a son who was now a stay-at-home dad. Steve wondered, "Had I let my dad down? Had I let myself down? Was I letting down my wife and kids? Or were the same values that told my father he should serve his country in time of war, regardless of personal consequences, directing my life now on a smaller scale?"

In light of his decision to become a stay-at-home dad, Steve considered the verse "Greater love hath no man than this, that a man lay down his life for his friends" (Jn 15:13 KJV). Realizing that many men have been willing to lay down their lives for their country, he wondered if one's children, as well as one's country, merited the giving up of certain individual rights. He concluded, "For a man, staying at home rarely seems like heroic service. It is, however, one way of laying down your life for another."

As the days rolled by Steve saw firsthand the benefits of willingly laying down some of his own personal drives and dreams for the good of his wife and children. Not only could Jamie begin her now flourishing career, but he learned that he could make contributions on the home front that only time and opportunity would allow. During the first summer, for example, he spent several hours each day with Nathan and Carey at a nearby pool teaching them how to swim. There were not many other fathers splashing around in the water in the afternoon, but by this time Steve was feeling less like an anomaly and more like a pioneer.

At first Steve confined them to the children's pool. However, Nathan kept looking longingly at the big pool and the diving board, which rose up and out over the water. By the middle of summer he could dog-paddle well enough to jump off the low board and swim back to the poolside. Noting Nathan's progress, Steve granted permission for him to attempt the high dive, and before long he was one of the few five-year-olds jumping off the high dive. Steve noticed that there were many mothers at the pool who would not let their sons go off the diving board, especially if they were just learning how to swim. But from Steve's perspective as a father, if a son wants to test his courage—the real attraction of leaping into thin air—Steve thought it ought to be encouraged in the right time and place. It was fine with him that fathers tend to define acceptable risks differently from mothers.

One evening in particular stands out in Steve's mind as a moment when the benefits of the choice he had made seemed particularly clear. It was a Thursday night, and Steve and the children were waiting for Jamie to come home while Steve's latest culinary wonder bubbled atop the stove. Nathan was playing with toys, and his fingers flew in virtuoso displays of manual dexterity. Carey watched her brother with her head draped comfortably over Steve's shoulder and her arms dangling around his neck.

She asked if they could play horsey, and soon Steve was crawling around the room singing "Happy trails to you." In that moment, recounts Steve, "it occurred to me that here was fatherly nurture in action. Nathan found affirmation and approval in his particular endeavor, while Carey's needs for acceptance, love and contact were being met as I played the role of horse and troubadour.

"For my part, I felt simple affection and love for these kids, sure that life offers few richer blessings than to be saddled up, sat upon and commanded to go 'giddy-up.' I couldn't help but wonder, *Who better to mold a healthy self-image through play and everyday activities like playing horsey? Who better than a father to teach his children that they are important and worthwhile by investing his time and energy in them? Who better than a father to nurture body, mind and spirit by showing that all of these parts are an integrated whole?*"

Benefits beyond Babyhood

Fathers who stay home with their children have the same goal as everyone else—to raise happy, well-adjusted children. But this modest goal is surely one of life's greatest challenges. When parenting is shared, however, the objective may be more easily attained. During Steve's three years of being a stay-at-home dad, he had the privilege of watching his son go through kindergarten, first grade and second grade. When Nathan returned home with his final second-grade report card, it indicated that he showed an above-average grasp of skills and concepts in all areas of study. In addition, he ranked at the 94th percentile in math in a nationally administered skills test. Steve feels a personal sense of accomplishment related to his son's academic achievement and healthy self-concept, realizing that the kind of nurturing that comes naturally to most fathers—physical, often athletic—is just what his son needed.

His experience is compatible with a study completed by Robert Blanchard and Henry Biller, which concluded that a father's availability or absence affects such things as later academic performance, an important area of parental concern. The study showed that among boys the superior academic performers came from homes where the father was present and highly available.[17] This is particularly noteworthy since among academic underachievers boys outnumber girls two to one.[18]

But boys are not the only ones who benefit from a father's more complete involvement in the parenting process. When Steve's daughter, Carey, went through preschool screening and was tested in three general areas—fine motor skills, verbal and cognitive ability, and gross motor skills—she emerged with a positive score in every category. As Steve says, "There is real satisfaction in moments such as these. You add up the peculiarities of your situation—the hurt and pain of social isolation and perhaps the slowing of your career progress that often goes along with taking this time to be with your kids—and you realize that your own momentary light affliction might just be working out a great good. To see a son or daughter strong in body, mind and spirit, and to think that being home with you helped them along that path is sufficient reward. For what is more important than family? What is more precious than the children we call our own?"

Steve looks back on his three years at home with great fondness, realizing that they were the best years of his life. He wonders why it seemed so painful during that time, why he often felt like he was drowning in anguish and self-doubt. Without minimizing the pain that was so real given the peculiar stereotypes and expectations inherent in our culture, he also realizes that hindsight is 20/20. He realizes now that if men, by being men, can successfully model those values that make for a better world, such as courage, commitment, honesty and sacrifice, then the traditional formula of exclusive mothering and marginal fathering is really not the most effective parenting model. If children need their fathers in concrete ways, and can benefit from having a competent male presence in the home, then masculinity is not at stake. What is at stake is how best to raise our kids.

Steve reflects on his pioneering experience: "As I look back on it now, I know I did something that was right, right for my children, my wife and even me. It makes me wonder why this opportunity isn't more palatable to other men. But as Isaiah the prophet said, 'Here am I, and the children the Lord has given me. We are signs and symbols in [the land]'" (Is 8:18 NIV).

Questions for Individuals or Groups

1. Early in this chapter the author states that in our society, motherhood has been "more defining and consuming for women than fatherhood is for men." Why do you think this is?

2. How has your responsibility as a parent affected your career? Has this been easy or difficult for you to accept?

3. How satisfied are you with your participation in the parenting of your children? Would you like to be more involved, less involved, involved in a different way?

4. What are the distinctive qualities that you and your spouse each bring to parenting? Does your parenting partnership make it possible for your children to receive the full benefits of the strengths that both of you have to offer?

11

Love, Sex & Friendship

For one human being to love another:
that is perhaps the most difficult of all our tasks,
the last test and proof, the work for which
all other work is but preparation.[1]
RAINER MARIA RILKE

Beloved, let us love one another;
because love is from God.
1 JOHN 4:7

A friend and I were sitting at a small coffee shop, enjoying a rare opportunity for leisurely conversation that was not associated with any task. For several weeks I had felt the need to apologize for a moment when I had become unfairly demanding. Because I had known men who shut women out of partnership and friendship due to their fears about sexuality, I was afraid that this friend might back away from our friendship at some point. Wanting to spare myself such a loss, I had said with some force, "Don't you ever do that to me!"

Later I realized that I had no right to make such a demand. A more loving approach would have been to express my desire that sexuality not be allowed to jeopardize our friendship, while at the same time assuring him that my role as a friend was to support him in doing whatever was best for himself at any moment. Certainly I could request that if he ever felt the need to back away, he would at least let me know what was going on so I would not be left to wonder. I could ask that he make the effort to deal with his issues and come back into the friendship, but I had no right to demand.

And so I seized upon this unhurried moment over coffee to apologize. Then these words slipped out: "You know, even if at some point you do have to back away, I will love you anyway."

Neither of us had ever used the "L-word" before in describing our friendship, and I certainly had not planned on using it, so we were both a bit surprised. He said, "Thank you," and then we sat for a moment in silence, not knowing what else to say. Eventually we let the moment pass and moved on to other topics, but as my friend confessed to me later, as he drove home later that day he began to feel a little nervous. He wondered, *How do I feel about this—a woman who's not my wife telling me that she loves me? Are we allowed to do this?*

I felt nervous too, but for different reasons. I felt vulnerable, wondering if I should have allowed such a personal admission to slip out so spontaneously. I doubted for a moment whether it was right and safe to acknowledge love in a friendship between a man and a woman. I worried about how he had interpreted it. As a come-on? As sappy sentimentality?

In the end, however, I had to acknowledge that I had grown to love him and to deeply desire God's best for him and his family. Often in times of wordless prayer he would come to mind, along with other friends and family members, and I would hold him in God's presence. As far as I was concerned, this kind of prayer and care was a normal progression in any friendship, and it was indeed about love. If it had been a woman friend sitting across from me (and it often is), I would not have given my words a second thought. By the same token, if it had been a guy sitting across the table from my friend saying "I love you, man," it would have been meaningful but probably not threatening. In contrast, my friend and I shared an unspoken fear that if we acknowledged love, no matter how appropriately, we might in some way weaken the boundaries protecting our marriages and our sexual integrity.

What's Love Got to Do with It?
Although there were a few moments when I might have wished that I could take back the acknowledgment of love that created that initial fear

and awkwardness, I was also glad for it because it brought into bold relief some of the core issues that men and women struggle with as they consider the possibility of friendship. Often framed as questions, they represent some of our deepest fears and concerns. We wonder, can men and women be friends without "the sex part" getting in the way? Do love and emotional connection make us hopelessly vulnerable to sexual failure? If men and women decide that they can be friends, what will these relationships look like? Most important, if men and women cannot love each other in any real sense of the word, what is it that we have to offer each other?

In this context, love is not sentimental slop that goes wherever emotion and physical urges take us. It is not the stoic and sometimes sterile way we often speak about "loving our neighbors as ourselves" while keeping our selves at a safe distance. Rather, it is the kind of love that engages with others on spiritual, emotional and physical levels. It is a love that opens us to the beauty in each other and compels us to reach out in meaningful and appropriate ways. Love calls us to hold each other in God's presence regularly and to take responsibility for ourselves so that we never intentionally do anything to hurt or defraud another person or their other significant relationships.

As disconcerting as it can be to experience an outpouring of God's love (Rom 5:5) in the context of male-female friendship, I have become convinced that I must not be ashamed that I love. I am called—we are all called—to love. Love that comes from God and finds its expression in working for the other's highest good is the best that we as men and women have to offer one another. It is a blessing to both the giver and the receiver. I would even say that women and men have the right and responsibility to give and receive love from each other. In this context love is the will to extend oneself for the purpose of one's or another's spiritual growth.[2] This willingness is characteristic of all love that is true love, and it is the only thing that will take us toward the healing, the community and the partnership for which we were created.

The Transformations of Friendship

In an article on male-female friendships Dennis Hiebert observes, "Current social structures and norms effectively separate and segregate the genders in all but association [interaction based on some common social interaction], leaving most adults with a collection of same-sex friends and perhaps a spouse in their personal circle. Conceivably, this scenario is both a cause and effect of gender alienation and antagonism, and the excessive modern pressure on marriage partners to be everything for the other."[3]

It should not surprise us that the segregation of the sexes into same-sex friendships has both caused and resulted in gender alienation and antagonism. If men and women are not free to share thoughts and ideas over lunch, if we cannot talk with enough privacy and safety to work through issues, if we cannot spend enough time together that we feel like we know each other, if we cannot have fun together, if we cannot open our hearts and love each other as friends do, we will keep a safe distance that permits us to communicate only over a chasm of apathy, misunderstanding and inadequate information.

Fortunately there are some courageous souls who are moving carefully and intentionally toward the better way. In her book *Friends and Strangers,* Karen Mains writes about beginning to discover the joy of male-female friendships through her relationship with a man she met on an overseas trip.

Properly chaperoned by a party of six people, but unaccompanied by our spouses, we traveled together for ten days. The trip thrust us into exotic locales and the drama of refugee camps. We shared hilarious adventures, met strange and courageous folk, enjoyed hours of conversation, and in the course of those ten days, we became friends. When I examined my feelings for this man, I realized I felt comfortable, as though I had discovered a long-lost brother. And I was glad, so glad. . . .

I am lonely for my brothers, I am lonely for this lost half of my female self. I want reconciliation. I am weary of the dividing wall of hostility Christ my brother came to tear down. I want to put away the world's ways, this damaging civil war of the sexes that rips apart our spiritual union.[4]

The loneliness and longing for connection that we experience in the absence of meaningful male-female friendships remind us of a goodness that we were created to experience. Our desire to embrace this goodness in our own lives can be used by God to motivate us to do the necessary work of reconciliation and community building. It has been in answer to these longings that God has led my path to cross with men who are courageous, wise and openhearted enough to move beyond fear and take the risk of friendship with women. They acknowledge their fear, but they are also willing to acknowledge their longing to be in comfortable, affirming relationships with women where they know that they are cared for.

When I asked one friend what he desires in relationships with women he said, "There is this longing to be heard and understood—maybe even to be forgiven for how we [men] have been trained in our culture—so that we can move forward. Even though I have what appears to be a cognitive approach to life, I want women to know that I do care. What women are asking of men is so new, but I want to be given a chance to figure it all out."

Another called it an "inarticulate gnawing" among Christian men who are trying to be obedient to the Scripture without any freedom to improvise: "I know that I have spent a lot of years wanting affirmation from women, looking for it, loving it when I get it and then judging myself for it. But as I have accepted more breadth of possibilities for relationships between men and women, I have come into a greater sense of wholeness because there is a fullness of imaging God. Being in meaningful relationships with women has brought healing for my own brokenness, redemption in my relationships and true shalom. And besides, it's so much more normal!"

In the Company of Friends

There is biblical and spiritual precedent for friendships between women and men that are characterized by love, commitment to each other's good and joy in one another's presence. Christ's personal circle of friends included Mary Magdalene and other women who accompanied him on his travels and cared for his material needs out of their love and gratitude. Also included were Mary and Martha of Bethany, two sisters who were distinct from each other in their approaches to life and also in the ways they interacted with Christ.

Christ's friendships with all of these women were characterized by a great deal of love and intimacy. The intimate nature of their relationships is evidenced by strong give-and-take in conversation (see especially Christ's conversation with Mary and Martha regarding Lazarus's death in John 11), the sharing of emotion and tears (Jn 11:28-36), freedom to share physical touch (Jn 12:1-8) and closeness (Lk 10:39), and a mutual desire to seek each other out in groups and in one-to-one interactions. For example, Christ felt free to seek out the welcoming presence of Mary, Martha and Lazarus whenever he was in the vicinity of their home; in fact, his most significant conversations seemed to take place not with Lazarus but with the two women. Similarly, Mary and Martha felt free to seek Christ out in their time of grief (Jn 11:3). After the resurrection, it was Mary Magdalene's tearful seeking and Christ's choice to appear to her first that gave them a few moments alone in the garden before spreading the good news to others (Jn 20:11-18). The love and regard between Christ and these friends is palpable throughout their interactions.

In case we are tempted to think that Christ's divinity was the only reason he was able to engage in such intimate friendships with women, it is helpful to learn about several significant friendships between men and women whom we have come to respect as spiritual leaders in the community of faith. One such example is the relationship between St. Francis of Assisi and Clare, whose work together laid the foundation for the worldwide Franciscan movement. Clare was only fourteen when she first heard about Francis and how he had withdrawn from the wealth of his upbringing to establish the order of the Poor Brothers. His reputation for charity toward all and his prophetic message of love drew Clare, a young, spiritually passionate girl, to want to meet him; Clare's reputation for purity, charity and piety preceded her and caused Francis to want to meet her as well.

Although their ages and stations in life were quite different, their initial meeting became the first of many in which Francis provided spiritual direction for Clare in her desire to find ways to give herself wholly to God. Clare became one of Francis's most faithful disciples and carried his ideals to new heights, especially in the founding of the Poor Sisters. The respective life callings of Francis and Clare became so intertwined that it is impossible for one to be understood without the other.

Clare loved Francis and Francis loved her ("Do not believe," he said, "that I do not love her with a perfect love"); and they used that love to refuel their own burning desire for God. One writer has said that "between them they invigorated not only Italy but also Christian Europe. They kindled a new poetry, a new art, a renewed religion."[5]

Letters from twelfth-century Cistercian monk and mystic, Bernard of Clairvaux, to a female friend named Ermengarde provide us with another glimpse into an invigorating male-female friendship. Although these letters contain the language of spiritual direction, they also reflect a deeply felt friendship that developed out of Ermengarde's interest in entering the religious life. Their correspondence reflected Bernard's support and input as Ermengarde explored monastic life, but they also included more personal expressions of love and friendship. In one letter Bernard writes, "Attribute to me as much love towards you as you find within yourself for me, so that you do not presume that you love more than I."[6] There even seems to be some attempt on his part to equalize the relationship away from spiritual director-directee to the mutuality of friendship: "It befits your modesty to think that the one who moved you to esteem me and choose me for consultation concerning your well-being will also have moved me in like manner to compliance and submission to your love and esteem."[7]

In another letter, he gives expression to his desire for physical presence: "Believe me, I am frustrated with the responsibilities by which I seem to be frequently prevented from seeing you, and I am delighted by those occasions in which I sometimes seem to be set free to see you. To be sure, few opportunities of this kind are given, but I confess, even the rarity itself is dear to me."[8]

One writer comments on the significance of this friendship in the context of Bernard's broader doctrinal work: "[Bernard's] view of the workings of grace is often sacramental—what we see, know, and experience can lead us to deeper and higher spiritual realities. Within the context of shared faith, shared life in the Body of Christ, human friendship—even friendship with a woman—can transform and be transformed. It, too, becomes a teacher in the school of love."[9]

Since there is still a great deal of reservation in some circles as to whether or not women and men can be friends without compromising themselves in some way, it is helpful to know that we are in good company as we explore the possibilities for such relationships.

Just Friends?

Friendship is a gift that often takes us by surprise. As C. S. Lewis describes it, friendship often begins with a discovery that leads us to say, "What? You too? I thought I was the only one!"[10] And if there is the opportunity and willingness on the part of both individuals, what develops thereafter may be a relationship that brings forth gratitude and reverence. As Caroline Simon writes in her book *The Disciplined Heart,* "A friendship that calls for reverence is a relationship in which the friend is valued as irreplaceable, as one for whom there is no double."[11]

There is no reason to think that women and men cannot forge friendships in which they become precious and irreplaceable to each other just as friends of the same sex do. While same-sex friendships offer us the comfort of being with others who are like us in body and life experience, there is also a great deal to be gained from cross-sex friendships. Not only do they open up new possibilities for reconciliation and full community (as I have already pointed out), they also foster another level of personal insight.

According to theologian and ethicist Stan Grenz, "When a man is around women he is far more conscious of his maleness. We act differently. It's quite intangible but it's important. It is the sense of being in the presence of the other that shows me who I am. It becomes an occasion for consciously acting out the meaning of genderedness in the presence of another." The same kind of awareness is available to women when they are in the presence of men. While we might be tempted to think that being around a spouse is enough of an occasion for this kind of awareness, Grenz goes on to observe that "a spouse can only provide a certain degree of input into our lives because he or she is finite. We need this kind of input from more than one person."[12]

While theological discussion, interpersonal skills and diversity training sessions are all important elements in the process of women and men pulling together in partnership, it is the love and care inherent in friendship that is truly transforming. When men and women open our hearts to each other as friends, we are changed in relationship to each other. We listen to each other with greater attention and concern because a friend's thoughts and opinions matter in different ways from those of mere acquaintances or coworkers. We find that we want to include each other not only because it is right but because we have grown to value and enjoy each other. When problems or misunderstandings occur, our commitment to working them through is deeper because we do not want to jeopardize a relationship that has become meaningful to us. An affection develops that makes us more tolerant of our friends' idiosyncrasies or moments when they are less than their best because, as the Scriptures tell us, love covers a multitude of sins. As we get to know each other's heart, we learn to attribute the best possible motives and meanings to interactions and actions that might otherwise be confusing or off-putting.

An openness to friendships across lines of gender does not necessitate that we become close friends with every individual of the other sex with whom we come in contact. However, those of us who choose to develop cross-sex friendships will find that our basic stance toward all members of the other sex will soften. Rather than experiencing each other as completely "other," we will come to know our friends (and thus all members of the other sex) as fellow human beings with whom we share the common experiences of joy and grief, strength and vulnerability, tears and laughter, success and failure. Rather than experiencing our differences as threatening, we will learn to delight in the richness of seeing the world from someone else's perspective. Even moments that require friends to navigate painful emotions and hard truths will instill in us the confidence that men and women can ride the waves of conflict and reach the other side with love and regard still intact. It is a confidence that we will take with us into every interaction. As we open the doors of our hearts in new ways to a few, we will begin to notice that our hearts are more welcoming to all. Such are the transformations of friendship.

But Is It Safe?

Inspiring stories and good reasons aside, in the context of male-female friendship we may still wonder, what makes a relationship safe? Of course, there are many ways in which a relationship can be safe or unsafe, but those asking this question are usually referring to safety from a sexual compromise or emotional bonding that would threaten the health of other significant relationships.

Rodney Clapp wisely reminds us that "relationships between men and women can never be entirely 'safe,' but following Jesus is not about being safe."[13] Love, if it is true love, always involves an element of risk as well as the possibility for great reward.

Because relationships are as diverse as personalities themselves, there is a sense in which each relationship is its own unique journey with its own lessons to teach. There are no simplistic formulas that can guarantee our safety. Having acknowledged this, however, let me hasten to add that there are degrees of safety. In a friendship where both parties take full responsibility for themselves by being self-aware, dealing with their own issues and being honest, loving and disciplined in their behavior, the degree of safety can be increased dramatically. On the other hand, when one or both parties renege on their personal responsibility by living an unexamined life, being undisciplined or placing blame on others, the relationship involves much more risk.

Bringing together two different personalities and collections of life experience into any kind of coherent relationship is a challenge under any circumstances. Male-female friendships present us with all of the challenges of same-sex friendships and more. In a study on cross-sex friendship, J. D. O'Meara identifies four primary negotiation challenges that are unique to these relationships: (1) determining the type of emotional bond represented by the relationship, (2) contending with the issue of sexuality, (3) dealing with the barrier of inequality and (4) dealing with the challenge of presenting the relationship as authentic to relevant audiences.[14] Developing "safe" relationships with members of the other sex revolves around the willingness and ability of both individuals to deal honestly and openly with these challenges.

Negotiating the Emotional Bond

The interaction I described at the beginning of this chapter was really a first pass at what some consider to be the greatest challenge of cross-sex friendship: trying to understand what it means for a man and a woman to be "just friends" and with what degree of emotional bonding we are comfortable. For me, putting my experience of this particular friendship into words was valuable because in so doing I became much clearer about who I was and what my commitment was in the friendship. Aside from the initial awkwardness, it gave me clarity and a greater feeling of safety in moving forward. It also gave my friend the opportunity to interact with what I had told him about myself and decide if he was comfortable with the way I envisioned our friendship or if some adjustment needed to be made.

It is important to acknowledge and accept emotional bonding as one of the defining characteristics of both same-sex and cross-sex friendship. Emotional bonding results naturally from the intimacy (which I am defining here as "reciprocal self-disclosure") that is central to friendship.

It is not helpful to deny the realities of emotional bonding or to attempt to keep it from happening; otherwise a conflict develops in which two people try to have a friendship without being friends. However, it is wise to be conscious about where we are on what Hiebert calls the "personal relationship continuum." He locates friendship on a "spectrum of personal relationships" that are differentiated based on degrees of interaction, intimacy and attachment. He identifies four different categories along a continuum moving from the least interaction, intimacy and attachment (acquaintance) to regular interactions based on common social involvement (associate) to increased positive interaction and intimacy based on the qualities of the person (friend) to the exclusive, institutionalized, domestic relationship of spouses.

> Where associates may be liked or disliked, friends are always loved, inasmuch as *philia* is added to *agape*. . . . Loving entails intimacy with, caring for, and attachment to the other. Attachment experienced as a powerful desire to be with the other is perhaps the most profound characteristic that separates the loving of friends from the liking of associates.[15]

How far we can safely allow a relationship to develop along this continuum is an individual matter that should be governed by the spiritual and psychological wellness of those involved, their sexual and relational histories, marital status (not only whether or not either friend is married but also the health of those marriages) and the support and accountability that both parties have for dealing with any issues raised by the relationship.

The challenge for cross-sex friends who are single is to sense if and when a relationship has moved to a point on the continuum where increased physical expressions of intimacy and considerations about marriage might be entertained. In this case, helpful questions revolve around whether or not the individuals desire total communion, whether any joint destiny that they might share is likely to enhance their own personal flourishing and whether both parties feel ready for the commitment and maturity that marriage requires.

The challenge in cross-sex friendships in which one or both persons are married to someone else is to keep the friendship from sliding to a place where the intimacy, interaction and attachment in the friendship overshadow one or both of the marriages. We need to be aware that it is possible to remain sexually faithful to a spouse yet at the same time maintain another relationship that threatens the primacy of the marital relationship. This awareness is not meant to engender inordinate fear or make us overly wary but rather to describe a creative tension that offers powerful possibilities for our own personal growth. Celia Allison Hahn describes this beautifully:

> A friendship between a man and woman, poised delicately in that role which is neither lover nor stranger, can provide one of life's most rewarding relationships. For both men and women here is a relationship that has no requirement for exclusivity and that therefore can touch many levels yet remain respectful of the larger context of both friends' lives. Perhaps it is just because friendships between men and women *are* so tensive that they have such a graced possibility of being one of those places where the holy shines through. Perhaps more than any other relationship, friendships between men and women are alive with ambiguity, contradiction, energy, paradox.[16]

This is, of course, the place where there are no simplistic, one-size-fits-all answers and we must find our own way along the continuum. Friendships can be many places on the continuum and still be good and safe. For instance, I have one friend whose work in the area of marriage and family counseling has given him the opportunity to work through issues related to his own marriage, intimacy needs, sexuality and friendships with women. He maintains a high level of daily communication and intimacy with his wife. The awareness of self and of others that he has developed in his life, the comfort level that he has with communication at deeper levels and the gut-level sense of safety we experience with each other has allowed us a great deal of freedom to move along the continuum fairly quickly. In fact, we joke about how our pattern of communication from our first private interaction onward has been to say hello and then move to the cutting edge with very few gradations in between. We have checked in with each other to see how that feels for both of us and have agreed that we are both comfortable with it, we enjoy it and we feel safe.

Other relationships move along the continuum more slowly. Different intimacy levels in our families of origin or marriages, different experiences and comfort levels regarding sexuality and intimacy in the context of male-female friendship, and different needs for processing relational issues all affect how fast and far we can safely move forward. In most cases I would recommend moving slower rather than faster as new friendships unfold; there is so much for friends to learn about each other that will affect the way they relate to each other, and there is no substitute for the time that this takes. The process of taking it slowly can communicate extraordinary respect for everyone involved. Giving each other time and space to process what is happening in the relationship, giving spouses the opportunity to understand the nature of the relationship and give input, and paying attention to any resistance that either party feels are all ways of honoring each person's individuality and life context. Relating to each other in group settings before moving into more personal one-to-one interactions is another way to give friendships a slower beginning, providing potential friends with an opportunity to observe each other, get to know each other and decide if this is someone with whom they feel comfortable and desirous of pursuing a more intimate relationship.

At whatever pace a friendship unfolds, there will probably be points along the way when it is good to discuss the issue of emotional bonding to make sure both friends are conscious of and comfortable with the level of intimacy they are experiencing. We can probably all use an occasional reminder that whatever love, compassion and warmth we are giving each other as friends, our spouses should be getting all that and more!

These questions can help us stay aware of what is happening in our cross-sex friendships in the area of emotional bonding:

1. Does either one of us believe that we are getting something from this relationship that we could not get from God, another friend, a spouse, a counseling session?

2. Is my marriage continuing to deepen even as this relationship deepens?

3. Do both respect each other's need to pull back at times in order to process the relationship?

4. Am I committed to what is best for the other person, or am I using the relationship to meet my own needs?

5. Are we able to be direct and forthright with each other about dynamics and concerns regarding the relationship?

6. What am I noticing and learning about myself, the other person, the human experience?

7. Am I willing to open up my experience of this relationship to a trusted friend or spiritual guide for their input and perspective?

8. Does this relationship contribute positively to my life in terms of enjoyment and personal growth, or does it drain energy from me?

9. Am I able to face these questions openly? Which words or phrases do I find myself resisting or challenging?

Contending with Sexual Attraction

Different people handle this challenge in different ways. Some disagreement exists among Christians as to whether or not it is wise for friends to acknowledge sexual attraction to each other. Many feel that this kind of acknowledgment increases vulnerability to sexual sin by making the situation more tempting. For those who have not learned to manage their sexuality openly and positively as described in chapter three, that is probably true. However, in a friendship where intimacy is growing between mature, self-aware individuals, it can be helpful to address this important challenge directly.

> It is unlikely that friends choose one another without being attracted in some way—physically, intellectually, emotionally. . . . The deeper the friendship becomes, the more friends find appealing. . . . Denial of the power of sexuality is far more risky than its acknowledgment. Naming the sexuality that draws intergender friends to one another can diffuse the temptations of the relationship and channel its energy to larger purposes.[17]

When friends are able to speak honestly and say, "There is some chemistry here and we are okay with that," they rob sexual attraction of its mystique. As one man says,

> When I acknowledge an attraction to myself, to my spouse, to a trusted friend and even to the person (if I have determined that the relationship can handle it) without acting on it sexually, the energy or the mystique goes out of it like air out of a balloon. For me this is about refusing to keep secrets or feel shame about who I am. When I acknowledge sexual attraction, I am much more able to connect emotionally with women because I am not ashamed of my own sexuality or afraid of theirs.

When friends use such acknowledgment as an opportunity to make a commitment out loud to each other that they will not cross the line into sexual expression (physical contact that is sexually motivated), they strengthen their mutual commitment to honor each other's sexuality. When such commitments are verbalized, they provide strong boundaries within which they become safer even as they deal with whatever sexual tensions exist between them. Such honest conversations can also be an opportunity to talk about what each individual can handle in terms of verbal intimacy, physical touch or time spent alone together. Since everyone is different in terms of what they mean and how they interpret the different overtures and avenues of friendship, what may create temptation or send mixed signals to one person may be an innocent display of affection or self-disclosure to another. For those who have worked carefully through their sexual issues, this is an opportunity for one friend to say to the other, "If something is a problem for you, I will honor that and refrain from doing it. I want to support your good intentions in every way I can."

Commitments about honoring sexuality are as sacred as commitments made to confidentiality or dealing directly with conflict. To push, to attempt to seduce, manipulate or even toy with the possibility of crossing these boundaries is a violation of the trust that is inherent in friendship.

The Equality Challenge
It is commonly understood that another characteristic of true friendship is equality or mutuality in the ability to give and receive influence. This presents an interesting challenge for men and women who are friends, because male dominance is still a way of life in much of society. Men still control a disproportionate amount of valued social resources such as money and power, so for men and women to find and maintain equality in their relationships, they may need to negotiate.

I reached such a negotiating point in my friendship with a colleague who would often invite me to hear him speak or preach. I was happy to accept his invitations when possible, because I enjoyed his style and wanted to support him as a friend. Eventually, however, I felt as if I was listening to him all the time and supporting him in groups where he was leading, but our roles were never reversed. I was playing the traditional woman's role of listening and following a man.

When I determined that this was bothering me enough that we needed to talk about it, I put it into the only words I could think of at the time: "If our friendship is going to continue, there is something you need to know. I am not going to be your groupie. I don't want to be the one listening and following all the time. Sometimes I want you to come hear me speak and support me in some of the things I am involved in."

As I shared my concerns, I was relieved that he listened without interrupting. When I finished, he sat quietly for a few minutes and took in the words but also the feelings behind what I said. Then he told me that my feelings made sense to him and agreed that we needed to be intentional about making our relationship more equitable. So the next time I spoke in our area he came to hear me and spent the day interacting with other participants and entering into my world. That expenditure of his time and energy meant a great deal to me because it demonstrated his support and his commitment to reciprocity in our relationship.

There is often negotiation that needs to take place around gender differences in relational style as well (although there are many friendships in which differences in men's and women's relational styles do not seem to create much difficulty). When this becomes evident, it may take some patience and openheartedness to negotiate a way of relating that gives equal value to both styles. An inequality that still exists in our culture is a belief, expressed consciously and unconsciously, that the way of men is the right way. While some in the feminist movement have attempted to describe women's ways of leading, communicating and using power as superior to men's, many of us still hold a fairly deep-seated belief that men's ways are more effective.

One example of a difference that might need to be negotiated in a male-female friendship is men's socialization toward individualism and separateness and women's socialization toward connection and dependence. In the development of a friendship it is not difficult to see how a man's attempts to stay independent and separate could leave a woman's need for meaningful connection unsatisfied, or how a woman's attempts at meaningful connection could feel threatening to a man who is more comfortable staying somewhat distant and less communicative.

Another difference that can cause tension is men's tendency to be led by thinking and women by feeling. Men may find it uncomfortable, embarrassing and even unnecessary to talk about feelings. Women, on the other hand, often associate the sharing of feelings with growing intimacy and concern about process. This may lead to times in friendship when a man gets frustrated that there is too much processing or a woman feels like there is not enough sharing for her to know what the man is experiencing.

We begin to eliminate inequality first by agreeing that in these and many other areas neither the woman's way nor the man's way of relating is better than the other; both have something valuable to offer. If gender differences become an issue, friends might then be able to negotiate a middle ground in which a man reaches beyond his comfort level to give what a woman needs in order to feel befriended (e.g., a phone call every so often just to check in, a willingness to talk at the feeling level when that would be truly helpful, an occasional verbalization that the relation- . ship matters) and a woman pulls back enough so that the man maintains the degree of separateness that he needs (i.e., "going with the flow" rather than probing and analyzing, participating in work or leisure together rather than always talking, giving physical or emotional space when he feels crowded by the relationship). Both friends should feel free to ask for what they need and to give only what they can joyfully give. When an adjustment or refusal is necessary, it is important to respond in a spirit of desiring what is best for the other.

When men and women can experience the tension associated with their differences while at the same time recognizing that both ways of being in the world emphasize aspects of the human experience that we all need, we have the opportunity to move into what Celia Hahn describes as "paradoxical caring space" in which we realize that

moving toward other people and moving apart are the basic steps in life's great dance. Whole and free, moving comfortably between autonomous and intimate activities, we may find joy in both tender- ness and adventure. The dance points beyond man and woman to the giver of a spacious love that embraces your freedom and mine. The One who *is* caring space can empower me to accept that gift and offer it to you.[18]

The Audience Challenge

Privacy is an essential part of any friendship, but it can arouse public suspicion when a friendship includes a man and a woman. This can create quite a dilemma for cross-sex friends. An inordinate concern over avoid- ing the appearance of evil has in many cases robbed us of meaningful connection as men and women. One author has gone so far as to say that by avoiding the appearance of evil we can avoid the evil itself![19] Surely it is this hope that has caused so many men and women to hold themselves at a distance from each other. How much better served we would be by concerning ourselves with how things really are than how they seem. Yet our culture's tendency to eroticize every interaction between men and women makes it necessary for us to deal with this challenge.

Spouses, parents, church family, coworkers are all parts of the audience with whom cross-sex friends might need to concern themselves. In the context of this audience friends might ask, Are we comfortable being seen alone together in a restaurant, on a walk, playing tennis? How much weight do we want to give to other people's concerns or to the issue of appearances? How can we create the privacy that it takes for a relationship to grow without giving others the wrong impression? These are personal decisions that only the two people involved can negotiate. We need to be relentless in monitoring how things really are so that our decisions about how things appear can flow out of that and so that there is integrity between the two. This monitoring can be done with God, with a spouse, with a spiritual friend, with the friend involved. If sexual energy in the relationship is strong, quiet dinners might not be a good idea. If friends have worked through sexual tension to a place where it is not a major issue, they may be able to give themselves more freedom without paying an inordinate amount of attention to appearances. Their comfort and ease can then become a model for others of what healthy friendships can look like.

If either or both of the friends are married, the spouses are the most relevant part of the audience and need to be brought into the loop in some fashion. Sometimes it can feel a bit unnatural or forced to bring two couples together just because a man and a woman happen to be friends. At other times this can work fine. What is more important is honest, open sharing with our spouses about our growth process and what we are learning in our friendships. Although for various reasons we might not choose to share every detail about our cross-sex friendships right at the moment (perhaps we need to process the relationship personally before trying to communicate with our spouse), it is important to be conscious of maintaining integrity, honesty and openness in our relationship with God, in marriage and in our friendship. As we work toward wholeness on all three levels, we support ourselves through this accountability. In addition, the insight and self-awareness gained through friendship can enliven each friend's marriage as new intimacies are shared over time.

Unless spouses come into a marriage with close cross-sex friendships already in place, it is possible and probable that the choice of either spouse to engage in such friendships after marriage will necessitate discussion and may even cause upheaval in the relationship. When a spouse chooses a friend of the other sex, especially if the friends are at all physically attractive to each other, it can be threatening for the spouse. This is a marital moment that can be difficult to negotiate, but it can also be an opportunity to face some of our fears and to be freed from them. It is almost certain that cross-sex friendships will raise issues that are beneath the surface and have not yet been discussed. Spouses must go slowly with each other at this point, because the issues raised are so tender: perhaps there are fears of abandonment, jealousy, feelings of inadequacy, inability to talk honestly about sexual issues or lack of trust. These are often the deepest issues in marriage, and we can be grateful for the opportunity to work through them, because there is greater freedom on the other side. Depending on the self-awareness, communication skills, and spiritual and psychological maturity of the two people involved, a couple may be able to handle these issues on their own and come up with guidelines for cross-sex friendship that are mutually agreeable. Other couples may find that they need help from a third party.

When your spouse develops a close cross-sex friendship, it is important to keep in mind that the discomfort you experience could be related to something about your spouse (maybe he or she is genuinely careless, shows a lack of wisdom or consideration, or leads an unexamined life) or it might be an unresolved issue within yourself that you are projecting onto your spouse. I understand now that the fears I had early in my marriage over my husband's working relationships with women were more about me than about him. I had so much fear about the power of sexuality, in addition to some deep-seated feelings of inadequacy, that the very idea of his being close to other women seemed unbelievably frightening. However, since he had always been completely trustworthy, I soon had to admit that my fears were about something inside me. Not until I worked consciously toward a healthier view of sexuality within myself was I freed from my fears about him.

We must be respectful of the time and effort that it takes for a husband and wife to achieve a comfort level with these things rather than settling into a reactionary fear that robs either one of the true blessings and growth inherent in cross-sex friendship. Different relationships can handle different freedoms. In one friendship there might be a great deal of freedom within both marriages and the trust and honesty in the friendship to go out to a restaurant together, to stop in and see each other, to go for a walk or to just hang out. In a friendship where the spouse is still processing these issues the options may be more limited. The important thing is that the friendship be allowed to unfold with respect for all involved. There must be a balance between consideration for the spouse who is feeling uncomfortable and the spouse who desires the freedom to receive the gift of friendship that God has provided.

Once we have negotiated concerns regarding the public perception of a particular friendship, we need to be prepared for people to question or express concern and to be appreciative when they do. Without getting defensive, we can use it as an opportunity to evaluate and make sure that everything is as aboveboard as we want others to think it is, to ask God if there is anything in their input to which he wants us to pay attention and, depending on the guidance we receive, to adjust or continue on.

The bottom line regarding all of these challenges is this: if we want to grow up in our ability to cultivate God-honoring, safe, satisfying cross-sex friendships, we have to talk about and work through the issues associated with them, keeping in mind these words from Paul: "Speaking the truth in love, we must grow up in every way into him who is the head, into Christ" (Eph 4:15). Our greatest progress in gender relations will be made as men and women who are friends care enough about each other to listen and do this kind of work in their relationships. It may be hard, it may feel awkward, we may wonder if it is worth it, but only those who accept the challenges will find out.

Giving You the Best That I've Got

Parker Palmer, an educator whose approach to truth and learning has been greatly influenced by his Quaker upbringing, has written an amazing little book titled *To Know As We Are Known: Education as a Spiritual Journey.* In this book Palmer describes the transformational power of relationships: "To search for truth is to reach out with our whole persons for relationships which can reform us and the world in the original image of love. To know the truth is to enter with our whole persons into relations of mutuality with the entire creation—relationships in which we not only know, but allow ourselves to be known."[20]

Surely this is what God is calling men and women to do in community—to reach out with our whole persons for relationships that can transform and heal us. Real transformation does not come from a set of rules imposed from the outside but from within relationships where we open our hearts to what is and to what God wants to do. We enter into life-changing relationships with a certain amount of not knowing; we do not know what it will feel like or who we will be when we emerge. This is frightening. But there is a Spirit that is strong enough to cast out fear (1 Jn 4:18); it is the Spirit of love, power and self-discipline (2 Tim 1:7).

This Spirit calls us as men and women to give each other the best that we have: a love that causes us to remain committed to God's will in the lives of everyone whom our lives touch. This love is not seductive, nor does it ask of others what they cannot or should not give. Sometimes love leads us to say so at appropriate times. Sometimes it leads to a hug or a touch or a tear. Sometimes love will call us to simple acts of human kindness or sincere affirmation. Sometimes love will give us the power to say a hard thing or to withdraw when we are vulnerable. Sometimes it will lead us to seek help regarding the issues relationships raise for us. Self-discipline might also require us to refrain from actions or words that bring us joy but would cause someone else to struggle.

Somewhere between the guideposts of "You shall not commit adultery" and "Beloved, let us love one another," there is a narrow path between two extremes: self-protective fear on one hand and a false sense of safety on the other. Fear will not do, because it is the opposite of the faith by which we are to walk. A false sense of safety is equally inadequate, because none of us will be completely safe until we are Home. The narrow way will require much more from us than leaving office doors open and making sure that men and women always socialize in groups of three or more. It will involve strong love, personal awareness and discipline. This more excellent way will lead us to the freedom to engage in the intimate relationships with persons, regardless of their sex, that will heal and invigorate us and our world.

Questions for Individuals or Groups

1. Do you feel comfortable in friendships with members of the other sex? What blessings have these friendships brought to your life? Have you found the issues and concerns in these relationships to be the same as or different from those in same-sex friendships?

2. What do you wish for in relationships with members of the other sex?

3. Which of the challenges of cross-sex friendship is most pressing for you at this time? What additional questions do you need to explore?

4. What fear does the Spirit need to cast out of your heart in order for you to enter into life-giving relationships with persons of the other sex?

Notes

Introduction

[1]John Dawson, *Healing America's Wounds* (Ventura, Calif.: Regal Books, 1994), p. 248.

[2]Henri J. M. Nouwen, *Reaching Out* (Garden City, N.Y.: Doubleday, 1975), p. 76.

[3]M. Scott Peck, *The Different Drum: Community Making and Peace* (New York: Simon & Schuster, 1987), p. 329.

Chapter 1: Created for Life Together

[1]Karen Mains, *Friends and Strangers* (Dallas, Tex.: Word, 1990), p. 128.

[2]As quoted in Sir Edward Cook, *The Life of Florence Nightingale* (New York: Macmillan, 1942), p. 57.

[3]Julie Gorman, *Community That Is Christian* (Wheaton, Ill.: Victor Books, 1993), pp. 29-30.

[4]For example, Moses named his son Eliezer because "the God of my father was my help *[ezer]*" (Ex 18:4), and in Psalm 40:17, as in many other places, the psalmist refers to God as "my help *[ezer]* and my deliverer."

[5]R. David Freedman, "Woman, a Power Equal to Man," *Biblical Archaeology Review* 9, no. 1 (January-February 1983): 56.

[6]Mary Stewart Van Leeuwen, *Gender and Grace* (Downers Grove, Ill.: InterVarsity Press, 1990), p. 42.

[7]Gareth Weldon Icenogle, *Biblical Foundations for Small Group Ministry* (Downers Grove, Ill.: InterVarsity Press, 1994), p. 117.

[8]Ibid., p. 10.

[9]Jon R. Katzenbach and Douglas K. Smith, *The Wisdom of Teams* (New York: HarperCollins, 1993), p. 45.

[10]Phil Jackson, *Sacred Hoops* (New York: Hyperion, 1995), p. 6.

[11]Ibid., p. 21.

[12]Kenneth Labich, "Elite Teams Get the Job Done," *Fortune,* February 19, 1996, p. 90.

[13]Katzenbach and Smith, *Wisdom of Teams,* p. 2.

[14]As quoted in Madeline Doubek, "Trying to Catch the Eye of Women Voters in Suburbs," *Arlington Heights (Ill.) Daily Herald,* October 10, 1996.

[15]Van Leeuwen, *Gender and Grace,* p. 155.

[16]Andrew Kimbrell, *The Masculine Mystique* (New York: Ballantine Books, 1995), p. 12.

[17]Van Leeuwen, *Gender and Grace,* pp. 45-46.

Chapter 2: The Disciplines of Biblical Community

[1]Stanley J. Grenz and Denise Muir Kjesbo, *Women in the Church: A Biblical Theology of Women in Ministry* (Downers Grove, Ill.: InterVarsity Press, 1995), p. 96.

[2]Klyne R. Snodgrass, "The Ordination of Women—Thirteen Years Later: Do We Really Value the Ministry of Women?" *Covenant Quarterly* 48, no. 3 (August 1990): 34-35.

[3]The Greek word used here is *prostatis.* Definition taken from Gerhard Kittel and Gerhard Friedrich, eds., *Theological Dictionary of the New Testament,* trans. Geoffrey W. Bromiley (Grand Rapids, Mich.: Eerdmans, 1985), p. 938.

[4]Aida Besançon Spencer, *Beyond the Curse* (Peabody, Mass.: Hendrickson, 1985), pp. 56-57.

[5]"Informed listeners customarily asked questions during lectures, but it was considered rude for the ignorant to do so. . . . Paul does not expect these uneducated women to refrain from learning (indeed, that most of their culture had kept them from learning was the *problem*). Instead he provides the most progressive model of their day; the husbands are to respect their intellectual capabilities and give them private instruction. He wants them to stop interrupting the teaching period of the church service, however, because until they know more, they are distracting everyone and disrupting church order." (From Craig S. Keener, *The IVP Bible Background Commentary* [Downers Grove, Ill.: InterVarsity Press, 1993], p. 483.)

[6]Richard and Catherine Clark Kroeger, *I Suffer Not a Woman* (Grand Rapids, Mich.: Baker Book House, 1992), p. 60.

[7]Spencer, *Beyond the Curse,* pp. 75, 79.

[8]W. E. Vine, Merrill F. Unger and William White Jr., eds., *Vine's Expository Dictionary of Biblical Words* (Nashville: Thomas Nelson, 1985), p. 503.

[9]Consistent with Vine's definition, *hēsuchia* is translated "quiet" in 2 Thessalonians 3:12, "Such persons we command and exhort in the Lord Jesus Christ to do their work quietly *(hēsuchia)*" and 1 Timothy 2:2 ". . . so that we may lead a quiet *(hēsuchia,* adjective form) and peaceable life."

[10]Spencer, *Beyond the Curse,* pp. 84-85.

[11]Ibid., pp. 91, 96.

[12]*Huperochē,* meaning "preeminence, superiority, excellency"; *exousia,* meaning "the right to exercise power"; *epitagē,* meaning "command, authority." (From *Vine's Expository Dictionary of Biblical Words.*)

[13]Kroeger and Kroeger, *I Suffer Not a Woman,* pp. 84, 102.

[14]Gareth Icenogle, *Biblical Foundations for Small Group Ministry* (Downers Grove, Ill.: InterVarsity Press, 1994), p. 63.

[15]As reported in Cheryl terHorst, "Is Anyone Telling the Truth Anymore?" *Arlington Heights (Ill.) Daily Herald,* July 18, 1996.

[16]Dwight Ozard, "A Feminist Agenda for Biblical Men," *Prism,* September/October 1995, p. 5.

[17]Ibid.

[18]John Dawson, *Healing America's Wounds* (Ventura, Calif.: Regal Books, 1994), p. 30.

Chapter 3: The Discipline of Honoring Sexuality

[1]Karen Mains, *Friends and Strangers* (Dallas: Word, 1990), p. 127.

[2]Tertullian, "On the Apparel of Women," as quoted in Paul Smith, *Is it OK to Call God Mother?* (Peabody, Mass.: Hendrickson, 1993), p.205.

[3]Carol Becker, *Leading Women* (Nashville: Abingdon, 1996), p. 78.

[4]James B. Nelson, *Body Theology* (Louisville, Ky.: Westminster/John Knox, 1992), p. 19.

[5]Ibid., 123.

[6]Joan H. Timmerman, *Sexuality and Spiritual Growth* (New York: Crossroad, 1992), p. 9.

[7]Lewis B. Smedes, *Sex for Christians* (Grand Rapids, Mich.: Eerdmans, 1976), p. 7.

[8]Dennis Hiebert, "Toward Adult Cross-Sex Friendship," *Journal of Psychology and Theology* 24, no. 4 (1996): 277.

[9]Gerhard Kittel and Gerhard Friedrich, eds., *Theological Dictionary of the New Testament,* trans. and abridg. Geoffrey W. Bromiley (Grand Rapids, Mich.: Eerdmans, 1985), p. 340.

[10]Stanley Grenz, *Sexual Ethics* (Louisville, Ky.: Westminster/John Knox, 1990), p. 21.

[11]Flora Slosson Wuellner, *Prayer and Our Bodies* (Nashville: Upper Room, 1987), p. 71.

[12]Quoted from a letter to the author.

[13]Celia Allison Hahn, *Sexual Paradox: Creative Tensions in our Lives and Congregations* (Cleveland, Ohio: Pilgrim, 1991), p. 11.

Chapter 4: Tearing Down Walls, Building Bridges

[1]M. Scott Peck, *The Different Drum: Community Making and Peace* (New York: Simon & Schuster, 1987), p. 257.

[2]Ibid., pp. 13-15.

[3]Ibid., p. 83.

[4]Ibid., p. 84.

[5]Stephen R. Covey, *The Seven Habits of Highly Effective People* (New York: Simon & Schuster, 1989), p. 252.

[6]Gerard Egan, *Interpersonal Living: A Skills/Contract Approach to Human-Relations Training in Groups* (Monterey, Calif.: Brooks/Cole, 1976), p. 147.

[7]Linda Himelstein, "Breaking Through," *Business Week,* February 17, 1997, p. 64.

[8]Deborah Tannen, *You Just Don't Understand* (New York: Ballantine Books, 1990), p. 48.

[9]Egan, *Interpersonal Living,* p. 97.

[10]Covey, *Seven Habits of Highly Effective People,* p. 239.

[11]Ibid., p. 243.

[12]Egan, *Interpersonal Living,* pp. 200-201.

Chapter 5: Beyond Stereotypes to Partnership

[1]Elaine Storkey, *The Search for Intimacy* (London: Hodder & Stoughton, 1995), p. 119.

[2]Kaye Cooke and Lance Lee, *Man and Woman Alone and Together* (Wheaton, Ill.: Victor Books, 1992), p. 77.

[3]As quoted in Gordon Walek, "Male Malaise," *Arlington Heights (Ill.) Daily Herald,* November 29, 1995.

[4]For a fuller description of these realities see Andrew Kimbrell, *The Masculine Mystique: The Politics of Masculinity* (New York: Ballantine Books, 1995), pp. 3-13.

[5]Ibid.

[6]Neil Chethik, "It's Time for Me to Quit Writing Columns and Chase a New Dream," *Arlington Heights {Ill.) Daily Herald,* September 30, 1996.

[7]As quoted in Cheryl terHorst, "Harriet to the Rescue," *Arlington Heights (Ill.) Daily Herald,* May 15, 1996.

[8]Carol Tavris, *The Mismeasure of Woman: Why Women Are Not the Better Sex, the Inferior Sex or the Opposite Sex* (New York: Simon & Schuster, 1992), p. 332.

[9]terHorst, "Harriet to the Rescue."

[10]Cooke and Lee, *Man and Woman Alone and Together,* p. 73.

Chapter 6: Improving Male-Female Communication

[1]Deborah Tannen, *You Just Don't Understand: Women and Men in Conversation* (New York: Ballantine Books, 1990), p. 42

[2]Kevin Maney, "Lost Dollars Take the Fun out of Language Blunder," *St. Cloud (Minn.) Times,* February 21, 1993.

[3]Tannen, *You Just Don't Understand,* pp. 47-48.

[4]Carol Gilligan, *In a Different Voice* (Cambridge, Mass.: Harvard University Press, 1982), p. 17.

[5]Ibid., pp. 7-8.

[6]Ibid., p. 173.

[7]Tannen, *You Just Don't Understand,* p. 52.

[8]John Gray, *Men Are from Mars, Women Are from Venus* (New York: HarperCollins, 1992), p. 5.

[9]Ibid., p. 67.

[10]Ibid.

[11]Ibid.

[12]Ibid., p. 69.

[13]Deborah Tannen, *Talking from Nine to Five: How Women's and Men's Conversational Styles Affect Who Gets Heard, Who Gets Credit and What Gets Done at Work* (New York: William Morrow, 1994), p. 23.

[14]Carol Tavris, *The Mismeasure of Woman: Why Women Are Not the Better Sex, the Inferior Sex or the Opposite Sex* (New York: Simon & Schuster, 1992), p. 65.

[15]Ibid.

[16]Peter M. Senge, *The Fifth Discipline: The Art and Practice of the Learning Organization* (New York: Currency Doubleday, 1990), p. 168.

[17]As quoted in Timothy D. Schellhardt, "The Other B-School: Watching Baseball Can Help Your Game," *Wall Street Journal,* October 28, 1996.

Chapter 7: Teaming Up to Get Things Done

[1]Phil Jackson, *Sacred Hoops* (New York: Hyperion, 1995), p. 5.

[2]Jon R. Katzenbach and Douglas K. Smith, *The Wisdom of Teams* (New York: HarperCollins, 1993), p. 22.

[3]Ibid., p. 50.

[4]Ibid., p. 48.

[5]Ibid., p. 59.

[6]Gareth Icenogle, "Women and Men Partnering in Small Groups: Conflict and Reconciliation," workshop presented at the National Small Groups Conference, Fuller Theological Seminary, June 1996.

[7]Ibid.

[8]Stephen Covey, *The Seven Habits of Highly Effective People* (New York: Simon & Schuster, 1990), pp. 269-70.

[9]Peter M. Senge, *The Fifth Discipline: The Art and Practice of the Learning Organization* (New York: Currency Doubleday, 1990), p. 257.

[10]Katzenbach and Smith, *Wisdom of Teams,* pp. 109, 111.

[11]Ibid., p. 4.

[12]Kenneth Labich, "Elite Teams Get the Job Done," *Fortune,* February 19, 1996, p. 92.

[13]Gareth Icenogle, *Biblical Foundations for Small Group Ministry* (Downers Grove, Ill.: InterVarsity Press, 1994), p. 24.

[14]Katzenbach and Smith, *Wisdom of Teams,* p. 126.

Chapter 8: Together at Work

[1]Letter to the author, July 17, 1997.

[2]Adapted from David A. Thomas and Robin J. Ely, "Making Differences Matter: A New Paradigm for Managing Diversity," *Harvard Business Review,* September/December 1996, p. 88.

[3]Vern Istock, "The Chairman's Corner," *First Chicago-NBD Forum,* February 1997, p. 2.

[4]Condensed from *The Drake Beam Morin Guide to Managing Diversity in the Global Workplace* (New York: Drake Beam Morin, 1994), pp. 28-37.

[5]Thomas and Ely, "Making Differences Matter," p. 80.

[6]Carol Becker, *Leading Women: How Church Women Can Avoid Leadership Traps and Negotiate the Gender Maze* (Nashville: Abingdon, 1996), p. 152.

[7]Peter M. Senge, *The Fifth Discipline: The Art and Practice of the Learning Organization* (New York: Currency Doubleday, 1990), p. 241.

[8]Anne Wilson Schaef, *Women's Reality: An Emerging Female System in a White Male Society* (San Francisco: Harper & Row, 1981), p. 2.

[9]Becker, *Leading Women*, p. 150.

[10]Ibid., p. 52.

[11]Carolyn Stahl Bohler, *When You Need to Take a Stand* (Louisville, Ky.: Westminster/John Knox Press, 1990), p. 63.

[12]Jeanie Daniel Duck, "Managing Change: The Art of Balancing," *Harvard Business Review,* November/December, 1993, p. 113.

[13]Ibid., pp. 114-15.

[14]Roger Fisher and Scott Brown, *Getting Together* (New York: Penguin Books, 1988), pp. 48-49.

[15]Ibid., pp. 54-55.

[16]The preceding section (pp. 140-42) was freely adapted from Ruth Haley Barton, *Becoming a Woman of Strength* (Wheaton, Ill.: Harold Shaw, 1994), pp. 255-60.

[17]An excellent resource on this subject from a Christian perspective is Jim and Sally Conway, *Sexual Harassment No More* (Downers Grove, Ill.: InterVarsity Press, 1993).

[18]Becker, *Leading Women*, p. 164.

[19]Ibid., p. 166.

[20]*First Chicago-NBD Express,* January 24, 1997, p. 3.

[21]*First Chicago-NBD Express,* February 4, 1997, p. 4.

[22]Statistics taken from a 1996 survey by Catalyst, a study group that works to advance women in business.

[23]Carin Rubenstein, "The Confident Generation," *Working Mother,* May 1994, p. 38.

[24]Miriam Neff and Debra Klingsporn, *Shattering Our Assumptions: Breaking Free of Expectations—Others' and Our Own* (Minneapolis: Bethany House, 1996), p. 34.

Chapter 9: Mutually Empowering Marriage

[1]Patrick and Claudette McDonald, "Marital Spirituality as Spiritual Companionship," *Spiritual Life,* Spring 1997, p. 43.

[2]James H. Olthuis, *I Pledge You My Troth* (San Francisco: Harper & Row, 1975), p. 36.

[3]Alvera Mickelsen, "An Egalitarian View: There Is Neither Male nor Female in Christ," in *Women in Ministry: Four Views,* ed. Bonnidell Clouse and Robert G. Clouse (Downers Grove, Ill.: InterVarsity Press, 1989), p. 183.

[4]Norman H. Murdoch, "Female Ministry in the Thought and Work of Catherine Booth," *Church History* 53 (September 1984): 351.

[5]Material on Catherine Booth adapted from Ruth A. Tucker and Walter Liefeld, *Daughters of the Church* (Grand Rapids, Mich.: Zondervan, 1987), pp. 264-67.

[6]Roger J. Green, *Catherine Booth: A Biography of the Cofounder of the Salvation Army* (Grand Rapids, Mich.: Baker Book House, 1996) pp. 294-96.

[7]Henrich Schlier, "κεφαλή κτλ.," in *Theological Dictionary of the New Testament,* ed. Gerhard Kittel and Gerhard Friedrich, 10 vols. (Grand Rapids, Mich.: Eerdmans, 1964-1976), 3:673-82.

[8]Gilbert Bilezikian, *Beyond Sex Roles* (Grand Rapids, Mich.: Baker Book House, 1985), p. 161.

[9]Ibid., pp. 212-14.

[10]Ibid.

[11]Miriam Neff and Debra Klingsporn, *Shattering Our Assumptions* (Minneapolis: Bethany House, 1996), pp. 112-13.

Chapter 10: Partners in Parenting

[1]Mary Stewart Van Leeuwen, "The Christian Mind and the Challenge of Gender Relations," *The Reformed Journal,* September 1987, p. 23

[2]Susan Moller Okin, *Justice, Gender and the Family* (New York: BasicBooks, 1989), p. 4.

[3]Ibid., pp. 4-5.

[4]Betsy Morris, "Is Your Family Wrecking Your Career?" *Fortune,* March 17, 1997, pp. 71-72.

[5]Mary Stewart Van Leeuwen, *Gender and Grace* (Downers Grove, Ill.: InterVarsity Press, 1990), pp. 176-77.

[6]Nancy Gibbs, "Shameful Bequests to the Next Generation," *Time,* October 8, 1990, p. 43.

[7]*Focus on the Family Bulletin,* June 1988.

[8]The preceding section (pp. 177-80) was freely adapted from Ruth Haley Barton, *Becoming a Woman of Strength* (Wheaton, Ill.: Harold Shaw, 1994), pp. 190-93, 209-10.

[9]Gerhard Kittel and Gerhard Friedrich, eds., *Theological Dictionary of the New Testament,* trans. and abridg. Geoffrey W. Bromiley (Grand Rapids, Mich.: Eerdmans, 1985), pp. 938-39.

[10]Rodney Clapp, *Families at the Crossroads* (Downers Grove, Ill.: InterVarsity Press, 1993), p. 148.

[11]Stephen R. Covey, *Principle-Centered Leadership* (New York: Summit Books, 1990), p. 62.

[12]I have adapted Steve's story from our conversations and from an unpublished article entitled "A Real He-Man: Three Years at Home with My Kids."

[13]The research findings noted in this paragraph are from Ross Parke, *Fathers* (Cambridge, Mass.: Harvard University Press, 1981), p. 38.

[14]Ibid.

[15]Ken Franckling, "The Mr. Mom Phenomenon is Real: More and More Dads Raise Their Kids," *Chicago Tribune,* October 13, 1985, sec. 3, p. 12.

[16]Tommie J. Hamner and Pauline H. Turner, *Parenting in Contemporary Society* (Englewood Cliffs, N.J.: Prentice-Hall, 1985), p. 47.

[17]As cited in Parke, *Fathers,* p. 72.

[18]Patricia Sexton, *The Feminized Male* (New York: Random House, 1969), p. 110.

Chapter 11: Love, Sex and Friendship

[1]Rainer Maria Rilke, *Letters to a Young Poet* (New York: W. W. Norton, 1934), pp. 53-54.

[2]M. Scott Peck, *The Road Less Traveled* (New York: Simon & Schuster, 1978), p. 81.

[3]Dennis W. Hiebert, "Toward Adult Cross-Sex Friendship," *Journal of Psychology and Theology* 24, no. 4 (1996): 275.

[4]Karen Mains, *Friends and Strangers: Divine Encounters in Lonely Places* (Dallas: Word, 1990), pp. 125-26.

[5]Ibid., pp. 128-29.

[6]As quoted in Shawn Madison Krahmer, "Interpreting the Letters of Bernard of Clairvaux to Ermengarde, Countess of Brittany: The Twelfth-Century Context and the Language of Friendship," *Cistercian Studies Quarterly* 27, no. 3 (1990): 218.

[7]Ibid., p. 219.

[8]Ibid.

[9]Ibid., p. 221.

[10]C. S. Lewis, *The Four Loves* (New York: Harcourt Brace Jovanovich, 1960), p. 96.

[11]Caroline Simon, *The Disciplined Heart: Love, Destiny and Imagination* (Grand Rapids, Mich.:

Eerdmans, 1997), p. 88.

[12]Quotations are from an interview with the author.

[13]Rodney Clapp, *Families at the Crossroads: Beyond Traditional and Modern Options* (Downers Grove, Ill.: InterVarsity Press, 1993), p. 110.

[14]J. D. O'Meara, "Cross-Sex Friendship: Four Basic Challenges of an Ignored Relationship," *Sex Roles* 21 (1989): 525-43.

[15]Hiebert, "Toward Adult Cross-Sex Friendship," pp. 272-73.

[16]Celia Allison Hahn, *Sexual Paradox: Creative Tensions in Our Lives and in Our Congregations* (Cleveland, Ohio: Pilgrim, 1991), p. 164.

[17]Richard B. Faris and Jeanne T. Finley, in "Letters," *The Christian Century,* May 7, 1997, p. 458.

[18]Hahn, *Sexual Paradox,* p. 27.

[19]Jerry B. Jenkins, *Hedges: Loving Your Marriage Enough to Protect It* (Brentwood, Tenn.: Wolgemuth & Hyatt, 1989), p. 75-76.

[20]Parker J. Palmer, *To Know As We Are Known: Education as a Spiritual Journey* (New York: HarperCollins, 1983, 1993), p. 54.

For Further Reading

Note: Inclusion of a work on this list does not signify my endorsement of everything in each one. Rather it is meant to indicate that the works listed here are signficant sources that warrant serious consideration.

Biblical Community

Bilezikian, Gilbert. *Community 101: Reclaiming the Local Church as Community of Oneness.* Grand Rapids, Mich.: Zondervan, 1997.

Crabb, Larry. *Connecting: Healing for Ourselves and Our Relationships.* Nashville: Word, 1997.

Dawson, John. *Healing America's Wounds.* Ventura, Calif.: Regal Books, 1994.

DeYoung, Curtiss Paul. *Reconciliation: Our Greatest Challenge—Our Only Hope.* Valley Forge, Penn.: Valley Forge, 1997.

Gorman, Julie. *Community That Is Christian.* Wheaton, Ill.: Victor Books, 1993.

Icenogle, Gareth Weldon. *Biblical Foundations for Small Group Ministry.* Downers Grove, Ill.: InterVarsity Press, 1994.

Peck, M. Scott. *The Different Drum: Community Making and Peace.* New York: Simon & Schuster, 1987.

Theology of Male and Female

Bilezikian, Gilbert. *Beyond Sex Roles.* Grand Rapids, Mich.: Baker Book House, 1985.

Bristow, John Temple. *What Paul Really Said About Women: An Apostle's Liberating Views on Equality in Marriage, Leadership and Love.* San Francisco: HarperCollins, 1988.

Grenz, Stanley J., and Denise Muir Kjesbo. *Women in the Church: A Biblical Theology of Women in Ministry.* Downers Grove, Ill.: InterVarsity Press, 1995.

Kroeger, Richard, and Catherine Clark. *I Suffer Not a Woman: Rethinking I Timothy 2:11-15, in Light of Ancient Evidence.* Grand Rapids, Mich.: Baker Book House, 1992.

Sanders, Cheryl J. *Ministry at the Margins: The Prophetic Ministry of Women, Youth and the Poor.* Downers Grove, Ill.: InterVarsity Press, 1997.

Spencer, Aida Besançon. *Beyond the Curse: Women Called to Ministry.* Peabody, Mass.: Hendrickson, 1985.

Tucker, Ruth A. *Women in the Maze: Questions and Answers on Biblical Equality.* Downers Grove, Ill.: InterVarsity Press, 1992.

Communication, Conflict and Interpersonal Effectiveness

Augsburger, David. *Caring Enough to Hear and Be Heard.* Ventura, Calif.: Regal Books, 1982.

Backus, William. *Telling Each Other the Truth.* Minneapolis: Bethany House, 1985.

Bohler, Carolyn Stahl. *When You Need to Take a Stand.* Louisville, Ky.: Westminster/John Knox, 1990.

Covey, Stephen. *The Seven Habits of Highly Effective People.* New York: Simon & Schuster, 1989.

Egan, Gerard. *Interpersonal Living: A Skills/Contract Approach to Human-Relations Training in Groups.* Monterey, Calif.: Brooks Cole, 1976.

Lerner, Harriet Goldor. *The Dance of Deception: Pretending and Truthtelling in the Lives of Women*. New York: HarperCollins, 1993.

Fisher, Roger, and Scott Brown. *Getting Together: Building Relationships as We Negotiate*. New York: Penguin Books, 1988.

Gilligan, Carol. *In a Different Voice*. Cambridge, Mass.: Harvard University Press, 1982.

Goleman, Daniel. *Emotional Intelligence*. New York: Bantam Books, 1995.

Tannen, Deborah. *You Just Don't Understand: Women and Men in Conversation*. New York: Ballantine Books, 1990.

Tavris, Carol. *Anger: The Misunderstood Emotion*. New York: Simon & Schuster, 1982.

Beyond Stereotypes

Baraff, Alvin. *Men Talk: How Men Really Feel About Women, Sex, Relationships and Themselves*. New York: Dutton, 1991.

Barton, R. Ruth. *Becoming a Woman of Strength: 14 Life Challenges for Women and the Men Who Love Them*. Wheaton, Ill.: Harold Shaw, 1994.

Becker, Verne. *The Real Man Inside*. Grand Rapids, Mich.: Zondervan, 1992.

Cook, Kaye, and Lance Lee. *Man and Woman Alone and Together: Gender Roles, Identity and Intimacy in a Changing Culture*. Wheaton, Ill.: Victor Books, 1992.

John Gray. *Men Are from Mars, Women Are from Venus*. New York: HarperCollins, 1992.

Groothuis, Rebecca Merrill. *Women Caught in the Conflict: The Culture War Between Traditionalism and Feminism*. Grand Rapids, Mich.: Baker Book House, 1994.

Kimbrell, Andrew. *The Masculine Mystique: The Politics of Masculinity*. New York: Ballantine Books, 1995.

Neff, Miriam, and Debra Klingsporn. *Shattering Our Assumptions: Breaking Free of Expectations—Others' and Our Own*. Minneapolis: Bethany House, 1996.

Malcolm, Kari Torjesen. *Women at the Crossroads: A Path Beyond Feminism and Traditionalism*. Downers Grove, Ill.: InterVarsity Press, 1982.

Tavris, Carol. *The Mismeasure of Woman: Why Women Are Not the Better Sex, the Inferior Sex or the Opposite Sex*. New York: Simon & Schuster, 1992.

Teamwork

Bennis, Warren G., and Patricia Ward Biederman. *Organizing Genius: The Secret of Creative Collaboration*. Reading, Mass.: Addison-Wesley, 1997.

Labich, Kenneth. "Elite Teams Get the Job Done." *Fortune*, February 19, 1996.

Katzenbach, Jon R., and Douglas K. Smith. *The Wisdom of Teams*. New York: HarperCollins, 1993.

Senge, Peter M. *The Fifth Discipline: The Art and Practice of the Learning Organization*. New York: Doubleday Currency, 1990.

Sexuality

Castleman, Robbie. *True Love in a World of False Hope: Sex, Romance and Real People*. Downers Grove, Ill.: InterVarsity Press, 1996.

Conway, Jim, and Sally Conway. *Sexual Harassment No More*. Downers Grove, Ill.: InterVarsity Press, 1993.

Dawn, Marva. *Sexual Character: Beyond Technique to Intimacy*. Grand Rapids, Mich.: Eerdmans, 1993.

Foster, Richard J. *The Challenge of the Disciplined Life: Christian Reflections on Money, Sex and Power*. New York: HarperCollins, 1985.

Grenz, Stanley J. *Sexual Ethics: An Evangelical Perspective*. Louisville, Ky.: Westminster/John

Knox, 1997.

Grenz, Stanley J., and Roy D. Bell. *Betrayal of Trust: Sexual Misconduct in the Pastorate.* Downers Grove, Ill.: InterVarsity Press, 1995.

Hahn, Celia Allison. *Sexual Paradox: Creative Tensions in Our Lives and Congregations.* Cleveland, Ohio: Pilgrim, 1991.

Nelson, James B. *Body Theology.* Louisville, Ky.: Westminster/John Knox, 1992.

———. *Embodiment: An Approach to Sexuality and Christian Theology.* Minneapolis: Augsburg, 1978.

Smedes, Lewis. *Sex for Christians.* Grand Rapids, Mich.: Eerdmans, 1976.

Starkey, Mike. *God, Sex and the Search for Lost Wonder.* Downers Grove, Ill.: InterVarsity Press, 1998.

Timmerman, Joan H. *Sexuality and Spiritual Growth.* New York: Crossroad, 1992.

Male-Female Friendship

Hahn, Celia Allison. *Sexual Paradox: Creative Tensions in Our Lives and Congregations* (chaps. 10-11). Cleveland, Ohio: Pilgrim, 1991.

Hiebert, Dennis W. "Toward Adult Cross-Sex Friendship." *Journal of Psychology and Theology* 24, no. 4 (1996): 275.

Mains, Karen Burton. *Friends and Strangers: Divine Encounters in Lonely Places* (chap. 19). Dallas: Word, 1990.

———. *Lonely No More.* Dallas: Word, 1993.

Olthuis, James H. *I Pledge You My Troth: A Christian View of Marriage, Family, Friendship* (chap. 5). New York: Harper & Row, 1975.

Simon, Caroline J. *The Disciplined Heart* (chap. 6). Grand Rapids, Mich.: Eerdmans, 1997.

Storkey, Elaine. *The Search for Intimacy.* London: Hodder & Stoughton, 1995.

Marriage and Parenting

Balswick, Jack. *Men at the Crossroads: Beyond Traditional Roles and Modern Options.* Downers Grove, Ill.: InterVarsity Press, 1992.

Balswick, Jack, and Judith Balswick. *The Dual Earner Marriage: The Elaborate Balancing Act.* Grand Rapids, Mich.: Revell, 1995.

———. *The Family: A Christian Perspective on the Home.* Grand Rapids, Mich.: Baker Book House, 1991.

Barton, R. Ruth. *Becoming a Woman of Strength: 14 Life Challenges for Women and the Men Who Love Them.* Wheaton, Ill.: Harold Shaw, 1994.

Clapp, Rodney. *Families at the Crossroads: Beyond Traditional Roles and Modern Options.* Downers Grove, Ill.: InterVarsity Press, 1993.

Gundry, Patricia. *Heirs Together: Mutual Submission in Marriage.* Grand Rapids, Mich.: Zondervan, 1980.

Okin, Susan Moller. *Justice, Gender, and the Family.* New York: BasicBooks, 1989.

Olthuis, James H. *I Pledge You My Troth: A Christian View of Marriage, Family, Friendship.* New York: Harper & Row, 1975.

Schwartz, Pepper. *Peer Marriage: How Love Between Equals Really Works.* New York: Free Press, 1994.

Spencer, Aida Besançon. *Beyond the Curse* (see especially "Equaling Eden: A Practical Male Afterword" by William David Spencer). Peabody, Mass.: Hendrickson, 1985.

Van Leeuwen, Mary Stewart. *Gender and Grace: Love, Work and Parenting in a Changing World.* Downers Grove, Ill.: InterVarsity Press, 1990.

Together at Work (including the church as a working environment)

Becker, Carol E. *Leading Women: How Church Women Can Avoid Leadership Traps and Negotiate the Gender Maze.* Nashville: Abingdon, 1996.

The Drake Beam Morin Guide to Managing Diversity in the Global Workplace. New York: Drake Beam Morin, 1994.

Hagberg, Janet O. *Real Power: Stages of Personal Power in Organizations.* San Francisco: HarperSanFrancisco, 1984.

Helgesen, Sally. *The Female Advantage: Women's Ways of Leading.* New York: Currency Doubleday, 1990.

Kotter, John P. *Leading Change.* Boston: Harvard Business School Press, 1996.

Kriter, Phyllis Beck. *Negotiating at an Uneven Table: A Practical Approach to Working with Difference and Diversity.* San Francisco: Jossey-Bass, 1994.

Noren, Carol M. *The Woman in the Pulpit.* Nashville: Abingdon, 1992.

Pierce, Carol, David Wagner and Bill Page. *A Male-Female Continuum: Paths to Colleagueship.* Expanded edition. Laconia, N.H.: New Dynamics Publications, 1994.

Schaef, Anne Wilson. *Women's Reality: An Emerging Female System in a White Male Society.* San Francisco: Harper & Row, 1981.

Tannen, Deborah. *Talking from Nine to Five: How Women's and Men's Conversational Styles Affect Who Gets Heard, Who Gets Credit and What Gets Done at Work.* New York: William Morrow, 1994.

Thomas, R. Roosevelt, Jr. *Differences Do Make a Difference.* Atlanta: American Institute for Managing Diversity, 1992.

White, Jane. *A Few Good Women: Breaking the Barriers to Top Management.* Englewood Cliffs, N.J.: Prentice-Hall, 1992.